PADDLING HAWAI'I

Why Paddle Hawai'i?

Twenty-three Reasons

1. Vacation for $5 a day in an oceanfront suite with a private waterfall.
2. Learn birds, plants, fish, and geology first hand.
3. Go with your three best friends.
4. Go solo, fitting into the wilderness.
5. Float those 60 pounds, rather than backpack them.
6. Try this remedy, "The cure for anything is salt water—sweat, tears, or the sea."
7. Develop your skills in warm water, then explore the world.
8. Take your children or someone else's. Kids don't yammer with a paddle in their hands.
9. Carry the scuba tanks and fishing gear out to the best spots.
10. Be a powerful paddler even if you have bum feet, ankles, knees, are paraplegic or an amputee.
11. Get to isolated areas without a motor, for solitude, for photography, for simplicity.
12. Experience quiet and peace and the shining sea.
13. Understand when you read Rachel Carson, Joseph Conrad, and Henry Beston.
14. Swim naked off shore; hang your suit on your kayak.
15. Troll your fishing line for papio, or snorkel, or pick opihi where no one goes.
16. Watch the sun rise out of the sea, and the sun set with a green flash.
17. Use a small kayak as a dinghy for your big boat.
18. Fly a kite with lots of space and no wires; sail a boat with no mooring fees.
19. Work out for the six-man canoe season.
20. Learn and feel how ancient Hawaiians lived, in places of village sites and old trails.
21. Play Robinson Crusoe on a small island.
22. Lose fears, develop self confidence and apply it to all your life.
23. Roll overboard and hear the whales sing.

PADDLING HAWAI'I

≋

Revised Edition

Audrey Sutherland

A Latitude 20 Book
University of Hawai'i Press
Honolulu

Copyright © 1988, 1998 by Audrey Sutherland
First edition by The Mountaineers 1988
Published by University of Hawai'i Press 1998
Printed in the United States of America
98 99 00 01 02 03   5 4 3 2 1

Library of Congress Cataloging-in-Publication Data

Sutherland, Audrey
Paddling Hawai'i / by Audrey Sutherland.—Rev. ed.
p.   cm.
Includes bibliographical references and index.
ISBN 0-8248-2041-X (pbk. : alk. paper)
1. Kayak touring   Hawaii.   2. Kayak touring—Hawaii—Guidebooks.
3. Hawaii—Guidebooks.   I. Title.
GV776.H3S88   1998
797.1'224'09969—dc21   77–48610
CIP

Maps by Nick Gregoric and revised by Julia Winslow.
Knot diagrams by Julia Winslow.

University of Hawai'i Press books are printed on acid-free
paper and meet the guidelines for permanence and
durability of the Council on Library Resources

Designed by David C. denBoer

Contents

Pronouncing Hawaiian Words

In the Hawaiian language, words look strangely repetitious because the Hawaiian alphabet contains only twelve letters: the five vowels and h, k, l, m, n, p, w. The vowels are pronounced as they are in Spanish (ah, ay, ee, oh, oo). W is often softened to a v sound. The macron over a letter (ā) gives it a longer stress. The glottal stop, marked by a reversed apostrophe, indicates a stopping sound where the voice pauses between letters, as in the English "oh-oh." Syllables always end with a vowel. There are no silent letters. Go ahead, try it, and pronounce everything.

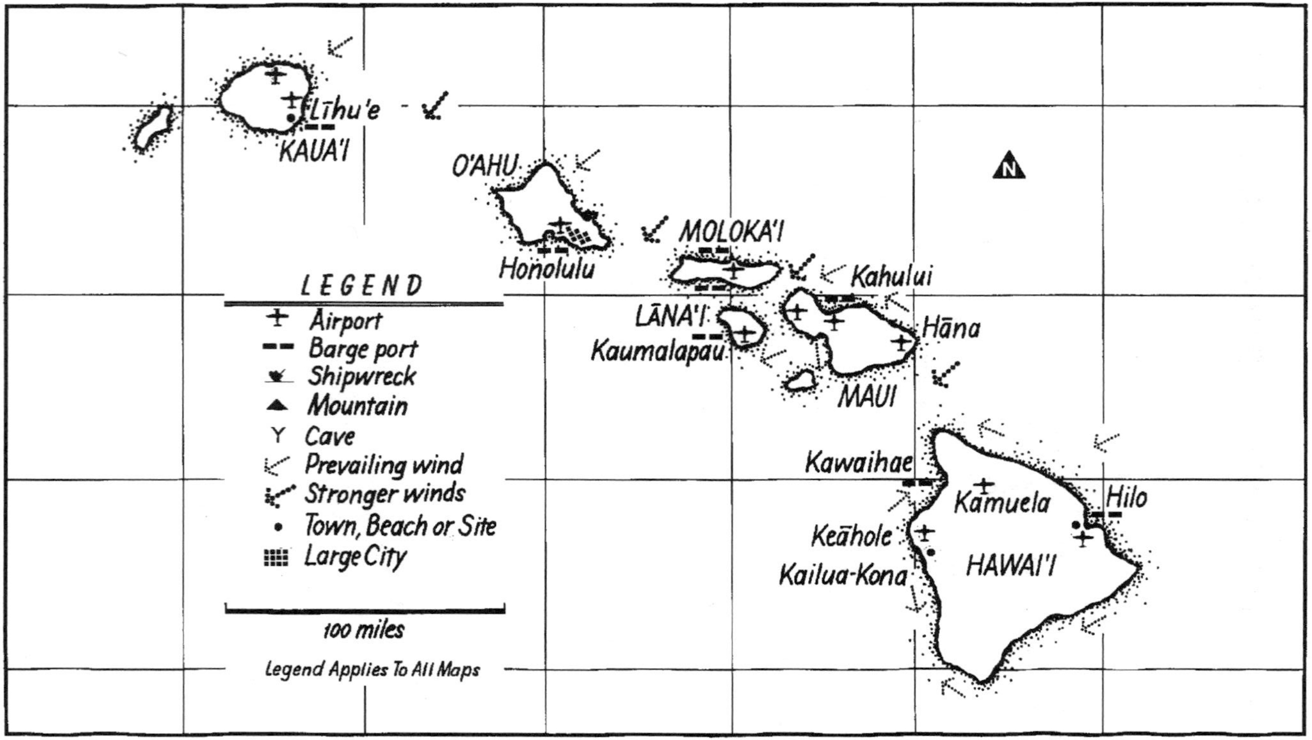
Līhu'e
KAUA'I
O'AHU
Honolulu
MOLOKA'I
LĀNA'I
Kaumalapau
Kahului
Hāna
MAUI
N
Kawaihae
Kamuela
Hilo
Keāhole
Kailua-Kona
HAWAI'I
LEGEND
Airport
Barge port
Shipwreck
Mountain
Cave
Prevailing wind
Stronger winds
Town, Beach or Site
Large City
100 miles
Legend Applies To All Maps

Part I

HOW TO

1

The Many Ways to Paddle
Boats and Paddles

This book is about cruising, exploring, seeing the Hawaiian islands and their coastal waters from small, paddle-powered boats. It touches also on racing and sailing. It is primarily about kayaks, but it also looks at other paddle craft. On the mainland (as we in Hawai'i call the rest of the United States) there are three broad categories of kayaks: those designed for cruising and sightseeing, those for flat-water racing, and those for running white-water rivers. We have adapted each of the three for use in Hawai'i, but the majority used here are in the cruising category, boats often called "sea kayaks."

One primary factor in choosing or designing a small boat for use in Hawai'i is our warm water: 78 degrees F in summer, 74 in winter. It's okay to get wet; to have water sloshing in and out of your boat; to fall out, laugh, and get back in; to paddle all day in a swimsuit. The most common hazard is not hypothermia but sunburn. Unlike Eskimo-influenced kayaks, boats here do not have to keep you dry and warm. You can even swim some trips and save the expense of a boat.

Surf is the second important consideration in Hawai'i. Landings are frequently wave-assisted (that is, only semi-controlled), and on some routes you must land on stony beaches. Fiberglass hulls won't take much of this abuse. Polyethylene ("plastic") hulls are tougher and you can drag them up over the rocks. Inflatable boats will bounce off rocks, but you must not drag them. Surf also dictates a boat that you can get into and out of fast, because the shore break is where you and your boat have the greatest chance of damage. If the next steep wave is approaching, you can't be struggling to get in or out of your boat; you have to be *moving*.

A third factor in choosing a boat is weight. A boat must be carried into or out of the water by its own crew, sometimes over uneven footing and in a hurry between sets of waves. Most kayaks carry one person and thus need to be carried by one. If you make solo trips, you need to be able to launch and land your boat by yourself. My own practical limit is a 30-pound boat. Even if you can carry a heavy boat alone, the difficulty of getting it out of storage, onto a car rack, and then into the water may mean that you just will not do it very often. If you go with friends, you may be able to partner up or group up on the carry, but even then a landing is often solo and fast.

Fourth, the boat should be fun to paddle. It should be reasonably fast, should steer easily in windy conditions, and should make you feel safe enough that you're not worried about survival, or staying upright, but can relax and enjoy the trip.

Finally, the boat should serve *your* purpose. Go back to the reasons for paddling given in the beginning of this book and decide why you, the unique person you, want to go paddling. Then choose a boat that will help you do it. Yes, I know, each paddler would like to own at least three kayaks to serve different purposes, but start with one. Bernard Moitessier said it well in comparing racing to cruising: "Our problems are not the same. Racing thinks performance at all cost. Cruising thinks simple, cheap, strong, durable."

Now let's look at how different designs reflect and make compromises among these partially incompatible criteria. Since so many boat designs are described and used, and since no experts I've talked to across the country agree on the definition of a kayak, I'll refer to them all as boats.

Cruising Kayaks

These fall into three groups: *hard shell*, *inflatable*, and *folding*. Veteran paddlers have favorite boats for cruising based on their own purposes and experience. John Dowd, for instance, used a Klepper folding boat for long-distance coastal paddles and sea crossings under nasty conditions. Among his long distance trips are hundred-mile crossings between islands on the two-thousand-mile paddle from Venezuela to Florida with his wife Bea as a paddling partner. Ed Gillet chose a 20-foot, 80-pound, Necky double hardshell for his solo California-to-Hawai'i 63-day crossing in 1987. Paul Caffyn used a hardshell, British-made, narrow Nordkapp for his voyages around New Zealand, Australia, and Japan, and for his two-summer trip along the whole coastline of Alaska from Ketchikan in the southeast to the far north border of Canada in the Beaufort Sea. My own main delight in paddling is to go on long, solo trips in a wilderness, much of it in open sea conditions, and that determines my choice of boat. It has to be light-weight, seaworthy, portable by air to other places in the world, and portable by me from shore to camp.

Hard Shell

Hard shell cruising kayaks here are of two types. The first are open-top, sit-upon, self-bailing craft, which make up at least 90 percent of cruising boats in use in Hawai'i. The second are enclosed, cockpit-type, Eskimo-style kayaks.

Open-top Hardshells: In the early 1980s fiberglass Ocean Kayaks, made here on O'ahu by Mike Cripps, were the ultimate in open-top design. They could be made in a one-man shop using a fairly simple mold and adapted to the individual. Those jewels were supplanted by the heavier, highly technical, rotomolded "plastic" boats, which can be bashed around in shipping, in rental fleets, and on rocks and, because of mass production, are cheaper. None are made in Hawai'i.

The two most often used open-top kayaks here are the Ocean Kayak Scupper or Scupper Pro and the Perception Aquaterra Prism. As John Enomoto says in the summer 1996 issue of *Hawai'i Skin Diver* magazine, "The plastic kayak gives us an extremely durable, stable, and easily repairable platform for surfing, camping, scuba diving, and fishing. . . . We have carried as much as 220 pounds of equipment with a 180 pound paddler on the 'Pro' in small craft advisory conditions. . . . An experienced paddler, with practice, can cover 25 miles (a day) of coastline with a fully loaded Scupper Pro."

An absolute beginner can also enjoy an open-top cruising boat. He feels safe, stable not tippy, can get in and out easily, can tie on an ice chest, can reach for sunscreen or water without needing to take off a

Tim Sawyer unhooks an ʻaha caught off Nā Pali coast. (Photo by Joseph Hu)

spray skirt. The boat is self-bailing through holes under his heels, and he can drag it up the beach.

Some models of open-top boats have molded insets for a scuba tank; others have hatches at each end for carrying tanks or camping gear inside. The double models for two paddlers are longer and heavier, with two molded inset seats. Both singles and doubles need a backrest for each seat. Backrests give you more power as you are braced into your foot rests, and they certainly ease the back strain. Backrests are made of heavy padded nylon and held in place with clips and straps in front and back. The back straps may have bungee or inner tube inserts. By adding thigh straps, which fasten by clips at toe and hip positions on each side of the boat, you can hook your knees under them and achieve greater control without sliding around in the seat.

What disadvantages do open-tops have? They are heavy—fifty-one pounds for the Prism single, fifty-five for the Scupper single, and sixty-five for the Ocean Kayak Zest Two double—and definitely not deflatable or folding. Thus, they are a hassle to ship to other islands for the best trips in Hawaiʻi, although lately Polynesian Air has been shipping hardshell kayaks as cargo to various airports. See "Sources."

And no, open-tops are not designed for cold water, although I've known of their use in Alaska with paddlers wearing a wet or a dry suit to keep warm. Open-tops sometimes have a design flaw, which can be a problem, no matter what the water temperature. Watch for and avoid any small threaded hatches between your knees near the water-line of the boat. These often leak disastrously if you are packing a heavy load that lowers the waterline.

What about the second type of hardshell, the enclosed Eskimo-Greenland type of kayak? According to the 1997 *Canoe and Kayak Buyer's Guide*, out of seventy kayak manufacturers, twenty-three were making open-top boats; fifty-six were making enclosed "sea touring" boats. They have a top deck, a bottom hull, a cockpit that you sit in-side with your legs under the top deck, and a spray skirt that cinches around your body and over the edge of the cockpit coaming to keep out the cold water. Jim Lelong of Kailua has a fiberglass 16-footer. He has modified it for fishing by installing rod holders on the front deck and adding a vertical hatch in a bulkhead just behind the seat so as to store the 30-pound *ulua* he catches. He shipped that same boat to Alaska two summers ago, where he caught salmon, cod, and halibut—plus crab in a folding trap—and stayed warm. Most enclosed kayaks are built of fiber-reinforced plastic (FRP) or fiberglass, but they also can be made with Kevlar or carbon fiber for the ultimate in light weight. Consider expense also—about $300 additional for part Kevlar and $3,000 for all carbon fiber.

My son, James, bought a well-used, mainland-style, plastic Hydra Sea Runner for $150, and he has added many more miles of fishing and cruising. Its 34-inch cockpit is long enough to get his knees in and out easily, certainly a reason to choose one of these boats in Hawai'i, where you need to get in and out for snorkeling and to land or launch quickly in surf. When measuring cockpit length measure from the seat-back to the front cockpit edge. That's your working distance. A cockpit less than 23 inches of leg-bending space with its small spray skirt may be fine for Eskimo rolls and waves that try to dump in your lap, but you have to shoe-horn your body into it while wishing you had knees that bent the other way.

Almost in a separate category are the wooden kit kayaks. If ever I shift to a hardshell boat it will most likely be to one of these. Inher-ently, a wooden boat floats; inherently a plastic or fiberglass boat sinks. A wooden kayak is beautiful, and can be made from scratch or bought in kit form. Either way, you have great satisfaction in creating your own. The kits cost about $500 to $600 including materials, approximately one-third of the cost of an enclosed pre-fab boat. Check the literature to see just what is included, partial or complete materials. A kit boat, the Pygmy Goldeneye 13, is at the top of my list. If I built it here in my garage, the only difficulty would be getting it from Hawai'i to Alaska, where I go each summer to paddle in a wilderness.

Three Pygmy Golden Eye wooden kit boats

Once there, I'd probably leave it with friends in Juneau. See "Sources" for boat kit addresses.

If minimizing weight is your number one requirement, you should consider the designs by Platt Monfort. His Geodesic Aerolite boat consists of a simple, wooden framework, braced with triangulated Kevlar roving strands. This tough, basketlike frame is then covered with Dacron, which is a heat-shrink, super-tough fabric like that used for modern sails. An example is the 14-foot Rob Roy, an adaptation of a cruising kayak design by L. Francis Herreshoff. It weighs between 20 and 25 pounds, depending on use of bulkheads. See "Sources" for catalog address.

Inflatable Boats

I've paddled over 10,000 miles in 12 models of inflatable boats since the first six-foot-long one in 1967, and I obviously prefer them. This book has more about inflatables because I know them well, and because you won't find the information elsewhere about using them on the ocean. So far, the books about them refer to white-water river boats or to dinghies. My favorite inflatable so far is a 13-foot Semperit Forelle III, which is no longer made but I bought it used for $300. (The closest to it available new is a Grabner Holiday.) The dimensions of my Forelle when it is rolled up are 18 inches long, 12 inches wide, and 6 inches high, for a total of one cubic foot. Its weight is 26 pounds, with an additional five pounds for rudder and custom-made spray deck.

Why are inflatables popular in Hawai'i? The most spectacular, least crowded places to paddle and explore are not on O'ahu, with its 800,000 residents, but on the other islands. With no bridges between islands and no ferries, the advantage goes to a boat you can roll up to carry in a duffel bag on a plane. Data are given in Table 1.

All boats except the Sevylor are made of triple layers, with, a layer of nylon or Dacron cloth sandwiched between layers of rubber or vinyl. This makes a tough hide that is not as subject to expansion in the sun or to abrasion as the single layer of PVC of the Sevylor.

Portability is another big plus for inflatables. I can carry one onto a plane or up a beach. A boat that weighs less than 30 pounds opens up the world of kayaking to women going solo. Why should they be

Table 1

Inflatable Boat Specifications (boats currently in production)

Maker	Model	Material	Decked?	Length	Width	Weight lbs	Capacity	Rudder
AIRE	Sea Tiger I	Urethane/nylon	No	16'9"	35"	46	1 person	yes
	Sea Tiger II	Urethane/nylon	No	19'9"	35"	51	2	yes
GRABNER	Explorer I	Hypalon/nylon	No*	12'8"	28"	37	1	yes
	Explorer II	Hypalon/nylon	No*	16'	31"	51	2	yes
	Holiday Economy	Hypalon/nylon	No	11'10"	31"	21	2	yes
	Holiday	Hypalon/nylon	No	12'10"	31"	33	2	yes
	Dolphin 1	Hypalon/nylon	Yes*	12'10"	29"	39	1	yes
	Dolphin 2	Hypalon/nylon	Yes*	13'10"	29"	42	2	yes
	Dolphin 2SL	Hypalon/nylon	Yes	15'1"	29"	44	2	yes
INNOVA	Helios 340	Rubber/nylon	No	11'	29"	24.3	1	no
	Helios 380	Rubber/nylon	No	12'5"	29"	28.6	2	no
	Junior	Rubber/nylon	Partial	8'	25"	11.5	1	no
JUMBO	Tramper	PVC/nylon	No	12'8"	31"	26.5	2	fixed skeg
SEVYLOR	K 79	PVC	No	10'7"	34"	25	1	no

*"Decked" means a full length, built-in top cover to keep out water. The Grabner boats marked with asterisks have a separate cover which can be fastened on. Grabner Explorer boats are available through U.S. dealers. Holiday and Dolphin boats are available through mail order.

Addresses to send for catalogs are given in "Sources." Aire is manufactured in the U.S. The others are all made in Europe and could probably be bought cheaper there, depending on customs and exchange rates. See also in "Sources," the full page on buying a boat direct from the manufacturer in Europe. Our experience is that it will save nearly half the cost, giving you a "free" trip to paddle the many places there.

Kids love inflatables. Here is a nine-foot boat.

excluded from this choice? Bart Hauthaway, a teacher, builder, and iconoclast from Massachusetts, is one of the few designers of hard-shells who has been building lightweight canoes and kayaks for years. He looked at my boat, snarled something about a sluggish rubber boat, took it out to sea, put it through all of his technical maneuvers, and came back muttering, "Surprisingly responsive."

One summer, after paddling my boat all spring in Hawai'i, I took it to Alaska, Maine, Scotland, Norway, and Washington state, traveling by plane, bus, ferry, train, subway, and rental car. Taking the boat along meant just sliding my arms through the duffel bag straps and walking off. Consider the logistical problems and the cost of shipping a hardshell boat to all those places in three months. Folding boats, such as the Feathercraft, also have portability advantages.

What about performance? This includes speed, comfort, packing ease and space, landing and launching, ease of repair, and handling in rough seas.

Speed? The more rigid the boat, the more efficiently it is propelled through the water. Fiberglass boats are fastest, plastic next, and inflat-able last, given comparable length and shape, and depending on the power and stamina of the paddler. I paddled my first 2,000 miles in a Sevylor Tahiti, first a six-footer, then a seven. I still own a nine-footer, which is great for quickie trips. One Alaska trip in it was 750 miles,

Top to bottom: *Metzeler Tramper (now Jumbo), Sevylor Tahiti, Innova Junior.*

good distance for the price of $150, though its high profile always made wind a problem. I admit that few people share my "Go light, go cheap, go low-tech" philosophy. My 13-foot Semperit is similar to the Grabner boats in shape and length, and both have rudders, needed because inflatables are vulnerable to wind. You get half again more miles in a day, because you don't need to paddle extra strokes on one side to keep going straight. With the rudder on my inflatable and at a three-knot cruising speed, I've done 35 miles in a day, and I average twenty, but that is still 7 to 12 hours of paddling.

Comfort? Inflatables are not soft and squishy. You have to pump them up hard to get maximum performance. For seating comfort in either a hardshell or an inflatable, use a softly inflated liner from a boxed wine as a cushion. It's great also for football games and dull lectures.

Packing ease? Here I mean packing your gear in the boat. An inflatable is just as easy to pack as an open-top hardshell, and much easier than one with hatches, but interior packing space may be a problem. Those inflated sides cut down on inside space, but in calm seas you can stack it up high, keeping the heavy items on the bottom for stability. The space in my boat is limited to five cubic feet, because I usually paddle with a custom-made, velcroed-on spray deck in place to keep out rain and choppy seas. On this list of inflatables only the Aire boats are self-bailing.

Landing and launching? Landing an inflatable is certainly easier. It bounces on rocky shores. You step out, tilt it up to empty any water, lift out the heavy bags, and quickly carry the boat up away from the shore break. On most boulder beaches, the rocks are rounded from tumbling in the surf. In quiet water, I step out when it's ankle deep, lift the bow of the boat up and onto shore, loop the lifeline/bow line around a big rock, unpack, then carry the boat up. Launching in surf is better in a hardshell, however; you can punch through waves, whereas an inflatable is so buoyant that a wave will often turn it sideways and carry it back to shore.

Repair? There is no big advantage here for any kayak. Prevention takes the least time. More maintenance time is required for an inflatable. A hardshell can just be hosed off, emptied out, and stored in hanging straps. The inflatable needs to be washed with fresh water and dried before rolling it up for storage. Rolled up wet, it mildews in a few days. With care and patching, my old boat lasted 14 years and 5,000 miles. To repair a PVC boat, use a glue with an acetone base. To repair hypalon, use a glue with a toluol base.

Handling in rough seas? Inflatables handle very well, and you don't need to worry about them filling with water and sinking. Folding boats with built-in air sponsons along the sides also have that advantage.

Mainland people are not going to buy a boat for just Hawai'i. They want to know how it will behave anywhere. One summer outside lower Baranof Island in Alaska, the tide out of Great Whale Arm was moving down from the northeast, the tide out of Chatham Strait was pushing up from the south, and a 30-knot wind blew in from the west. On that rock cliff coast there were few places to duck into, and the confused, eight-foot seas made for two nasty hours. I snatched off my wool cap and tucked it under the spray deck of my inflatable, to better hear over which shoulder the hiss of the curling crest astern was coming, and to know which way to rudder and stroke to keep at right angles to the breaking seas. I would not want to have been there in a less responsive boat. "My, she was yare," Katharine Hepburn once said of a small sailing yacht. Yare means responding quickly and truly to the helm. "This one, too," I thought. Eight years later I had the same boat

out in a full gale (45-knot winds) in Boca de Quadra, south of
Ketchikan. It was a beam wind, and she still behaved beautifully.

No inflatables are truly built for the sea. Most of them are river
boats, with high bow and stern for diving in and out of river rapids.
Broad as bath tubs and without rudders, those are slow on the open sea
and track abominably. In the table above I've selected the few inflatables that are more suited than most for ocean use. We need a manufacturer to build to these specifications: 14 feet long, 26 inches wide at
the center outside, 20 inches inside, nine inches above the water line
(unloaded), thin ovals of tube-over-tube construction on the sides, a
removable spray deck, a simple, removable rudder, a boat weight of 25
pounds. Several makers boast that their boat will carry 800 pounds. I
don't know of anyone who needs to carry more than 400 in a single;
better to make the sides thinner for more interior space. The problem
is the bulk of the gear, not the weight.

Folding Boats

These boats have a rigid framework of folding, lengthwise struts
clipped to cross frames of wood or tough plastic and are covered with
a tough top deck skin of nylon or other material plus a rubber or synthetic bottom hull. Certainly they are the closest of any kayak to the
original form developed in Greenland and the Aleutians as hunting
craft. Five companies manufacture about twenty-one different models. The best source of information about these boats is Ralph Diaz,
who first published the bimonthly newsletter *Folding Kayaker*, and
then wrote a book *The Complete Folding Kayaker*. As he says, "Bear in
mind that they have a long, rich tradition of seafaring. For nearly a
century, hundreds of thousands of folding kayaks have been leaving
their wakes on every waterway from the Arctic to Antarctica. They
have crossed oceans and other major bodies of water, in frozen climes
and in balmy tropics. . . . foldability is just the frosting on the cake . . .
you should consider having a folding kayak primarily for its superior
seaworthiness and reliability."

Paul Theroux, in the foreword to Diaz's book, mentions that he
owns three kayaks, two of them foldables—a Klepper Expedition single and a Feathercraft K-1. He used a folding boat to paddle through-

A Klepper folding boat near Waimānalo.

out the South Pacific for his book *The Happy Isles of Oceania,* and he recently took a folding boat with him to Africa.

John Dowd paddled not only across the Caribbean, but also in Chilean Patagonia and from Singapore to Java. Kleppers were also twice sailed across the Atlantic. My own choice of the five companies would be the Feathercraft, for its engineering and its relatively light weight. Ralph Diaz's book compares the models of folding boats as I've done for inflatables. His book includes prices, which in 1994 ranged from $1,200 to $4,400, with an average of $3,211 for full-size singles.

Racing Kayaks and Canoes

Flat-water Olympic-style racing kayaks have been in Hawai'i since the 1950s. We had two paddlers in the 1996 Olympics, but many more people paddle the surf ski. It is a long (19 feet), narrow (19 inches), open-top kayak designed for racing in rough open ocean—not just the flat water of the Ala Wai Canal in Waikīkī. The term *surf ski* is a misnomer, since the boat is a kayak, not a water ski, and is used primarily for day cruising and racing, not surf riding. The name comes from the

Class day. Front to back: *Scupper Pro cruising kayak, Wave Witch wave ski, two surf skis, Wave Witch double, Scupper Pro, several inflatables.*

original Australian craft, which had an upturned bow like a ski. These boats are designed for straight-ahead speed, not quick turns. Like a bicycle, the surf ski must be moving for you to balance on it. Part of the boat's potential speed is achieved as it slides down the face of a big ocean swell while you paddle. The record time for the annual 30 miles Moloka'i-to-O'ahu channel race is three and a half hours, with racers averaging 90 strokes a minute.

Several of these boats are built locally, from pure race boats to those with a bit more stability. Some even have hatches to store gear in the hull for cruising the coasts of the islands. The big advantage to local manufacture is being able to work with the designer to get a boat that just suits you.

The newest boat on the Hawai'i scene, the one-person canoe, has simply exploded in its use and popularity. It is even longer than a surf ski (22 feet), but it has an outrigger (*ama*) and two curved connector bars ('*iako*), so it really is an outrigger canoe. There are three reasons it has so endeared itself: First, you don't have to spend weeks learning to balance, the outrigger does it for you. Second, you use the same stroke, with a single-bladed paddle, as in the traditional six-person racing outrigger canoes, so, without waiting for the other five people, you can go out and improve your conditioning for the six-man season. And third, the boat weighs less than 30 pounds. Recently, four women of the North Shore Canoe Club went paddling by my house. I met them at Hale'iwa Beach Park and took photos as each woman lifted her canoe out of the water, unscrewed the *ama* and *'iako,* and put the hull atop her car—all with easy power and grace. And, of course, the boats should be named not one-man but one-paddler canoes, *hoekāhi.*

In the summer 1996, six teams of two men each, using one-person canoes and changing places at will, paddled the whole 42 miles of the north coast of Moloka'i. The teams finished with less than 14 minutes between first and last, with a winning time of 4:32:32. Seeing the photos of that race in *Hawai'i Paddler Magazine* brought back memories of my own 18 trips along that coast. No matter where in the world I'm paddling, when the headwind builds to 25 knots, and the swells seem huge, I build up courage with my old Moloka'i chant, *"Hoe aku i ka wa'a."* "Paddle ahead the canoe," each word grunted with one stroke

Folly Murdock trains in a one-paddler canoe for the state races with her North Shore Canoe Club.

to make another six inches' headway. That's a long way from the ten miles per hour of the racing times.

I once had a 12-foot Samoan outrigger fishing canoe, a *paopao*, built of *ufalele*, a Samoan hardwood, but it was for utility not speed like these fiberglass, more fragile beauties. See *Canoes of Oceania* under "Further Reading."

Surfing Kayaks

White-water kayaking on mainland rivers is a big performance sport. In Hawai'i there are no navigable white-water rivers, but we have lots of white ocean surf, so we've adapted the idea. White-water river waves curl up stream, opposite of the river flow, and I've watched experts ride that continuous upstream curl as if it were Hawaiian surf. Surfing waves go the same direction as the water flow, toward the shore, and dissipate on the sand. The wave ski meets the concept of a performance kayak. It's like a short, thick surfboard with toe straps and a molded seat, and uses a short kayak paddle. It has a planing hull instead of a displacement hull. This makes the shorter boards sluggish to paddle until they get up to speed as they slide down the face of the wave. The longer ones, with a back rest or with a clipped-on pack containing your camping gear, can be used for short cruises. My favorite day or weekend small cruiser, which is also good for surfing is Hunt Johnsen's Wave Witch. It just feels right. For you, with a different purpose and a different body size and strength, some other boat may fit you better.

Other Craft

The islands' most well-known ethnic, traditional, and historic boat is the outrigger canoe, which, in the form of large, double-hulled sailing canoes, brought the first inhabitants to Hawai'i over 1,500 years ago. Of course the voyagers also brought with them the knowledge of the craft in all its forms—from a one-person fishing canoe to giant, double-hulled war canoes. Now the six-person canoes are used mostly for the highly competitive sport of canoe racing. Fifty or more clubs compete throughout the islands, and the season culminates in a state championship and a 40-mile race in September across the Ka'iwi Channel from Moloka'i to O'ahu.

Another craft for voyaging is the surfboard, not the little six-foot, eight-pound boards for performance on six-foot waves. Those don't have enough buoyancy to hold a paddler high enough for distance paddling. You need a twelve-foot tanker, or a rescue board used by lifeguards, or one of the long, slim paddleboards used for distance racing. You can carry gear by stretching two bicycle inner tubes around the board and clipping your gear to the tubes. A small pack can be positioned as a chin rest. Unless surfers are in excellent condition for distance paddling, they cannot keep up with kayakers for even an hour, much less a whole day, especially in rough seas, so it is better not to try a mix of the two craft during trips.

Swimming It

The cheapest and most basic way to see the island shores is to become an amphibian and swim your trip. You walk where you can, and when the cliffs or the jungle make walking impossible, you put your pack in a waterproof floating bag and take to the sea with fins, mask, and snorkel. (See *Paddling My Own Canoe* under "Further Reading.") A requisite for this traveling method is long-distance swimming ability. It's different from being a speed champ in a pool. You need to be at ease in surf and currents and adept at using fins, mask, and snorkel. There may be three miles or more between possible landings. On a boat trip, you need to know wind and current; when swimming, only current is a major factor. Tides in Hawai'i are not a problem, though changing tides may cause shifting currents around points of land. The range between highest and lowest tide is less than three feet.

The minimum equipment for a swimming expedition is asterisked on the gear list (see chapter 2). The waterproof bag could be the same kind you use in a kayak, but it should be lashed to a pack frame with a hip belt for carrying it on land. Lash on some strips of styrofoam for added flotation, and use plastic bags inside the dry bag. Test it to see whether you can really tow it without leaks. Another gear carrier is a garbage bag inside a styrene box, again on a pack frame. Toni Withington and two friends swam Nā Pali coast on Kaua'i in 1967, pushing a large truck inner tube with a plywood floor lashed in the center. It wasn't streamlined, but it *was* easy to rest on en route. A tough air mattress, a body-surfing boogie board, a kid's inflatable boat—there are many possible floats for your gear. This would be the simplest way to cross Kealakekua Bay on the Big Island. Swim the mile over to the snorkeling area with just a pair of tennies tucked in your swim suit for walking on rocks and thorns, or tow a gourmet lunch in a styrofoam ice chest lashed to a boogie board. I swam Moloka'i, Nā Pali, and Waipi'o to Waimanu. Later, traveling in a kayak, I missed that underwater scene and oneness with the sea.

Paddles

Before choosing a paddle, decide on your purpose, your probable speed, and what boat you'll be using. Know whether you'll be paddling on ocean, surf, calm or rough water, racing or cruising. Long paddles with large blades require more power from the paddler; they give more distance per stroke but wear you out sooner. Paddle lengths are given in centimeters.

Many paddles are imported to the islands, and Hawai'i boat designers often make good ones to go with their specific craft. Consulting the builder of your boat has many advantages. You can talk over your purpose, the boat design, your size and strength, whether you'll be racing or cruising, and the cost. For selecting a paddle you cannot surpass the general advice in John Dowd's *Sea Kayaking* (see "Further Reading").

If you will be paddling long distances and long hours, the weight of a paddle matters. An extra pound that you push through an arc for five hours of paddling adds up to 9,000 pounds a day. A paddle needs to be very efficient in the water to justify that tonnage. Some inflatables need a longer paddle to reach over the fat sides. Narrow surf skis take a shorter paddle to swing through the arc of the stroke faster.

If portability while traveling is a big factor in your choice, you may want one with a center joint and detachable blades. One high-tech paddle I used on a 300-mile trip was made of carbon graphite and Kevlar. It broke down into four pieces, could be feathered left- or right-hand control, and weighed only 29 ounces. It cost $227. The efficiency was about 15 percent greater than that of an aluminum-shaft, plastic-blade paddle made by Sevylor. The Sevylor paddle has been modified by several people in Hawai'i. Its lightweight aluminum-tube shaft has been replaced with a stronger one, and the center plastic joint has been replaced with a foot-long inner core of aluminum tubing. Each end of that core has an added push-in button that lets you rotate the outer shaft and change the angle of the curved blade in order to shift quickly from an unfeathered to a feathered position of the blades, with either right-hand or left-hand control. The blades unscrew from the shaft, so they can be set at whatever angle you choose, usually 80 degrees from vertical. The whole paddle breaks down into five parts, which are easily packed in a duffel bag. Weight is 36 ounces and cost is $27.

Only you can decide which is best for you, balancing the difference in cost, the weight, and the efficiency. If I'm going high-tech, and also need a four-piece take-apart to fit in a duffel bag for plane travel, I've been pleased with the paddles from Aqua-Bound Technology (see "Sources"). Some local builders are making single-blade canoe paddles of all graphite, and probably within a year we'll have kayak paddles to match that light weight. Buying a locally made paddle gives you the advantage of conferring with the maker to get one perfectly suited for your needs.

What does "feather" mean in paddles? Experts can skip ahead. An unfeathered paddle has two blades parallel to each other. A feathered paddle has blades at right angles so that as one blade is in the water, the other is slicing through the air to minimize resistance. The control hand holds tight (not a death grip) and raises and lowers the wrist joint to turn the shaft in the loose ring of thumb and fingers of the other hand. An unfeathered paddle will give you a slight push from the wind if you're traveling downwind, as all of the trips in this book are designed to do. It is also less likely to afflict you with tendinitis from all that wrist flexing. Even going upwind, the feathered paddles are advisable only in winds of 10 to 25 knots. Below 10 you don't need to feather; above 25, the wind can spin a feathered paddle right out of your grasp or, if you're gripping tightly, can flip you and your boat. One blade at 80 degrees to the other seems to give most of the advantages of feathering without the drawbacks. If you have a paddle that changes from feathered to unfeathered by pushing a button and rotating one-half of the shaft, make sure that the center joint moves easily as it rotates. One of the well-known paddle brands has such a tight joint that I have to lie on my back and brace the paddle blade between both feet in order to rotate it to a feathered position. That's hard to do in your boat at sea.

People who race the narrow, tippy surf skis nearly always keep their paddles feathered with a right-hand control, so that they always know exactly where each paddle blade is in relation to the water surface for a fast brace or other control stroke.

This book is not intended to teach you how to paddle. Taking a class or individual lessons is strongly advised, but Table 2 gives a summary of strokes. David Seidman's book, *The Essential Sea Kayaker,* has excellent chapters, sketches, and photos on all aspects of paddling. Even after lessons, you'll need Seidman's book for continuing to practice.

Rental Boats

Ten years ago you could only rent boats to go down Nā Pali coast on Kaua'i. Now, O'ahu, Moloka'i, Maui, and the Big Island all have sources, and each island has companies or clubs that also lead trips. Check "Sources" in this book, and also check the Yellow Pages under "Boats."

Shipping Your Boat

If you live on the mainland, already own a hardshell boat, and plan to paddle in Hawai'i, is it worthwhile to ship your boat over here? That depends on how long you will be paddling here, how strongly you prefer your own boat, and how the cost to rent or buy a boat in Hawai'i compares to the cost to ship your own.

Shipping conditions and companies change rapidly. You'll need to start phoning in your own city to learn the current costs. Look under "Freight" in the Yellow Pages. You might check with kayak builders here and on the mainland to see if they get a cheaper rate.

What is the best way to ship your boat between the islands? No question here if it's by water. We have only one tug and barge company, and happily, Young Brothers is reasonably priced, prompt, and honest. You can tie your hardshell to the overhead beams of the company's shipping container so the boat will not be mashed by shifting

Table 2

Stroke Review

Stroke Name	Use to	Main execution points to remember
Beginning Forward Power stroke—*(other technique points become important AFTER you have become comfortable with this stroke in your boat.)*	Move forward/ make easy turns	SET-UP: Bottom arm fully extended Top hand starts 1 ft. outside of eyes POWER: Keep blade face perpendicular to your line of pull AT ALL TIMES. Pull with the bottom arm and push with the top—ONLY till blade gets to your side, then lift blade out to the side.
Reverse Power stroke	Stop, move back, slow and turn simultaneously	Begin with blade flat on the water behind you. Do not "over-rotate" the blade face.
Forward Sweep	Turn more quickly than with a forward stroke	Plant blade close to the boat. Keep top hand low. Push water to the side rather than pulling back.
Reverse Sweep	Turn more quickly than with a forward stroke	Plant blade close to the boat. Keep top hand low. Push water to the side rather than pushing forward.
Low Brace	Provide stability/ recover from imbalances	Back of blade flat to the water. After the slap, twist blade (knuckles up!) to exit water.
Sculling Low Brace	Provide stability/ recover from imbalances	Keep leading edge elevated only SLIGHTLY. Abrupt twist at the end of each sweep.
Draw	Pull your boat sideways	Fore-arm on Fore-head. Abrupt 90° twist at end of power phase.
Sculling Draw	Pull your boat sideways	Fore-arm on Fore-head. Tilt leading edge of blade out SLIGHTLY on each sweep. Abrupt twist at end of each sweep.

Courtesy of Bob Twogood

cargo in rough seas. When you make a reservation, get a booking number. Otherwise your freight can be bumped. Also get the bill of lading number so that your boat's arrival and unloading can be tracked on the company's computer. Currently a 14- to 19-foot hard-shell travels for about $30 each way from Oʻahu to the Big Island.

See the table on kayak shipment between the islands in "Sources" for a listing of ports and airports. The best sources of information on shipping boats are the local designers and dealers who do it most often. Check also with Polynesian Air, which ships cargo and boats by air.

2

꠸

Gear

What You Need to Paddle Hawai'i

In the 1960s, Mike Doyle and Rusty Miller, two iron man surfers, as they were called then, before a triathlon took the name, swam the length of Nā Pali coast on Kaua'i in three days. They had only swim trunks and one knife apiece. At the other extreme, a group of kayakers took the same route a few years later, and on the first night had a five-course dinner with five wines, candles, tablecloth, and place cards. The second night they all showered under a waterfall and dressed up for a Chinese dinner. The third night they were entertained by a Tahitian dancer, who was one of the group's leaders.

Only you can decide what paddling equipment is essential, useful, or just nice to have. Safety comes first. After that, you can be spartan or luxurious. To choose the right equipment for your trip, you (one, two, or more) must be clear on the purpose of the journey, its length, your probable paddling speed, and whether this is to be a deluxe expedition or a minimum gear and foraging trip.

The list of equipment includes more items than you will need on any single trip described in the "Where To" section. To stretch your paddling budget when buying gear, follow the TS principle—use thrift shops. You can probably get all but 12 items on the list at garage sales, swap meets, or one of the 60 thrift shops on O'ahu and the other islands. Of course you also have to balance out the time involved. If you are just visiting Hawai'i, you probably won't want to spend time assembling gear here, so do it before you arrive. Boats might be one exception. It certainly is possible to buy a used kayak here, which can cost less than half the price of a new one. On your return to the mainland, you can sell it here and save shipping costs. On every island now it is possible to rent a kayak for about $25 to $40 a day, but you should arrange rental in advance if for more than one day. You might contact people in one of the local kayak clubs about rentals, or if you have time, place an ad in their newsletter for what you want. Spend money on plane fare and the boat, and save on or improvise other gear. George Dyson, in his great book *Baidarka*, says, "Don't buy anything you can make, and don't make anything you can find."

Hawai'i doesn't have the big camping and mail order stores found in mainland cities. Discount, chain, and department stores carry an assortment of sports gear, but some of it is useful only for car camping. Where specialized gear is not available in Hawai'i, I'll say so. Then you'll need to bring your own, borrow it locally, or buy it in advance. The "Sources" section at the end of the book lists addresses.

GEAR LIST
This is the deluxe list. Add or subtract as you see fit.
Items with an apostrophe(*) are needed for a swimming trip
without a boat.

SHELTER AND SLEEPING
  *tarp or plastic sheet
  *nylon cord
  tent and seam sealant
  hammock
  sleeping bag or substitute
  air mattress or mat
CLOTHING
  *fast drying shoes, reef walkers, or strap sandals
  felt-soled tabis
  zori (for camp)
  *swimsuit/underwear
  T shirt, part synthetic
  long sleeve shirt, synthetic
  *jacket and pants, foul weather jacket
  shorts

*wet suit vest
pareu/lava lava/sarong
hat and gloves
bandanna

PERSONAL
towel
*sunscreen
toiletries kit
*first aid kit
portable toilet
sunglasses, polarized with UV filter

PHOTOGRAPHY
camera and film
waterproof containers
tripod

TRANSPORTATION
boat and paddle
life line
*fins, mask, snorkel
air pump (if inflatable boat)
water pump (if boat is decked or has hatches)
repair kit
maps and map case
tide chart
compass
tow line (floating line like polypropylene)
life jacket
self rescue system, float bag
drogue
emergency signals
VHF radio
*waterproof bags, stuff sacks
duffel-type travel bags for plane
cartop racks and line
kayak wheels

MISCELLANY
weather radio
notebook, pencil, pen

binoculars
*small flashlight
underwater flashlight
extra batteries and bulbs
candles
lantern and fuel
fishing gear
lighters
magnifying glass
small pickax, machete, saw
sheath knife
*Swiss Army knife
books
waterproof watch
KITCHEN
stove and fuel
fuel bottle with spout
stove pump if needed
grate for open fire
water bags
bowl, cup, spoon
cooking pots
nylon net
detergent
roll-up table
*food
*water purification system
rubbish bags
kitchen box
coconut grater

Shelter and Sleeping

By the time you go off camping from a kayak you have probably done car camping and backpacking. If you're unfamiliar with the fundamentals, see "Further Reading," and start with one night in your own backyard or in a nearby camping park.

In Hawai'i some kind of *tarp* is a basic necessity. It will shelter your kitchen and gear from rain, wind, and sun. It will be a place for your friends to meet and to eat, a place to put your pants on in the morning instead of standing on your head in a tent, a place to cook and to store gear out of the rain, a place to study maps and to make reasonable, considered decisions, not soggy ones. For years, going solo without a tent, I used only a sheet of heavy, clear plastic, rolling a rock in each corner as a knob to tie a cord around. I've even got by with a painters' drop cloth, $1.50 at the local chain drug store. Opened to its flimsy extent, it measures nine by twelve feet, but you can leave it a six by nine double thickness and use it as a cover for a simple lean-to made of slanted driftwood and covered with more fallen branches to hold the drop cloth in place. No, it isn't tall enough to stand under, but solo, you can sleep and cook out of the wind and rain.

You can buy proper tarps of lightweight, coated, ripstop nylon with grommets along the sides, but I've never seen them in the stores in Hawai'i. Locally, you would need to either mail order them from catalogs or order the material and make your own. Campmor of Saddle River, New Jersey, carries a variety of sizes, and REI carries one (addresses in "Sources"). I make my own from ripstop coated nylon yardage, a grommet kit, and ribbon ties. Seal your felled seams. Ten by sixteen feet is a useful size. You can buy reinforced blue plastic or the more durable gray tarps in Hawai'i but they are bulky for a kayak. My stuffed tarp sack is five by eleven inches and weighs four pounds, including lines and tarp.

Whether you make or buy a tarp, it should have a loop of cloth tape sewn in the center on the top side so you can tie one end of a 20-foot cord to the loop, tie the other end of the cord to a rock, and toss the rock over a high branch. Then you pull on the rock to lift the center of the tarp into a roof peak to shed those sagging puddles before tying off the corners to trees. You could get the same shape by using your paddle as the center pole of a four-sided roof, and thus eliminate the need for an overhead center tie, but a sudden gust of wind could lift the tarp and drop the paddle into your pot of simmering stew. A center tape loop on the inside would enable you to hook in a light bungee cord around the paddle.

Another rig is to drop the tarp's windward side low to the ground as a windbreak, stake the corners down, drape the center across a 12-foot

An easy way to rig a tarp is to use your paddle as a center pole.

stick or across a line lashed horizontally about five feet off the ground between two trees, and raise the other side high enough to walk under. Rigging tarps can be great fun for the engineers in your group, who may rig a whole village of parabolas, domes, wings, and walls—hut building like Saharan nomads—while your chef cooks dinner. With two basic knots, the bowline and the taut line or rolling hitch, you can slack off or tighten up quickly on the rigging lines. Carry at least 10 lengths of *nylon cord*. It doesn't need to be huge stuff. One hundred feet of one-eighth-inch line will do. I usually cut two 20-foot lengths, five 10-foot lengths, and two 5-foot ones. If you're super organized, you can color code the different lengths with tape or paint. Melt the ends so they won't unravel.

On a kayak trip the *tent* is probably only for shelter from bugs and rain while you sleep. If you are car camping at a beach park as a base for day trips in your boat, then a big, standing-room tent that you carry in the car trunk, and that will sleep six is practical. But if all the gear is going into two duffel bags as luggage on an airplane and through the hatches of your boat, then you need to get down to sausage sizes. My current tent is the L. L. Bean Ultralight, free-standing, needing no stakes except for the rainfly; it is great for Alaska, but I'd

Rig your tarp with a back wall for shade or for wind-blown rain.

prefer one with more ventilation for Hawai'i. This one costs $150, weighs six pounds, and fits in a five by 22 inch sack. It's possible to find tents at four pounds with shorter poles. Research those by Sierra Designs, REI, and Walrus. Make sure it has no-see-um fine-mesh netting; Hawai'i mosquitoes are small. *Seal the seams* of any tent and carry extra sealant goop with you.

If you need branches for tent stakes or a lean-to, use guava when available. It's a hard, useful wood, but it proliferates like a weed and crowds out native plants that may already be endangered. If you don't know guava, ask someone or look it up in one of the books listed under "Further Reading," chapter 5.

A small selection of tents is for sale in Hawai'i. The locally run Bike Shop, a Honolulu sports shop, and several department stores carry a limited variety. Most of us here get ours by mail order. As an alternative to a tent, consider a tarp plus a small netting rig that fits over only your head and shoulders, the ultimate in ventilation. Hawaii Outdoor World carries them for about $30.

If you don't carry a tent and are concerned about small critters that scamper or undulate on the ground (like cockroaches and centipedes), you may want to sleep off the ground in a *hammock*. Small

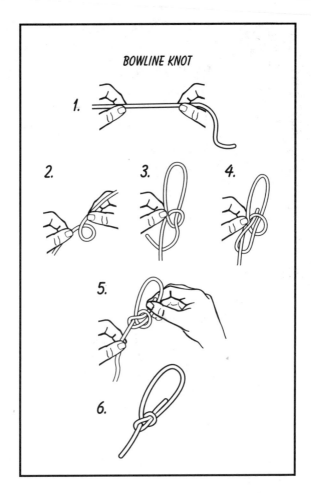

Bowline Knot

1. Hold the line between the thumb and forefinger of each hand, with about three inches of line between your hands and about five inches of the line beyond your right hand.
2. Bring your right hand in front of your left, making a loop an inch in diameter. Hold it between the thumb and forefinger of your left hand.
3. With your right hand bring the right end of the line into the loop from the back, then behind the standing part.
4. Put the end of the line back through the loop. Let go with your left thumb and forefinger.
5. Hold the standing part with your left hand. Pull the larger loop and the end of the line with your right hand.
6. The finished knot.

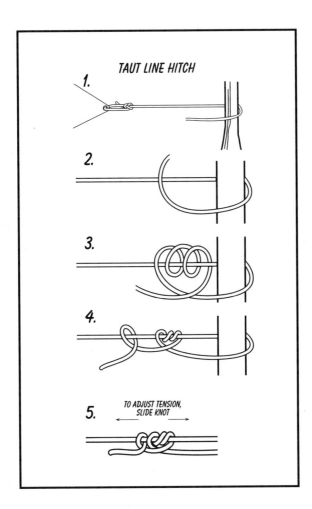

TAUT LINE HITCH

1.

2.

3.

4.

5. TO ADJUST TENSION, SLIDE KNOT

Taut Line Hitch (Rolling Hitch)

1. Use a bowline to fasten the line to the grommet in the corner of the tarp.
2. Bring the end of the line around the tree.
3. Wrap the line around itself once, twice, and three times.
4. Take the end of the line back toward the tarp and wrap it around the taut line, making a half hitch. Tighten all the turns around the taut line.
5. Now you have a knot you can slide along the taut line, making it tighter or looser, to tighten the tarp or to slack it in order to tighten another corner. It's a useful knot for adjusting the lines to a rudder or in places where you need to have a knot that will slide when you want it to, but will grip tight when you let go.

nylon mesh ones are fist sized and cost about $8; they are available locally. You could get cold when the wind blows so you will need insulation under and over.

When it comes to *sleeping bags* and improvisations, you don't need much. At sea level in Hawai'i the temperature rarely drops below 65 F. Most mainland-style bags are too hot and far too bulky. One choice is a zip-around-pile bag, sold through catalogs for about $40. You could make your own sewn-around bag for about $20. An army poncho liner works well if you can find one. So does an old lightweight polyester quilt that you sew up around the foot and side. You may sleep warm enough in just sweatshirt and pants. I made a bivy sack to keep my sleeping bag drier and cleaner on three-month trips in Alaska; I use it in Hawai'i by itself as a warm weather sleeping bag. The top is uncoated ripstop nylon, the bottom is coated ripstop—in different colors to easily tell the difference. If it rains in the night and I'm not under tarp or tent, I just roll over.

You don't need much ground insulation, but some softening of sand and lava is necessary. Some people are addicted to their self-inflating *mats*. I wouldn't travel without my three-quarter-length *air mattress*. Stebco made the best ones, but lately it has made only six-pound full-length ones. Watch for used ones.

Clothing

You need some kind of *shoes*. Leaping out of a boat onto thorns, coral, or rough lava doesn't work, even with the thick calluses that Hawaiian kids get from going barefoot. Fast-drying, synthetic running shoes or tennies and *socks* work fine. Hightops save your ankles from boulders and keep out more sand and gravel. Leather never dries, nor do cotton socks. If your route requires scramble landings on slippery boulder shores with surf, you'll need the gripping quality of *felt-soled tabi*, available in local fishing supply and kayak stores for $15 to $40. Some have sock tops and split toes, which may chafe the tops of your feet. You'll also need to wear some soft split-toe socks underneath (stocked here at Japanese-style department stores); otherwise, tape molefoam or moleskin around your toes. In camp or on the plane, the all-Hawaiian footwear is a pair of thongs, also known as *zori*, slippers, or go-aheads, sold everywhere for as little as three dollars. Be aware that the all-rubber ones are lethally slippery when wet, and that kiawe thorns go through half-inch soles with ease. The tougher, thicker zori with wide nylon straps are best.

All-nylon racing *swimsuits* dry fast and can double as underwear. If you are too shy to appear in Speedos or a bikini, then try nylon or Supplex jogging shorts with a drawstring tie for use in peeling surf. You'll probably want a V-neck *T-shirt* for coolness, and a *long-sleeved shirt* for sun protection. My favorite is the Patagonia silkweight, Capilene crew neck. White shirts keep you cooler but show dirt faster, a reasonable tradeoff. Again, choose a fast-drying material. You will get wet while paddling, so take one outfit, *jacket and pants*, that you wear on the plane and carry in waterproof bags during the day, then put on in the evening. Even 70 degrees is cool when it's windy. A nylon knit warmup suit works well. Mine is TS. Jeans are a poor choice—bulky and slow to dry. On one September trip along the north Moloka'i coast, I was glad to be wearing my hooded *foul weather jacket*, which kept me warm and dry while paddling in rain and wind and twelve-foot seas.

Shorts are practically a uniform in Hawai'i. They should be loose, stretchy, fast drying (nylon or Supplex material), and have deep pockets. Don't carry your car keys there: If you *huli*, no more keys unless you've attached them with a big safety pin.

If you plan to do much diving, or if it is to be a swimming voyage, then a sleeveless *wet-suit vest* is worth taking. It will keep you warm during several hours in the water, will increase buoyancy, and can be used as a sleeping pad at night. Because of its buoyancy, I sometimes grab three or four rocks and stuff them inside the vest when diving as an instant, disposable weight belt.

An all-purpose garment is the *pareu*, the Tahitian version of the Samoan lava lava and the Indonesian sarong. It is simply two yards of cotton/polyester cloth that you (male or female) wrap around your hips or (female) drape in a dozen different ways from neck and shoulders. If you have been in Tahiti or Samoa, you will know that in various styles and materials, it is a formal and informal garment for males. Large Samoan chiefs, legislators, and football players wear them; so does my six-foot fireman son, and no one calls their pareu a skirt. You can use a pareu as a towel, as a flowered tablecloth, as sun protection

A pareu is an all-purpose garment for male and female.

for your legs while paddling, or in ten other ways. It is a good example of making everything you take do triple duty.

You'll need some kind of *hat* to keep the sun off. If your hair is long enough to cover pate and nape, then a visor cap may be enough. If not, a brimmed hat is advisable. Rig a line with a spring-loaded cord lock to cinch it under your chin on windy days.

Most people need a pair of *gloves* to prevent blisters. Polypropylene glove liners dry fast and work well. You can also prevent blisters by taping the bases of your thumbs with moleskin or molefoam.

A *bandanna* is also multipurpose. You have to fold it double for an effective coffee filter. Red or orange ones are colorful in photographs, as signal flags, and as placemats.

Summary on clothing: it is the easiest, bulkiest stuff to cut down on, so when the pile of gear won't fit in the kayak, start reducing here.

Personal

This list is also brief. The *towel* can be part-synthetic for quicker drying, or thin and all-cotton to better dry you, or you can use the pareu. An all-synthetic Pak towel can also be used as a sponge in your boat. For half the price try a synthetic chamois from an auto supply store. *Sunscreen* should be protection factor 15 or higher, and waterproof. Check *Consumer Reports* and talk with local lifeguards for recommendations. I like a local product called Beaver. Keep it accessible while you're paddling and don't forget to apply it under your chin—water reflects the sun upward. Remember that skin damage from the sun is cumulative and permanent. I'm blonde, have had three basal cell carcinomas removed surgically, and am always alert. You'll probably want a separate lip salve with sunscreen. A *toiletries kit* can be very simple.

A *first aid kit* should first of all include the knowledge you get from going through some kind of certification course. You can improvise a lot on a trip, but not that. Repeat the course often. A five-year-old CPR course is more than half-forgotten and a quarter-outdated. If you are a group leader, you need more than the basics: Take at least an advanced course, and preferably have some EMT training. My own kit also includes a tube of antiseptic ointment, a prescribed pain killer, butterfly tape closures, gauze pads, tape, and hydrogen peroxide to scrub coral cuts. I have also added Sting-Aid, which contains ammonium sulfate and gives relief from nearly all bites and stings. It certainly worked on a recent wasp sting. Include a mosquito repellent to smear or spray on, and a pack of the local mosquito coils (pyrethrin) to burn for their repellent smoke. Also in my kit is the four-by-six inch, two-ounce booklet *The Pocket Doctor*, by Stephen Bezruchka, M.D., published by The Mountaineers of Seattle.

Polarized, ultraviolet-filter *sunglasses* are both necessary protection and useful to cut the glare on the water so you can see the rocks and fish. Mine, purchased from L. L. Bean's fishing department, have magnifying lenses in the lower half, and let me read my maps without shifting to reading glasses.

A portable toilet can be as simple as a Tupperware box or a PVC tube with one solid end and one screw-cap. See chapter 7 for a more complete discussion. You can't just crap on the beach anymore. Hawai'i isn't big enough and the beaches just can't handle that kind of impact. One person, once a year, on a mile-long beach was once possible. No more.

Photography

For some people this is the main purpose of kayaking, the boat only a platform for the camera or a way to take it to some spectacular place. You have several choices for a *camera*: one that's waterproof, or a non-waterproof one with a housing or carefully protected from moisture. My workhorse camera for years was a Fujica HDS, but now the company no longer makes or repairs it. Your waterproof choices have a wide range in price and sophistication. For about $14, you can buy a plastic-boxed instant camera made by Fuji or Kodak, which is designed for use in snorkeling and in bright sun. You turn it in, camera-and-all, for development. The top of the line at over $200 may well be the Pentax 1QZoom 90 WR (for water-resistant). You may want one camera with color slide *film*, and a second camera with black-and-white or color print film.

A dedicated photographer who is kayaking primarily to take photos will have several cameras and lenses, and a variety of *waterproof containers* to keep the cameras and film dry—ammo boxes, plastic boxes with a seal, plastic envelopes with finger insets, and inflated pouches. So far there is no waterproof camera that will take a long telephoto lens, though some such as the Pentax 1QZoom 90 WR and the Olympus Stylus will give you about two times magnification. "Waterproof" is a relative term. Read the instructions carefully to see if it only means splashproof. Some go down to ten feet deep, the Minolta Weathermatic to thirty, but as far as I know only the Nikonos goes deeper without a housing.

A *tripod* can be as simple as a two-ounce, $10 one with a Velcro strap to wrap around a stick or branch if the camera needs to be higher than the tripod's four inch legs. Some tripods are as heavy and bulky as your tent. For serious work on shore with an 80 to 300 mm zoom lens I use a monopod that weighs ten ounces and telescopes down to 20 inches long. Check also on the tripod Slik 5006, which is one and a half pounds, and is eighteen inches long when closed.

Light meter and housing, a variety of cameras and lenses—photography can dominate a trip. Some people opt to leave all cameras and all food (horrors!) at home and go only with a clean, aware mind.

Transportation and Navigation

Fins, mask, and *snorkel* are essential to nearly every small boat expedition in Hawai'i. Aside from snorkeling and scuba diving, you'll use them for anchoring, for retrieving items dropped overboard, for food gathering, for teaching beginners to swim (it's much easier with mask and snorkel), and for body surfing (fins only). Finally, chopping onions for that giant bouillabaisse is tearless if you wear the mask, and smoke from the cooking fire doesn't get in your eyes.

Fins can be small and flexible or huge and stiff. Suit yourself. Unless you're scuba diving, you don't need big stiff ones. It's better if they float. Masks need to have a soft edge and to "suck on," stick on, when you put them on your face without the strap and inhale. Snorkel Bob has a store on each island in the tourist areas where you can find a hundred masks hanging on the wall ready for you to try on and to buy or rent. To keep masks from fogging up as you go into the sea, rub the inside of the glass with a bit of seaweed, tobacco, or the always-with-you spit, then rinse. Masks come with a glass lens that is nearly unbreakable. Don't buy a mask with a plastic lens; it always fogs. They are supposedly safer, but they don't work. Snorkels need to fit your mouth; some are for megamouths and are a strain to hold in your teeth. I have rarely found a snorkel with a purge valve (which supposedly lets water out the bottom) that didn't leak more than it purged, but perhaps you have. Experts insist that it is worth spending $40 for a mask that really fits, but for years I happily used a thrift shop

$2 Squale. Most dive or snorkel shops will have information about masks with prescription lenses built into the glass. Tie your mask to your body or clothes in some way if you're coming in through surf, because masks don't float, and without the mask you can't see to find it on the bottom. Most fins don't float either, but a pair of fin keepers will attach them to your ankles. You can buy these or improvise.

Boats and paddles are covered in chapter 1.

If you have an inflatable boat, you'll need an *air pump*. You have two choices, a bellows-type foot pump or a tall, cylindrical hand pump. The foot pump may need a lot of weight to force enough pressure. For my hypalon boat, which requires four psi, I'd have to pick up a 50-pound rock to make me heavy enough, so I use a cylinder type. On trips, because of bulk, I carry a smaller version, which takes up half the space and takes twice as long (about 10 minutes) to inflate my 13-foot boat.

When your car is at the put-in spot, you can use a pump that attaches to a 12-volt battery or plugs into the cigarette lighter. It is faster and requires less effort, but you must still carry a nonelectric pump with you for field repairs.Make sure you have the nozzles to fit all the valves on your boat. Tahitis have three valve sizes on a single boat.

Unless you have a totally self-bailing kayak without bulkheads and hatches, you'll also need a *water pump* for leaks or flooding. They cost about $14 and are very lightweight. Test out different models for efficiency.

Obviously, the *repair kit* contents will vary with the type of boat you're using. No matter whether it is fiberglass, folding, inflatable, wood, or plastic, you'll probably need the following items, in addition to appropriate patching material: duct tape, electrical tape, a small pair of vise grips, a couple of bronze snap hooks, spare stove parts and manual, dental floss to use as strong sewing thread, a small can of lubricant, and assorted screws, nuts and bolts, D-rings, plugs and cotter pins.

Going solo means being self-reliant, so every March I assemble the gear, do repairs, buy replacements, and make up the repair kit. See Annie Getchell's book in "Further Reading" for how-to and check lists. And yes, I do carry an unusual repair item, condoms, which are useful to replace the rubber in a spear gun, waterproof your watch or film, or make a slingshot. You can use an orange one as a crab trap

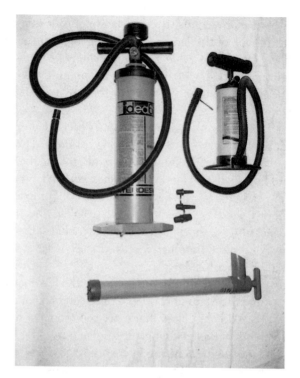

Large and small air pumps for inflatable boats, end valves for the tubes, and a bilge pump to get water out of your boat.

float, or tie several together end-to-end as a long, super strong rubber band.

Maps could be a chapter in themselves. Some people take one to bed with them and fall asleep poring over the contour lines around that little hidden cove and waterfall. In Hawai'i the NOAA (National Oceanic and Atmospheric Administration) sea charts are not nearly as useful for kayakers as the USGS (United States Geological Survey) topographic land maps. The charts are mostly of the harbors in the cities, or of such a small scale that they aren't useful for daily planning. I really don't need to know if the depth below me out at sea is 60 or 600 feet. At six feet I can see the bottom. Deeper than that I can drown.

The maps, though, show both urban and wilderness areas and are 1 to 24,000 scale (about two and a half inches to a mile), giving very good detail. On many charts, the first land contour line is 200 feet high, but the shape of the land is of absolute importance to a small-boat paddler. The larger scale topographical maps usually have a 40-foot contour interval, which is an improvement even if it doesn't indicate whether you can land or whether those 40 feet are straight up from the water.

For overall route planning, start with James Bier's reference maps of each island, published by University of Hawai'i Press. They are regularly updated, show a detailed network of roads, hiking trails, beaches, and parks. They spell the Hawaiian names with all pronunciation marks, which can change the meaning of a word. For example, *lanai* means stubborn, *lana'i* is a veranda, and *Lāna'i* is the name of an island. The meanings of some place names are included in the "Where To" section. For a more thorough discussion, see *Place Names of Hawaii*, listed in "Further Reading."

When you have decided on a route, refer to the Geological Survey Index to Topographic Maps of Hawai'i, American Samoa, and Guam. It is free for the asking at places that carry the topo maps. On it you can find the names of the quadrangle maps you'll need for your route. You'll also find a quad maps listing in each voyage description in the "Where To" section of this book. All of these maps are available in Hawai'i. See "Local Sources" for the address of Pacific Map Center on O'ahu, the best local source for maps of all kinds.

You will need a *map case* to carry them and to keep them dry but visible for constant reference while you paddle. The simplest case is a two gallon ziplock plastic freezer bag, with a tab of duct tape to put a grommet in, or you could buy a heavier, longer-lasting one with foldover closures and attachment grommets. Some map cases are designed for yachts, three by four feet, too big for the deck of a kayak. You can buy fancy waterproofing for your maps, or you can use a hardware store waterseal, brushing it on both sides and letting it dry thoroughly.

Unless you're an old hand at interpreting maps, get the USGS Symbols and Abbreviations key, free at map stores, and take it along so you can translate all those little squiggles and colors. For example, what is the symbol for a cave, for an intermittant stream, an abandoned building, a coral reef?

The extreme tidal range in Hawai'i is less than three feet, so tides are not a major consideration. Still, it's good to have a *tide chart* with you for the calendar and moon phases. The charts also show the increase or decrease in tide time at different locales in the islands, which varies as much as two hours.

You won't often need a *compass* while kayaking in Hawai'i. We have no fog, but you might be caught in a downpour that cuts visibility to less than a mile. The compass will be of most use in land explorations, since a jungle can be very confusing.

A 1,000-pound test *towline*, 30 feet long, should be carried, at least by the leader of a group. Short lines are fine for rigging tarps and securing gear, but you need a long, strong line if towing should ever be necesssary. Towing, *life jackets*, a *self-rescue system*, a *drogue*, *emergency signals*, a *VHF radio*, a *cellular phone*, and an *EPIRB* are covered in chapter 3, Safety, and chapter 4, Wind and Surf. A GPS (global positioning system) would only be necessary if you're doing a Pacific crossing like Ed Gillet, who used a sextant, before a GPS was available.

Whether you're using an enclosed, cockpit craft, an open deck kayak, an outrigger canoe, a folding boat, or an inflatable, you will need *waterproof bags* for gear. Enclosed boats with bulkheads require bags small enough to fit through the hatches. Bag varieties include heavy six mil garbage bags or trash compactor bags with tops folded over and then tied; PVC or coated nylon bags in various brands and sizes with foldover tops and straps with quick release buckles; and heavy, clear vinyl bags, some with tubes you blow into to inflate the bags for flotation after packing gear inside. I've found that the coated nylon ones fold smaller and last longer than those of PVC.

Use several sizes of nylon *stuff sacks* with drawstrings and cord locks inside the waterproof bags to separate gear, to stuff sleeping bags, and perhaps to organize by color. For example, pack breakfasts in yellow, lunches in green, dinners in blue, emergency gear in red. Stuff sacks can be homemade for a tenth of the commercial cost.

To carry your gear on airplanes you'll need *travel bags*. Large, army-style duffel bags, or long, side zipper, cylindrical bags, or waterproof raft bags with backpack straps all work well. Some newer ones have wheels at one end, a great help when the bag contains boat, food, tent, and gear for a week and weighs 60 pounds. A lightweight nylon zip bag that measures only one foot by two can be used to carry your smaller items from shore to campsite, leaving your hands free for larger bags. All travel bags should have wide straps to fit over your

Boat bag with wheels, folded duffel bag with zipper, and boat wheels for the end of your kayak.

shoulders. Use the big, bulky bags on the plane but leave them in the car or with your land transportation support team. The small nylon bag rolls up fist size to take along.

To transport a hardshell kayak on any island, you will need *cartop racks*. Soft racks have foam rollers, straps, and gutter hooks and are easily transported in your luggage when you fly to another island. If you are going to rent a car, specify one with gutters. Take *line*, at least 1,000-pound test, to tie down the bow and stern of the boat to the car's bumpers. Soft racks are not enough. Only specifically designed boat racks, professionally fitted to your own car, such as those by Yakima and Thule may be used without tie downs at the end of the boat. Recently a car with a 19-foot surf ski on top, traveling at 45 miles an hour, lost racks that were riveted through the roof of the car. The rivets pulled out, the boat uplifted like an airplane wing, lost its cords, handspringed down the road, and speared through the windshield of an oncoming car, neatly between the driver and passenger. It was not tied bow and stern and this is not an advisable part of the sport.

Cart wheels that attach to one end or fit under the center of your kayak are very useful if you'll be doing much solo wheeling around on pavement or down boat ramps; they're less useful on soft sand or boulders.

Miscellany

A *weather radio* costs about $15 and gives detailed forecasts for land and marine weather wherever you can receive the local NOAA weather service broadcast.

You can buy little rainproof *notebooks* made for surveyors, or carry a journal, or write on the back of a map, but some way of recording the trip to remember it years later is well worth the effort if the trip is. Besides, you may want to write a guide book.

Binoculars are not only fun to use; they add to your safety. From an angle out at sea you can watch the surf break on shore and decide if it is a level you can handle, find the opening in a reef, or spot the missing paddler in a group. Watching whales, porpoises, and birds is much better with binoculars. The price of waterproof ones used to be in the $300 range, but now those with a magnification of 8x30 are about $170 and a 7x21 pair at $90. Many companies make waterproof binoculars in different weights, power, and prices. Canon, Fujinon, and Zeiss also make them with an image stabilizer, so you can use them even when your kayak is bouncing in choppy seas. You'll need to research price, weight, and cost of batteries, and balance these factors against your own needs. IS binoculars may cost as much as your kayak. As with cameras, you can always check the discount stores.

Flashlights have gone high-tech—lithium, cadmium, Krypton, indestructible, waterproof. When shopping for one, compare the number of hours they burn on one set of batteries. With a Halogen bulb, you get a brighter light but shorter battery time. With a Krypton bulb, you get a softer light and double the battery time. Some flashlights have one bulb of each type so you can switch according to your need of the moment. Princeton and Petzl are two of the high-tech brands. To free your hands for cooking or for reading in bed and to stop drooling around one held in your teeth, try a flashlight with a three strap headband. You might also try to choose a flashlight that uses batteries the same size as those that power your camera and your VHF radio, so you can carry one size spares for all three.

Night diving requires a lot of light. *Underwater flashlights* have also improved in the last 10 years. You can find a wide assortment at local dive shops. No, the price hasn't gone down.

Candles are romantic but don't give much light. The little lanterns with spring-loaded candles carried by most outdoor stores for about $16 give protection from the wind. Your spares are useful to drip onto wood as a fire starter. It takes four candles to read by.

Lanterns are far more necessary in Hawai'i than in higher latitudes where summer twilights are long and it may not get dark until 11 P.M. When the sun goes down in Hawai'i, you need to be parked for the night, because it will be dark in half an hour. The latest sunset in summer is at 7:15 P.M. and the earliest in winter is 6 P.M.

Your lantern should be fuel-compatible with your stove if possible. Be aware that airlines have strict rules about carrying flammable fluids and gases or even empty stoves and lanterns. Call for guidelines before you fly. Alcohol for stoves is usually permitted. Carry spare mantles and have a case for your lantern. The shield around the lantern is glass, so wrap a piece of foam around it inside the case. I then put mine—a Gaz lantern without the cannister—in a plastic bag inside the sleeping bag. Try out the fluorescent lanterns that run on batteries. They are less fragile and don't have fuel supply or airline problems. Batteries take less space and are safer than fuel, but more expensive. Consider choosing a headlamp instead of a lantern. A new stove/lantern combination by Primus has a metal mesh latern top—no glass, but still has fragile mantles—and weighs less than one pound. It uses a butane-propane cartridge and costs $150.

Fishing is such a major sport and livelihood in Hawai'i that it is hard to recommend specific gear. Stop at the nearest fishing supply store and get advice, then talk to all the people you see fishing en route. Rod and reel, throw nets, spears, hand lines, and traps are a few of the many methods. Buy a copy of *Hawai'i Fishing News,* on sale at newsstands and at many country grocery stores. I've successfully trolled a lure that dives as you tow it but floats to the surface when you stop so that it doesn't snag on coral. Several kinds of rod holders that fasten to the kayak are available. Keep in mind that all Hawai'i is overfished, so don't expect great results.

For a look at what you're trying to catch, go to the Aquarium in Waikīkī or to Tamashiro's Market on North King Street. Check also with the State Fish and Game office for a handy digest of regulations to take along.

Lighters are superior to matches. I prefer BIC for longevity and reliability and hate childproof ones. Carry one in your emergency kit, one double-bagged in a pocket of your life jacket, one with your stove, one with the lantern, and one in the repair kit.

A folding, multi-lens *magnifying glass* is an addition worth carrying. After days of thousand foot cliffs it is a relief to have the perspective of examining a spider's eye. A glass with 5x to 20x lenses takes a cubic inch of space, weighs one ounce, costs about $12, and goes in your first aid kit for removing thorns.

The small *pickax* is used for husking coconuts (see chapter 5), and a *machete* is generally useful, though dangerous in unskilled hands. A folding buck *saw* or pruning saw is more versatile than a hatchet. The "Sawvivor" folding saw is the most efficient one I've used. It weighs 10 ounces and costs $30. A *coconut grater* with its seat can be taken along, or you can unscrew the metal grater part and find a piece of driftwood to screw it onto once you have found the coconuts en route.

A knife seems to be a very emotional object, a weapon not a tool, maybe because of an atavistic human desire for claws or talons. One kayaker says, "There are good reasons for a *sheath knife*. First, on boats, you don't need two hands to get the blade out, and there can be situations where you don't have two hands available because you are hanging on with one, and you need to cut a jammed knot, *fast*. Second, they are safer in use. The grip is larger and more secure, especially with the modern, contoured, non slip surface." If you have a favorite knife, take it, or take more than one for special jobs. On any kayak trip, I am attached, literally, to my *Swiss Army knife* by a lanyard to a belt loop. You borrow it, I come with it (after one snapped-off blade and one total loss). A simple tool for cleaning it after you get home is a Water Pik. Used full blast with warm water, it will clean out sand, dirt, and hardened peanut butter; it also gets the lint out of pocket corners.

A *wrist watch* is essential. Mine is a $10 Casio, "water-resistant to 50 meters," adequate for snorkeling. A 25-meter resistance was okay for a shower but not for even a 10-foot-deep dive.

Some people carry a library of *books* on anthropology, plant and fish identification, cuisine, coconut weaving, and other references. Some take novels while others prefer to simply absorb the surroundings. The only books I think essential are John R. K. Clark's four-volume series *Beaches of Oʻahu, Beaches of Maui County, Beaches of the Big Island,* and *Beaches of Kauaʻi.* Packed with history, legend, beach conditions, and safety information, they are the best addition to this small guide. See "Further Reading" for publication information. My copies are all salted, battered, frequently borrowed, and treasured.

Kitchen

Local people may take only fishing gear, a grate, and a pot to cook rice. Others may carry only granola, a bowl, a spoon, and powdered milk. But for cooking a variety of food on long trips, you need some kind of *stove,* because the supply of driftwood on the beaches is scanty. Many trips are on the wet sides of the islands, and trying to cook with wet wood under a tarp in the rain and wind is difficult. Every camper has a favorite type of stove, ranging from a pocket-size heat tablet stove ($3) to a two-burner gasoline or propane one. Basically, there are four types: alcohol, white gas, bottled gas, and multifuel. Alcohol stoves burn clean, silent, and slow, and you can carry the fuel on a plane. Trangia is one brand. Kerosene stoves are safe; they don't explode, as gasoline stoves supposedly do, but I haven't seen a pure kerosene stove for a long time. See "Further Reading" for more discussion. Also, the October 1996 issue of *Backpacker* has a fine comparative article on multifuel stoves. My square box, white gas Optimus 8R has been with me for 24 years. It has never exploded, does not simmer well, and is more reliable with fewer dangling parts than any I've used. It weighs two pounds, a bit heavy but worth its weight. I will probably wear out before it does. My son uses a 1952 Optimus, older than he is. Another favorite with many campers is the MSR WhisperLite Internationale 600, a white gas stove weighing only 14 ounces and using a fuel bottle as its tank.

If you are using liquid fuel, you will need a *fuel bottle.* Yes, it's worth buying a proper anodized aluminum one instead of using a rusty, recycled paint thinner can. If the fuel has to be poured into an integral stove tank, a pouring *spout* ($3) that screws onto the fuel bottle works well and saves carrying a separate, fuming filter funnel.

Paddling solo, you'll find that a quart of fuel a week is plenty, even with heating water for a shower. Yes, most gasoline stoves now can use the cheapest unleaded automobile gas. It will burn with more smoke and soot and less heat, but is one-fourth the price of Coleman or Blazo. If a pump is not built into your gasoline stove, a *mini stove pump* ($8) makes the stove easier to light so you don't have to play Aladdin by warming it in your hands.

Richard McMahon (*Camping Hawai'i*), among others, prefers butane stoves. His reasons are clearly explained in the book, along with much more information on shoreline campgrounds than I've included. I find the cost and the bulk of carrying out canisters prohibitive on two-month trips, but their efficient simplicity makes them preferable for a week. Pair your butane stove with a butane lantern that uses the same size canister. See the note under *lanterns* for a combination.

Some people who combine car camping and kayaking do all their cooking on charcoal in a hibachi. Lightweight ones, not cast iron, are in many stores in Hawai'i. Other people take a small fuel stove for pot cooking and do all their fish on a grate over campfire coals. If you do build a fire, make it on sand or rocks below the tide line and, below the vegetation line. Like the peat of Ireland, the organic soil of the forest floor burns; a smoldering fire can travel underground for weeks and then burst into a forest fire. When through with your fire, put it *out*, until you can stir the remains with your bare hand. Too many little kids have walked into a bed of hot coals on the beach that was only lightly covered with sand. Turn over the sooty rocks, and scatter or burn up any charred wood. You don't need a big *grate* for one or two people; one by two feet is enough. But you do need one-inch mesh for 'opihi (see chapter 5).

Save and recycle the aluminized plastic bags inside bulk wine boxes for use as *water bags*. See chapters 1 and 5 for more uses. Make your own cloth sack to hold the wine bag, with a handle for carrying and a hole for the spout. Using black material makes the sack a solar heater for a warm shower.

A *bowl*, *cup*, and *spoon* are minimum eating utensils. Plastic wine glasses are a nice touch, and fish really needs a plate if accompanied by rice or fruit. Check the menus and carry whatever cooking pots you will need. On a month-long solo trip I carry two nesting pots; the lid

Boxed wine bags are tough! Here, one is inserted in a carrying bag for water, one is air-inflated for a seat, and a spare is rolled up.

of the larger one serves as a skillet. On group trips you can divide larger skillets, pots, griddles, and a kettle among several boats. Aluminum is lightweight, and Consumer's Union research has shown that it would take 900 years of using aluminum to accumulate any discernible amount of it in your body. The research has found no connection between aluminum and Alzheimer's disease, either. Even though in a hundred years cast iron might benefit me, I'm not carrying that.

Nylon net serves as scrubber and bug strainer. Buy a yard of it at your local dry goods store (80 cents) and cut off a square foot. A *mild detergent* can be used for dishes, shampoo, and showers.

You may want to carry a *roll-up table* if there are several kayaks. A table is very handy to cook on if you can't find a plank or piece of plywood for a kitchen counter. They cost about $35, weigh 10 pounds, and roll up to 6 by 32 inches. They are not available locally.

A *water purification system* is necessary. See chapter 5. *Food* is happily described in chapter 5 and packing it is covered in chapter 6.

Rubbish bags are necessary to carry back everything you don't eat or burn. Carry assorted sizes, some with ziplock tops for wet garbage. You could even be a noble kid and bring back 10 items of other people's trash. If a place is dirty after you leave, all kayakers look bad, though kayakers really don't have space in their boats to bring in cases of beer and spray paint for graffiti as one park official alleged. People remember a kayak and forget who else was there.

Make or improvise a soft-sided *kitchen box* to contain stove, cooking pots, implements, and basic breakfast items. Inside, use small snap-lid plastic boxes hold an assortment of instant soups, beverages, and condiments. What size kitchen box will fit through the hatches or slide in from the cockpit? Most of the boats I paddle have an open top

Top: *Two kitchen boxes. A stove is inside the sooty, square pot at left. At bottom and right are food bags with cord-locks.*

with velcroed-on pack-cloth top decks, a real advantage if you're load-
ing almost daily on a three-month trip. Use a lidded wooden box, a
tackle box, a tool box, a soft-sided cooler, or sew your own with inside
pockets. It really helps to have all the basic gear in one place so you
can stop mid-morning or mid-afternoon for tea or espresso, or have
the first course of soup or beverage ready twenty minutes after you
land for supper.

Getting It All in the Boat

Gear freaks could go on forever. Do a sample packing of your boat at
home, well before an expedition, not the night before, to see what fits
in. See chapter 6. A beamy single kayak in a calm sea or a double can
carry a load of 300 pounds plus paddlers. Some boats can carry only
half that, and towing a second kayak as a trailer doesn't work.

3

≋

Safety
Rules, Hazards, Rescues

A mainlander might ask, "How there can be safety problems in Hawai'i? The water is warm, the winds blow from one direction, the tide range is only three feet, there is no fog at sea level, and it must be calm in those tropical lagoons and inside those reefs in the 'pacific' ocean." All of those statements show some degree of misconception.

Three major dangers exist in Hawai'i for kayakers: wind, surf, and sun. Going back to the preceding paragraph: Yes, the water averages 72 degrees F, but that is 26 degrees below body temperature. Immersed, you might last 10 hours. In a kayak where you're wet in the spray and rain, and the wind is blowing, hypothermia is certain, but will just take a little more time than in more northern waters. An air temperature of 65 with a 30-knot wind equals a wind-chill temperature of 51 Fahrenheit, 47 degrees below body temperature, which is certainly enough to make you lose consciousness if you have no waterproof, windproof clothing. This is on dry skin. What are the calculations for wet skin?

Yes, the winds often blow from one direction. On the windward side of an island you will be blown toward shore. On the other three sides you'll be blown out to sea. One channel is aptly named Kealaikahiki, the way to Tahiti. Other wind directions and full gales are not uncommon, and each year the National Weather Service issues many small craft advisories. In anything more than a 20-knot wind, any kayaker less than expert is advised to stay ashore. More about wind is in the next chapter.

To me or to a tree, the boat is always secured.

4. LEARN TO SWIM IN ALL CONDITIONS: in surf, in rough water out at sea, in currents. Be at ease using fins, mask, and snorkel. The fins give you three times the speed and power, the mask lets you see the rocks under the surface and keeps water out of your eyes, and the snorkel lets you get a breath between the waves washing over your head. In Hawaiʻi my fins, mask, and snorkel are always clipped in the boat close at hand, or else I'm wearing them. The mask is tied to a shoulder strap and is often on my forehead while I'm paddling. Some fins float. Masks sink. I've said this already. Someday I'll learn it.

Rip currents, where water flows out to sea in a channel, often occur between two surf breaks. To get out of a rip current, angle across it and come in where the breaking surf is moving toward shore and can push you in. When you do get your feet on the sand, there can be a strong backwash of receding waves on a steep beach, but an "undertow" that pulls you down is a myth.

Body surfing is a good skill to learn in case you lose your boat in the surf. It teaches you to handle yourself in breaking seas and in rough landings. Turning seaward to dive under a breaking wave allows you to escape most of its impact. If you do lose your kayak don't get between it and the shore. When being washed ashore onto boulders, try tucking into a ball to help protect your vital organs. Keep one hand over your mask to protect the glass, the other arm behind your head. It's also useful to go limp like a piece of *limu* (seaweed) until the wave washes you up on the rocks, then grab them and scramble up higher before the next wave. On boulder beaches, most of the rocks are rounded from tumbling in the surf. Watch that your ankles, toes, and head are protected from these basalt bowling balls. Next time, plan a better landing place. Nearly always some jutting point will have a lee of calmer water. Be especially wary of ledges when swimming. A wave can wash you onto one and scrape you off like a grater. A sheer cliff in calm seas is safer to swim beside. The water level just rises and falls with some cushion effect as the water washes back, but stay well clear of the turbulence of breaking waves against cliffs.

Is it absolutely necessary to be an excellent swimmer before you go kayaking? At the risk of loud shouts of protest, I say that it's not. I would take my sister Marge anywhere, in her life jacket, and in calm conditions. She is only a fair swimmer, but her judgment is excellent, her panic button is nonexistent, and she follows directions precisely. And in my boats, all guests follow Rule 2, Life Lines.

5. KNOW THE BASIC FIVE OF FIRST AID. Restore breathing and heartbeat. Control bleeding. Dilute poisons. Immobilize fractures. Treat for shock. For more confidence, for leading a group, for going solo, and for sorting out major injuries from minor, get advanced certification.

6. LEARN TO USE THE EMERGENCY SIGNALING GEAR. Practice in advance. The items on the gear list in chapter 2 are discussed later in this chapter under Rescues.

7. DO A SHAKEDOWN CRUISE BEFORE AN EXPEDITION. With any new assortment of paddlers, or with a new boat, you need at least a brief precruise. If you are the leader, you need to assess each member's boat handling skill, swimming ability, self-rescue skills, gear, and general attitude. You may need to wash someone out of the trip rather than endanger the group.

8. GET THE LOCAL KNOWLEDGE about currents, winds, landing, and camping sites. Asking humbly for advice makes allies. Be aware though, that powerful motor boats, deep-keeled sailboats, and six-man canoes are not kayaks. Ask "What if you were in a small dinghy?" and "What if you were in a boat 24 inches wide with a six-inch draft?" and "Who are the local kayak and one-man canoe experts?" Check with lifeguards and kayak rental shop personnel. They know where people and boats get crunched.

9. GET THE WEATHER REPORTS before you go, and tune in your weather radio frequently en route. It's the marine forecast you want.

10. FILE A FLOAT PLAN. Keep one copy of a detailed itinerary with you, and leave one copy with a local friend or family. Leave instructions on what to do, whom to call, and how many hours leeway to allow if you do not get back on time. Include in your float plan the names and phone numbers of the paddlers, a description of the boat(s) with length, color, identifying hull names or numbers, and a list of the emergency gear you have on board. Even if you are only going for a

day, leave a note of launching and landing places and your planned return time. Add all the above information if your trip is for more than
a day or if it is to include open sea conditions. Your float plan should
also include where your car will be parked. If the car's gone after the
time you're supposed to be back, your family or the police will assume
you got back and neglected to close out your float plan.

11. GO THROUGH THE "WHAT IFS." Each time you prepare for
launching, go through a list of the horrible possibilities. What are the
alternative landing sites? Brainstorm to come up with all the worst
scenarios, and then prepare for them.

12. STAY WARY. That is how animals survive. You, too. Conditions
change rapidly. Surf can go from two feet high to 10 feet in an hour.
Rain can fall at six inches an hour, turning a gurgling stream into a
muddy torrent, and slamming whole trees into your campsite. Flash
floods in Hawai'i kill people. Be triply cautious if you are paddling
solo.

Hazards

What hazards are there in Hawai'i? They are the same here as in a
small boat anywhere in the world, though some hazards are less severe
because it's not as cold in the islands. You can drown, get bashed, be
harmed by excess heat or cold, or by animals or plants. Your gear can
get banged up, wet, lost, or stolen. Here is a look at dangerous land
and marine animals, at harmful land plants, then at some of the other
perils that you're likely to find in Hawai'i. Wind and surf will be discussed in chapter 4.

Land Animals, Small to Large

Mosquitoes here are Aedes and Culex, not Anopheles; they do not
spread malaria. We have bees and wasps; use the same precautions as
elsewhere. The islands have no ticks that carry human diseases and
there are no chiggers, no-see-ums, or sand fleas. Cockroaches are numerous. They're best controlled in a long-term camp by sprinkling

boric acid tablets, and short term by using insecticide or stomping. Spiders? Not to worry unless you have phobias. The big, brown house or cane spider is shy and gentle and eats mosquitoes. Like the golden orb garden spider and the small red-shelled spiny spider, the cane spider is nonvenomous. We do have an occasional centipede. Its bite is painful, so avoid putting bare hands and feet in piles of old lumber, leaves, and rocks, and shake out your shoes if you've left them outside your tent. I put the big ones I find in the freezer to show my kayak classes. They bite with two curved front "claws" next to their mouths, not like the rare and tiny local scorpion, whose tail hook makes a very mild sting.

As a paddler you are unlikely to meet wild pigs. They live back in the forests and will try to avoid you, attacking only if cornered.

The largest land animal dangerous to man is man, but no more so in Hawai'i than elsewhere. In beach parks or other inhabited areas, pitch your tent inconspicuously, away from entry roads, and near local families. Take special care on Friday and Saturday nights, when most beach parties take place. When you get your camping permit, ask for advice about that particular park. It is the young guys who are on drugs or drive in with three cases of beer in the trunk who are going to cause problems, if anyone is.

Newcomers always ask about "growers," but marijuana does not flourish near salt water, and growers want to avoid you, so they are not a threat to paddlers.

Thefts from parked cars, especially rented ones, are a major problem. Often you can arrange with a local family to leave your car in their yard at your launch site. Or talk to a hotel manager about leaving it in a patrolled hotel parking lot. Just don't ever leave anything of value in a parked car, not even in a locked trunk.

Most local people are amazingly helpful. The concept of *aloha* is real and true, not just a tourist word. Many of us who live here feel that the drawn-out, fakey pronunciation "alooooha" is repulsive, but we still use the real word tenderly, among ourselves.

Marine Animals, Small to Large

The most dangerous marine animal in Hawai'i is less than two inches long. Ten times more deaths have been caused by the 'opihi, the Hawaiian limpet prized for its flavor, than by all other marine animals combined. The story is repeated several times each year. Someone climbs down a cliff or out on a rocky point to pick the treasured *'opihi*, where it clings at tide line in the surf; an unexpected large wave washes him off the rocks, and he is smashed by succeeding waves or drowned for lack of swimming ability in a rough surge. If you want *'opihi*, look for some in a quiet cove on a very low tide. More on these limpets in chapter 5, Food.

You can learn to recognize the two poisonous cone shells (*Conus textile* and *Conus striatus*) and the various scorpion fish, and avoid them. If you do pick up any unidentified cone shell, hold it by the large end, since the poisonous barb is at the small, mouth end. Their poison is as strong as rattlesnake venom, but they are rare.

Three other small dangerous marine animals are more frequent. One is the little Portuguese man-of-war, a deep blue, two-inch jellyfish with tentacles below and a transparent bubble on top that acts as a float and a sail. Since it has one tentacle up to 10 feet long and several shorter ones, and each one has thousands of stinging nematocysts, contact can be very painful. You may swim into one, or even pick one up on your paddle, but you are more likely to step on one on the beach where they are blown ashore. The standard remedy for its sting has always been to apply a paste of unseasoned meat tenderizer (on the spice shelf in most grocery stores). The tenderizer contains the enzyme papain, the digestant found in papayas. It was believed to soften the protein of the tentacles and stinging cells. A newer and more effective remedy is a product called Sting-Aid, containing aluminum sulfate. It comes in a spray bottle or in a smaller daub-on tube, $6 and $3. Many dive shops and kayak stores now carry it for use on all types of marine organism stings. One writer suggests applying shaving cream and gently shaving the area to get rid of the clinging cells.

A second common injury in the islands comes from stepping on or washing against a spiny sea urchin. One small species, *'ina*, lives on the reefs and in the tide pools. A larger species with short black spines, *hāwa'e*, lives in deeper water, collects debris on its back, and can be picked up by hand. A third type, *wana*, pronounced "vuhnah," has long black or striped spines, which have a nasty habit of penetrating skin and then breaking off. They are found most often in rocky cracks in deeper water, but sometimes in wading depth as well—an-

delicious. Just handle them with gloves or have someone else peel them. The fruit is not toxic, only the skin, and only to a few people. Eating the fruit seems to gradually diminish the skin sensitivity.

Oleanders and milky sap shrubs are poisonous. Don't use them for hot dog or shish kabob skewers.

The most common plant injury is a punctured foot from stepping on thorns of the kiawe ("kee-ah-vay"), the most common tree on the dry sides of the islands. Wear shoes or thick slippers.

Sunburn

The most frequent injury to visitors and to kayakers, and the most easily prevented, is sunburn. Cover up and goop on one of the water-proof and effective sunscreens now available. Here in Hawai'i close to the equator and with no smog, you'll burn twice as fast as in most mainland areas. Recoat after swimming or sweating. Beaver and Banana Boat are two effective brands.

The minimum PF, protection factor, depends on your skin. A factor of 15 is usually enough, but consider the length of time you'll be out, your previous exposure, and your skin type.

Sarah Preble and author cover up against sunburn.

Traffic

If you're going to do a lot of paddling around Oʻahu, or in and out of boat harbors, stay aware of marine traffic. Keep to the edges of channels, watch for the wakes and courses of powerboats and sailboats. Jet skis have increased and often are not in responsible, skilled hands. Those plus wind surfers and water skiers racing around, mean that the kayaker has to be very wary in congested areas. Go Bananas Kayak shop near Waikīkī sells a flag holder that attaches to your kayak to hold a diver's flag or a fluorescent orange banner for visibility. Unloop the life line, stay visible, wear a red cap, and when all else fails and collision seems imminent, dive deep or try an intentional *huli* (capsize) to get your boat hull between you and that propeller.

Earthquakes and Tsunamis

A few years ago a group of us hiked into Halapē on the southeast coast of the Big Island within the Hawaiʻi Volcanoes National Park and checked it out as a landing site for a possible voyage down that very rough coast. A week after we left, another group of campers there was awakened by an earthquake. When it settled down, so did the campers. An hour later the strongest earthquake of this century in Hawaiʻi shook the ground with a magnitude of 7.2 on the Richter scale. Within a minute, the first of five high surges of a locally generated tsunami washed over the site. Two of the campers were killed, one by a rockfall, the other washed out to sea and was never found. The land subsided 10 feet, wiping out the coconut grove where we had camped the week before.

Episodes like this are extremely rare, only three in 40 years, but it is wise to remember that it can happen. If you are on shore in a severe earthquake or if you see the water suddenly receding from its normal level, you should head immediately for higher ground. Most people have the comic-strip concept of a tsunami as a single, hundred-foot wall of water. Except in a funnel-shaped bay, where you might have an upward compressed force with you at the small end of the funnel, the tsunami will probably be a series of water rises with the prevailing surf height on top of that water level. In March of 1957, 11 different waves in two hours came up into my North Shore yard, went under the

learn if BCs and inflatable belts have been approved. You may have to choose between what's approved and what is most suitable for your purpose.

Here is a step-by-step method of getting back in your boat. Practice in calm water until it becomes automatic. After you capsize, swim to the side opposite the point where your life line is clipped on, leading the line over the top center of the upside-down hull. Put one knee up on the hull, a pull of the line rights the boat. Next, bail or pump enough water out of the boat so that it will not roll like a log when you need it stable for reentry. This is not a problem with surf skis, wave skis, sit-on-tops and other self-bailing boats, or with most inflatables since they don't ship much water. If your boat is beamy and flat-bottomed with a large cockpit or if it is an open top, reentry is easier. The basic idea is to kick your legs up to a horizontal position, push down on the far gunwale with one hand, and boost and slide your body in on the near side with the aid of the other arm. If you have a mainland-style, enclosed sea kayak, you may need to get onto the rear deck of the kayak on your belly, facing the stern; then slide your feet and legs into the cockpit and roll from a face-down to a face-up sitting position. The object is to avoid flipping the boat upside-down again. If you have a long, narrow enclosed craft or even an open surf ski, it may be very difficult to get back aboard without doing just that. Then, you'll need some kind of outrigger to stabilize the hull while you get in.

Several paddle float systems are possible. Basically the float keeps one end of your paddle supported in the water; the other paddle blade lies flat across the boat and is attached at right angles just behind the seat. Because I prefer a system that doesn't require three minutes or more of inflating a float by mouth while treading in cold or rough water, I carry a waterproof bag of coated nylon with a roll down edge and a Fastex buckle on the back deck of my kayak. Unstuffed, it measures 21 by 34 inches. Stuffed, its first purpose is a back rest; its second is as a waterproof sack for sleeping bag, Ensolite pad, and clothing. Since these items need to stay dry, they get the best waterproof bag; they are lightweight and can be carried on deck without compromising stability; they are bulky so I need to get their bulk out of the limited space in the 13-foot boat; they contain enough air to allow the bag to float high in the water as an outrigger/paddle support when it is released from its bungee cord. The bungee is hooked at each end to a

Here, a life line is rigged as a stirrup for reentry. The far side needs to be steadied by another paddler.

An inflatable kayak rigged for rough seas with a spray deck. A gear bag is lashed on behind the seat.

D-ring on each side of the boat. The bag itself has a six-foot cord that is coiled beneath the bag and has a snap hook on each end. One end is atttached to a grommet on a bottom corner of the bag and the other to a D-ring on the side of the boat.

After capsizing, right the boat. Assess whether or not you'll need the extra stability of a paddle float. Nearly always, yes. Unhook one end of the bungee cord to let the bag float free, tethered by its six-foot line. Rehook the free end of the bungee. Place one paddle blade under the bungee cord on top of the boat and the other blade on top of the floating bag, tucked under its carrying strap. So now you have an out-rigger, a small double hull, which steadies the kayak and keeps it from rolling. You place one hand on the far gunwale of the boat and the other hand on the paddle shaft. Boost yourself into the boat, keeping your weight on the float side so as not to roll over on the unsupported side. A paddle float reentry is shown on page 127 of Randel Wash-burne's book, *The Coastal Kayaker's Manual.* You can adapt the basics of this system for other boats and floats. Refer to "Further Reading" for other books with chapters on self-rescue.

In lieu of that bag on deck, I have used an Ensolite pad that folds flat in six layers. A pair of big rubber bands (made from an old inner tube) go around the pad, and the paddle blade slips between the lay-ers. A no-cost float is made of two slightly inflated boxed wine bags with their edges sewn loosley together on three sides. Those single

A waterproof gear bag as a paddle-float for self-rescue. Note the clipped-on life line.

bags can serve as a seat, as spare water bags, as floats for your folding fish trap, as buoyancy bags in the bow and stern of a hardshell kayak, and as a dozen other useful items. They can be folded into a tenth the size of the stiff plastic water jugs, and their price is right. Opinions of the original contents vary considerably.

When you practice self-rescues, start in shallow water or in a warm swimming pool with an empty boat. Then progress to actual rough water self-rescues with all your gear. I practiced with clothes, boots, foul weather gear, and a fully loaded boat out in the seas in front of my house in 25 knot winds until I could dump and get back in 10 times out of 10. The water was warm enough for continued practice. After 3,000 solo miles, I did capsize in iceberg waters in Alaska, and the self-rescue did work. Yes, I had clipped the paddle to the boat, the boat to me, and the float to the boat, and no, I was not strangled or tangled in the three lines. In 23 seconds I was back in the boat. Then I pulled the float bag onto my lap, paddled to shore, changed clothes, and got warm. Practice!

Group Rescues

These have been covered in other publications, and the ones that work elsewhere also work in Hawai'i, and without the urgency of getting the victim out of 50 degree water. Practice group rescues, including towing, on your shakedown cruise. Towing seems to work best from two boats or from one boat with the tow line fastened to two cleats, with one on each side of the rescue paddler, with the two Y-arms of the tow line meeting behind the rudder of the rescue boat. A bicycle inner tube tied between two sections of tow line seems to take up some of the jerking caused by wave action. If the person being rescued is totally unable to steer or control his boat, it will be necessary to put another paddler alongside to steady the rescuee's boat. If a double kayak is on the trip, shifting the incapacitated paddler into the bow of the double may be necessary.

Rescue from Other Sources

Under horrible conditions or in case of severe injury, you may have to look for rescue from outside your own resources. Smoke and aerial flares, dye markers, a waterproof flashlight, a VHF radio, a mirror, a cellular phone, and an EPIRB (emergency position indicator radio beacon) cover most of your choices for alerting rescuers. The smoke and aerial flares should be the kind you can hold in your hand. Aerial flares are more visible at night; they only last about 10 seconds but shoot up 100 feet or more. Parachute flares last longer. Orange smoke flares may be better for daytime use. Don't just shoot off flares blindly. Wait until you see someone who will probably see you. Along many coast lines in Hawai'i there are daily commercial planes and helicopters, and on other routes there are small commuter airlines. Check your route in advance and compare it to scheduled plane routes. Before paddling from Hāna to Kahului route I phoned a pilot friend who flew that route, so he could look for any distress signals. Remember that pilots have the nose of the plane in front of them. You have to signal while they are still able to see down, that is, when they are at least a mile away. In most cases they are going to be looking up and around for other planes, not down at the sea for kayaks.

The county fire departments in Hawai'i usually handle rescues within a mile of shore; they are alerted by a dispatcher in response to a 911 emergency phone call. The Coast Guard handles offshore searches and rescues. The agencies work together and overlap when necessary. They cannot help if they don't know that you are in trouble, or where you are. A VHF radio enables you to have two-way communication with a boat or plane or the Coast Guard. The November 1996 issue of *Practical Sailor* gives results of testing of eight "waterproof" VHF radios. Some were *not*. According to the article, "a waterproof warranty does not necessarily mean that a product is waterproof, only that it will be repaired under warranty should it be damaged by water." A lot of good that will do you, holding a flooded radio in your hands when your life depends on getting a message out. The clear winner in the *Practical Sailor* article was the Icom IC-M1. Look in the Yellow Pages under "Marine Electronics." Kems Kewalo on North Nimitz Highway in Honolulu carries them for about $310.

An EPIRB simply sends out a distress signal on international emergency frequencies and pinpoints your location. EPIRBs are expensive ($200 to $800 plus) and are rarely used by kayakers here in Hawai'i, where other faster, simpler communication is available. A newly available EPIRB conveys to the Coast Guard rescue center by computer your boat name and description, your name and home address, and will get an immediate response by rescue teams. Price is about $800.

Several kayakers now carry a cellular phone in a waterproof bag. If you already own one, bring it along, remembering that they are not equipped for direction finders to locate them. Unless you know where you are and can tell your rescuers, they won't know where to look. Cellular phones also have a limited distance range. The signaling devices described are available at marine supply stores in Hawai'i and at kayak shops. In any real emergency you'll want all seven rescue systems.

The fire department and the Coast Guard are primarily concerned with saving your life. Depending on conditions and the size of the rescue boat, they may be able to tow or carry your kayak. Certainly it will help if you have an accessible tow line and a strong fitting on the bow for attaching a line. A *de*flatable kayak has an advantage.

Final Thoughts on Safety

Follow the rules and suggestions. Add more of your own. Carefully evaluate your experience and ability. Err on the safe side. Drive carefully. The automobile trip to and from shore is the most dangerous part of your kayak journey.

A drogue can slow your wind-blown drift out to sea. (Photo courtesy of Rick Warshauer)

off the hillside at unpredictable intervals. I had a hard time clawing
back to shore in my high-performance fiberglass boat—had I been in
an inflatable, I don't think I could have made it." It may have been
the Āpaʻapaʻa wind of Kohala. Ask paddlers of the outrigger canoes
and crews of the sailing canoes at Kawaihae about the *mumuku* wind.

A Hawaiʻi Bound wilderness program crew in a four-man outrigger
canoe farther south on the Kona coast of the Big Island *was* blown out
to sea several years ago. They simply could not make headway against
a strong, offshore wind at 6 P.M. Seen from shore and rescued by a
small fire department boat, they had to abandon the canoe. A rumor
said it washed up in the Marshall Islands, months later. Captain Cook
rescued even native Hawaiians who were being blown out to sea in
their canoe off the Kona coast.

In Hawaiʻi you should not be far at sea. Island hopping across channels is not a reasonable kayaking endeavor here. Fom Maui to Lānaʻi,
eight miles downwind, is feasible for experienced paddlers who carefully consider wind and seas that are higher once out of the lee of
Maui. Crossing between other islands means 10 to 60 miles of fun-
neled and accelerated channel winds and seas that can squirt you out
to oblivion. Crossings have been done, but the kayaks and outrigger

canoes that race across the Moloka'i Channel have escort boats. Greg Blanchette waited three weeks for summer weather to be calm enough for his overnight, 32-hour crossing to Kaua'i from Mākaha on O'ahu.

The safest route is to hug the coast when on the leeward side of an island, and to come ashore before the wind builds to a dangerous velocity. How close is hugging? It's as close as you can get without being in the surf or on the rocks, usually no more than 50 yards out. If you are being blown offshore in spite of your strongest paddling, first put out an anchor if the water is shallow enough. Too deep? Then hang some kind of drogue. You can make one that folds up small and is carried on deck to always have at hand. If you don't have one when you need it, improvise. Hang an open gear bag overboard or your paddle on its leash or yourself, anything to slow down that increasing distance from land. Then get busy with your VHF radio broadcasts, and get the flares and flashlight ready. You are always clipped to the boat with the life line, yes? And you did file a float plan so someone will come searching when you're overdue?

You can make the wind more of an ally if you use it cautiously for sailing. Some kayaks, Klepper folding boats in particular, are designed with sailing rigs, including mast, stays, step, leeboards, rudder, sail, and sheet. Other craft have been modified by their owners, and *Sea Kayaker* magazine has ads for furling spinnakers, for stability floats, and for kayak outriggers. Randel Washburne, author of *The Coastal Kayaker's Manual*, built a 12 square foot, reefable Chinese lugsail with a folding mast step that lies flat on the deck. He uses it along the channels and outer coasts of British Columbia and southeast Alaska, and says it does best across the wind.

George Dyson, author of the book *Baidarka,* has experimented with many different sail shapes for his *baidarka* (Russian for kayak). One of them, a fan-shaped sail, has two halves raised separately from a short cedar mast. His aluminum and nylon boats are longer than most kayaks, faster and more stable, but they still are keelless, narrow craft. In his book he writes, "These craft are designed for paddling directly into the wind and waves, and for running downwind at high speed under sail, rather than compromising these qualities in favor of all-around performance under sail." In other words, he doesn't plan to tack upwind or to sail crosswind.

A swell is not a problem until the wind blows the crests into breaking seas.

The best rule for getting in and out through surf is *don't*. Nearly always you can find an alternative—a bay with a channel, a hook of land that provides quieter water on its lee side, or even just a rip current in a channel where the waves are smaller but the current is not so strong that you cannot paddle against it to shore. Playing around in small surf for fun, when your boat has no gear in it and you have planned the whole caper as a learning process, is one thing. It is quite another matter when the surf is more than six feet high, your boat is loaded with all your supplies for a month, and the shore is solid rock. Another quote from the old salt, "Do not attempt to land on a rocky shore in surf unless all hope for life has already been abandoned." He was thinking of landings in big, wooden lifeboats in storm surf, but the advice indicates the danger.

Planning your route and landing places in advance should make surf bashing unnecessary. Studying the detailed topographic maps and the photographs in the many tourist guides and coffee table books, and making a few phone calls to people who have been over that route, should give you some other choices.

A few people in Hawai'i, such as Bob Twogood, ride surf for fun. That takes a proper boat and experience. The place with the best rideable surf isn't the place they would choose to come ashore to camp.

The surfboards are 11 feet long. How high is the wave? Waimea Bay winter surf with Jock Sutherland sitting casually at left.

Surf Landings

Whether to make a solo or a group landing through surf depends on several factors. What are the options? How far is it to a better landing? How long is it until dark? What is the ability of each member of the group? Is it a rock or a sand beach? What kind of boats do you have, and will they bounce or break? How important is it to get ashore then and there? Do you have the ability to repair a battered boat or body? And finally, can you get back out? What if the surf gets bigger? If it's the middle of September on a north shore, the surf may very well get bigger. If you cannot get back out, is there another exit by land, or is it a cliff-locked shore? Have you time to wait for three days or more until the surf goes down?

Coming in to a shore is harder than going out because you cannot judge the waves as well from the back side and from a sitting position in your kayak, where your eye level is only three feet above the water. To the inexperienced, it may look easier from out at sea, but your view is of the smooth back side of a wave instead of the crashing front side.

If you dump, but you and the paddle are clipped on, you will come in together, even if upside down. Would you be safer not clipped on? It is your choice of course, depending on the size of the surf, the shore line, your clothing, the water temperature, and the boat you're using. In Hawai'i, where so many of the most spectacular, isolated coastlines also have steep, rocky shores, I prefer to come ashore with my boat, in it as long as possible, being towed behind it if necessary. The three-foot loop on the life line makes it easy to slip out of and just hang onto. You might be wiser to unclip the life line and tuck the snap hook end into your swimsuit before entering the surf zone so that you're ready to grab the stern in case you capsize. A toggle handle on the boat's grab loop at bow and stern enables you to grab or let go easily instead of having your hand in a loop that could twist around your wrist. I made my toggle handle from a T-joint of plastic plumbing pipe. One danger of staying clipped on is being dead (figuratively) in the water while attached to a boat filled with 200 pounds of water when said boat is picked up and thrown shoreward or onto the rocks by a few tons of white water. One cubic yard of water weighs one ton. Damage to you could happen before you slip out of the loop. If an inflatable boat bashes you, you survive. Not necessarily so with rigid boats. Unclip the paddle also. It's less likely to be damaged if you're carrying it than if it's fastened to an uncontrolled boat in the surf. Also, your spare paddle needs to be thoroughly attached or, better yet, inside a hatch.

On rocky shores it helps to be wearing wet-suit bottoms and bootees as padding. Shore boulders are usually rounded from tumbling in winter surf. Beware of ledges, as in Safety Rule Four. They are giant graters. You and boat, together or separately, can be washed up and across a ledge by a wave, then scraped and tumbled across sharp rock, coral, and spiny urchins as the wave sluices you back off. I relate this experience, about a Moloka'i cliff and ledge, in *Paddling My Own Canoe*.

All of these dire warnings about surf should be tempered by the words of an experienced paddler who loves surfing his kayak. John Enomoto writes in the Summer 1996 issue of *Hawai'i Skin Diver*:

> Over the years, we have been honing our skills in serious surf conditions, always looking for the best surfing kayaks for Hawai'i. . . . This

their voyages with full awareness of what time of year it is and which side of the island they will be on. Read the previous chapter, evaluate your own ability, and go on an easy trip with an experienced group or commercial trip if you're not certain.

As I was writing the first edition of this book, the mail brought a letter from a man in Iowa who planned to paddle in Hawaiʻi in December and January in a beamy 10-foot inflatable, from Oʻahu to Molokaʻi to Maui to the Big Island. He would have been paddling upwind and crossing 90 miles of channels as rough as any in the world, in the worst choice of boat for those conditions, and at the worst possible time of year. He got a kindly letter back (I still have a copy) about seasonal surf, wind direction, channel conditions, and some alternate shoreline routes. I found out later from a newspaper item that he did come, limited his paddle to the sheltered side of Lānaʻi, and still smashed up on a cliff, lost his boat, and had to be rescued.

Wind and surf and sea are bound together in Hawaiʻi, but the unceasing miracle of a warm ocean, our warm weather, and the great variety of shore lines all make our islands a great place to paddle.

5

~

Food

From Land and Sea to Haute Cuisine

Some of us delight in the textures, colors, and flavors of eating, have a passion for building kitchens from driftwood, smile back at the prismatic rainbows seen through a chilled glass of wine at sunset, and believe that cooking is a great creative art form. We go kayaking in order to find new native foods, new sites to construct a kitchen, new views from an outdoor dining room—and to work off all the calories.

Some backpackers have even taken up sea kayaking because it is so much easier to float the weight of food than to carry it. They forgo fishing, photography, and all the other camping gadgetry in order to make room for their Craig Claiborne recipes, some adapted dishes of Julia Child, the ice chests, and the omelet pan. If you are a kayaker who subsists on Gatorade and granola, you may as well move on to the next chapter, because we are going to talk about *food.* We will forage for some, select from local sources, and look at taking along a five-course dinner. But before you skip over this chapter, read the section on water. We all need that.

This chapter offers only a taste of the possibilities. A bibliography called "Ethnic Culinary Art in Hawai'i" issued by the Hawai'i State Library lists 146 books. One of the great things about the islands is the mixture of races and nationalities. Most grocery stores stock items from local farms, from the whole Pacific rim and islands, from Europe, and from the U.S. mainland. Powdered coconut milk, dried shiitake mushrooms, Italian pasta, Portuguese sausage, passion fruit juice, dried mango, Thai curry—the list is endless. Browsing in a good grocery store is next best to a bookstore.

Basics

Most paddlers have breakfast in camp and have a cold lunch either on shore or while pausing and rafting up together in a quiet cove. You might each take a sack of creative gorp and one of fruit for the trip, so you are free to eat whenever you feel a munchie attack. Remember that in the tropics chocolate bits have a way of melting and gluing the contents to the side of a sack, and that fresh coconut turns rancid in three days at Hawaiian sea-level temperature.

Water

You should also carry your own one or two quart water bottle. You need to put water stops on a schedule so that you will drink frequently. "If you are thirsty, you are already two quarts dehydrated," say sports medicine doctors. Flavoring the water with one of the powdered fruit drink mixes such as Crystal-Lite or Koolaid makes you more likely to keep up your fluid intake, especially if the water came from a doubtful source and you have added purifying tablets or boiled it with the resultant flat taste.

Do you need to treat the water? Unless it's from a municipal source, an unqualified yes. "Three categories of creatures can make you sick if you ingest them: protozoans, bacteria, and viruses." So states an article in the December 1996 issue of *Backpacker*, the best and most up-to-date coverage of the subject I've seen. Most of the information in this paragraph comes from it. Water filter pumps are now available in a variety of sizes, speed, and cost. In *Backpacker*'s survey, the highest rated pump was the PUR Hiker. Boiling works for all three categories of contaminants; you need only bring it to a rolling boil, then turn off the fire. Iodine is still the lightest, simplest, and cheapest method of water purification. It's available as a solution, in crystals, or as a tablet. Iodine, however, is not effective against Cryptosporidium, a protozoan similar to Giardia, but without the cure. It usually runs its course in seven to ten days. Twenty years ago I drank from the streams. Then I read the accumulating literature, and I also found a dead pig carcass upstream. Now I carry a safe supply or carefully treat it.

The municipal water supplies in Hawai'i are safe. Much of our drinking water comes from deep underground sources and requires less chlorination than the river water that supplies many mainland cities. Ours tastes good. Rainwater collected on your tarp is an excellent source, unless you have a very grungy tarp. Collect it from the uncoated side of the tarp.

Utensils

What kitchen items will you need in addition to the basics listed in chapter 2? Check your menus. Some people take their thick aluminum omelet pan, crystal wine glasses packed in foam inside a mailing tube, and a hand grinder for coffee. Be wary of the new little coffee grinders advertised in catalogs. The one I tried took 10 minutes to grind a tablespoon of coffee, so I sent it back. You may want to take a small pressure cooker to save fuel. It sure speeds up the brown rice and the goat stew. Also, John Dowd's *Sea Kayaking* tells how to make a desalinator with a pressure cooker to convert sea water to fresh drinking water.

Shish kabobs are delicious grilled over kiawe coals. On one trip I took along my two-foot-long wood-handled skewers, inserting each one into the hollow aluminum shaft of my take-apart paddle. Each night we had a different kabob, using skewered chunks of fish and shellfish plus varied veggies such as onions and zucchini. Dessert was fruit gathered on the route, skewered, grilled, and flamed with a brandy sauce.

You could take a styrofoam ice chest, using frozen gel packs or filling the chest with frozen supplies, but the cold will only last about three days. If resupplies of ice or places to refreeze your gel packs are not possible, it is still worth hauling the chest. Free foam shipping boxes are often throwaways from hospitals or electronic stores. They are lightweight enough to pack out empty or full of other gear, for reuse on the next trip. Thrift stores and department stores carry soft-side nylon cloth coolers that fold flat when empty. After three days you'll probably be enchanted enough by the wilderness to give up amenities, and you can shift from chilled white wine to beach-temperature red.

Wine bags as utensils are a subject in themselves. What is a wine bag? It's the inside bladder, made of plastic and aluminum foil, which contains the wine in the boxes of drinking wine made by such vintners as Franzia, Summit, and Almaden. The basic size is four or five liters, but in the last two or three years, they've been available in retail stores in one-and-a-half and three liter sizes and in better quality varietals. You don't have to drink all that wine yourself. Have a party, make a wine pot roast using two quarts of a basic red as a marinade. Or better yet, get bags free from restaurants or bars which use these as their "house" wines. Some vintners even have 18-liter sizes; two of those will make a full-length air mattress. Sometimes you can find apple juice in similar containers. Carefully cut away the box, snap off the valve cover, and rinse the bag out with water. Leave the cover off long enough for the bag to air out. See chapter 2 for more uses.

Foraging from the Sea

Many foods grow wild on or near the shore, and they don't freeze and disappear in the Hawaiian "winter." Euell Gibbons, whose book *Stalking the Blue Eyed Scallop* is the best foraging guide for the coasts of Maine and Alaska, came to Hawai'i in 1950. He planned to stay here only long enough to learn about tropical foods and then to move on to the South Pacific. But he met a local family who told him that in the islands farther south every coconut belongs to someone because people depend on them as food and as a cash crop, but here in Hawai'i the population has a supermarket mentality, and much of the food growing wild goes to waste. Gibbons stayed in Hawai'i, learned the local ways to eat cheaply, and wrote *The Beachcomber's Handbook*, which is still the best single source of information on how to find and use free food here in the islands (see "Further Reading"). His thatched shack has been replaced by a hotel and a golf course in Kāhala, and Gibbons died several years ago, but his book and his teachings live on.

Suppose you want to live as a beachcomber on some remote coast or do a walk-swim shoreline trip, towing a tiny pack with only your dry clothes and a plane ticket. What can you find to eat on the islands that will sustain you and still not exterminate any endangered species? Be aware that I've tried it, and found that it would take eight hours a day of skillful, knowledgeable foraging to find enough calories for sustenance.

When you take your kayak on an extended trip, you may not be able to carry enough food for the whole journey and will need to add a bit more from the land to your own chow bag. You may even be on a fully supplied short trip but will find it delightful to add local culinary touches such as drinking coconuts, fresh papaya, and flavorful seaweed.

Remember that just as the rainfall varies from 10 inches a year on one side of an island to 150 on the other side, so does the food available from the land. Most fruits are seasonal. Food from the sea will pretty much stay the same year round, varying mainly in relation to the number of people fishing in the area.

From the sea and streams you can get a healthy meal of fish, shellfish, and seaweed. Fishing is complex and does not provide easy, instant results. The best fishing strategy I've found is to take an expert along on the trip, a capable fisherman who will provide the main course for breakfast and dinner. Your expert will know that many reef fish are subject to Ciguatera, poisonous to humans, and know which ones not to bring in. The Hawai'i State Department of Health has a free brochure listing the affected fish, along with a map showing the shores where poisoning has occurred. None of the deep-sea fish such as tuna, marlin, mahimahi, and ono have been found to carry it, but reef fish such as ulua, palani, kole, wrasse, weke, and menpachi are subject to it. You should clean the fish very well, eat only small portions of those that might have the poison, and not eat the roe, liver, head or guts. Ciguatera poisoning is not common, but it does occur.

What are some island styles of cooking the various fish you get? The simplest method is *pūlehu*. Just score the skin, salt it lightly, preferably with red Hawaiian salt, and lay the fish directly on a bed of kiawe coals—skin, head, guts, and all. In a few minutes turn it over— few culinary items are sadder than good fish overcooked. Lift it off the coals onto several layers of fresh leaves, peel off the charred skin, and eat the juicy chunks with your fingers, washing it down with a frosty bottle of Maui lager. There's minimum preparation, no pots, no dirty dishes. Burn the skin, guts, and bones. Erase your fireplace before you leave the site.

Another method is to fillet your fish and lay the pieces on squares of foil. Cover the fish with slices of fresh ginger root, minced garlic, a

A *small* pāpio. *Good eating.*

slosh of sesame oil, some chopped cilantro or dried dill weed, and a dollop of shoyu (soy sauce). Wrap it snug and set the packets on the coals. In 10 minutes an inch-thick fillet will be done.

You may have more skill in grabbing things that don't move as fast as fish and can be cornered, such as lobster. On Oʻahu most of them are gone, overfished without regard for season or size, but on the remote coasts of other islands you can still see those waving antennae deep in a cave, or find lobsters crawling around the bottom on moonless nights when they come out from the holes to feed. Here is the second use for your pair of gloves. Hawaiian lobsters are not the big-clawed Maine variety, but the spiny kind with most of the meat in the tail. They are photophobic—will move away from light—so use your underwater flashlight only to spot them, and then turn it aside as you dive down to grab. They move backward by flipping their tails, so keep your gloved hand ready to clutch from the back. Getting them out of a cave is more difficult because two long antennae are in the way of your grab, and two sharp spines protrude above their eyes. Be doubly wary if one antenna is pointed back into a hole behind the lobster. Local lore says that it means a large eel is behind it in the cave, and the lobster is keeping track of you with one feeler and of that sharp-

Spiny lobster, minimum size.

toothed eel with the other. I ignored the lore only once. The lobster kept backing up, and I kept reaching without being able to see into the darkness. Result: one finger shredded into three julienne strips.

It is always illegal to take a lobster with eggs, even if you net or trap. Thus, spearing is illegal because you cannot see whether the lobster has eggs until after you've pronged it. If you catch one with eggs, that glob of tiny red beads tucked under the curve of her tail, put her back. Minimum legal size for spiny lobster is about a pound in weight, and with a carapace (from eye to beginning of tail joint) measuring at least three and a quarter inches long. I've seen them as large as 14 pounds. The season is closed between June 1 and September 1, the lobster's primary breeding season.

Crabs are not as populous as in many mainland areas; the seas of Hawai'i are too warm for abalone; there are few oysters or scallops; and the ocean shrimp are too deep. The most prized shellfish are limpets ('opihi). These little flattened-dome single shells cling to the rocky cliffs just at tideline and can be pried off by quickly sliding a knife blade between the 'opihi's strong stomach-foot and the rock. A putty knife or a flexible sandwich spreader is a safer tool. Make a lanyard to attach the knife or spreader to your wrist so you don't lose it when it slips from your grasp. 'Opihi must be at least one and a quarter inches long to be of breeding size and to reproduce themselves, so take only the ones larger that that. See chapter 3 for the dangers of 'opihi picking.

How do you eat an 'opihi? They're best raw, preferably alive and squirming, and they are sweeter and chewier than an oyster. If you insist on cooking your seafood, here are two methods. Put the 'opihi shell-down on your one-inch-mesh grate. Slather each 'opihi with a mixture of butter, minced garlic, and chopped parsley. No parsley? Use ulva, the bright green sea lettuce known in Hawai'i as *limu pālahalaha*. Put the grate over hot coals until the 'opihi comes loose from its shell and the butter sizzles. Lift the grate off the heat, and let the 'opihi cool just enough that you can lift the shell with your fingers. Slide the buttery morsel into your mouth and close your eyes. No other senses should compete with that heavenly taste and texture. No grate? Put the same sauce mix into a flat pan and simmer the 'opihi belly down. Either way it is 'Opihi a l'Escargot and it is 'ono, delicious. Limpets occur worldwide, and I have used these cooking methods in Alaska, France, Scotland, and the South Pacific. I look forward to Chilean limpets.

Another edible shoreline shell is the tiny, round black nerite, the *pipipi*. You can scrape off a potful, steam them briefly in water to cover, then laboriously pick out the meat with a safety pin, and in half an hour have a quarter cupful. The broth is the best part.

Hā'uke'uke is the little, flat purplish-black petal urchin that clings to rocks in the splash zone. Out in deeper water are two larger species of urchin, more worth the effort of gathering them. As with all sea urchins, it is the orange eggs you're after. When you talk of urchins, you'll be better understood if you use the Hawaiian names. The short-spined *hāwa'e*, the collector urchin, can be picked up with bare hands. The longer-spined ones, *wana*, should be carefully avoided, unless you have a spear or a long pair of tongs or two long sticks. See chapter 3 for the perils of *wana*. Use a thick burlap sack to carry them ashore, and shake them in the sack until the spines are broken off. Holding a *wana* with gloves, turn it mouth-side up and break away the top third of the shell with a rock or knife. Pull out the five-part center mouth structure and appreciate the complexity. Its name of "Aristotle's lantern" refers to the philosopher who first described it, who was also one of the first marine biologists, carefully studying and describing the sea animals of ancient Greece. Rinse out the watery, brown membranes until you get down to the five golden-orange sacs of eggs that cling to the inside of the shell. Both James Beard and John McPhee have written of the delicate flavor of urchin eggs. Think caviar, think high protein, and carry a small spoon. I asked a local fisherman once about the best time of year for *wana*, and he replied in Hawaiian, "When the *kiawe* tree blooms, then the *wana* is sweet to eat."

'Opihi, pipipi, hā'uke'uke, and *wana* are not usually found in stores. These delicacies do and should require your own effort.

In Hawai'i you may need to know five names for each of the many plants and animals. Consider, for example, what we call "octopus" in English. It's *Polypus ornatus* in Latin, *tako* in Japanese, *he'e* or *pūloa* in Hawaiian, and "squid" (pronounced "squeed") in the common denominator of pidgin English.

The most difficult part of catching an octopus is seeing it. Its protective coloration is a mottled brown, closely matching the rocky holes where it lives. Spearing is the usual hunting method, though some skilled fishermen prefer to cruise on their motorized surf boards, watching through a mask as they lower down a weighted yellow ball from a surfboard to a spot in front of the hole. The octopus comes out to fight off the invader and is pulled up to the fisherman's bag.

How do you prepare and eat an octopus? The time-honored way to kill one is to bite it between the eyes. Actually you have to take both eyes into your mouth and bite down behind the eyes. Meanwhile, you must avoid the strong parrot-like beak, which can nip a chunk out of your lip or fingers. You can also quickly kill and clean an octopus by grasping the head openings in your fingers, placing your thumbs on top of the head, and turning it inside out. The guts and ink sac are then easily removed.

Sprinkle coarse salt on the body and massage it well to get rid of the slimy coating. For tenderizing it, a simple method is to put a few inches of water in a washing machine and agitate the octopus for about five minutes. If you aren't carrying a washing machine in your kayak, slam the octopus repeatedly on a big rock until it is limp. Then

Left to right: Wāwae'iole *seaweed, urchin eggs in their shells, other* limu.

Cleaning an octopus.

you can dry the meat, eat it raw, or simmer it for half an hour in a pressure cooker. You could also cut it into small pieces and saute it quickly, for about three minutes. Serve the chunks with a dipping sauce of shoyu, grated ginger root, and garlic. You can buy ginger, garlic pulp, and *wasabi* (powerful green horseradish) in small tubes for easy transportation and preparation.

Then again, since the octopus is the most intelligent of the mollusks and such a graceful underwater ballet dancer, you may want to just watch instead of spear.

Several species of sea turtle live in Hawaiian seas. You used to be able to find turtle steak on restaurant menus, but now the animals are protected, and possession of any part of a turtle subjects you to a stiff fine. Most residents are in favor of saving turtles and will report violations. Endearing is not how one would usually describe a reptile, but a sea turtle is both startling and delightful when she comes up alongside and whuffles a greeting.

From the sea you also get the vegetables for dinner—*limu*, the local seaweed. Most of the island fish markets and some grocery stores stock a variety of seaweeds, both fresh and dried. Browsing through is a good way to learn what the common edible *limu* looks like. My own favorite is *wāwae'iole*, translated literally as "rat's foot," a succulent, dark-green plant. Its thick stems are delicious as is, with the tang of the

Cooked octopus on a paddle platter.

sea. For an appetizer, you can dip them in mayonnaise spiked with a sharp mustard. For salad or relish, you chop them with green onion, tomato, fresh ginger, and shoyu to make *gulamon*, the Filipino word for seaweed.

Foraging from the Land

You can also find food on land. Up in the valleys there are sometimes remains of the old Hawaiian taro terraces, and some of the plants still grow along the streams. Learn to differentiate between taro and the nonedible *'ape*. Taro (*kalo* in Hawaiian) leaves can be wrapped around fish and a fatty chunk of pork or bacon, then overwrapped in *ti* leaves and steamed for an hour to make the *laulau* that are popular Hawaiian fare. Make sure to cook the taro leaves or roots an hour or more to destroy the calcium oxalate crystals, which will irritate your throat. If you have never seen *laulau*, you can purchase them at many local markets to get a better idea of their structure. You can also combine fish with other greens, such as sweet potato leaves, pigweed (Amaranthus) or New Zealand spinach (Tetragonia). Add coconut cream to cooked leaves and octopus or calamari to make "squid" *lauau*. Delicious. The New Zealand spinach is so easily available that you need to know how to identify it. It's *kokihi* in the Maori language and is in the iceplant family. It grows at the edge of sandy beaches and has an arrowhead-shaped, thick leaf which feels like scratchy velvet. The small yellow-green flowers and the hard seeds are at the base of the leaves. Pull off and cook just the leaves. They aren't good raw, but are just fine stir-fried with garlic and olive oil, then simmered a few minutes with a tablespoon of water or wine and served with crisp, crumbled bacon. No, I haven't tried them in Oysters Rockefeller—no oysters.

Taro root can be cooked and eaten like potatoes or pounded into poi, but if you have a yen for poi you can buy it in the markets. You mix it with water to thin it to the consistency you prefer. One-finger poi is thick—you can pick up a mouthful with one finger. Three-finger is thin, and takes three fingers to scoop a bite. After three days poi becomes sour and pink and bubbly—just right to some tastes.

Mushrooms are magic, and I don't mean the ones that cause a mind-altered state by the destruction of brain cells. Dozens of edible species grow wild in Hawai'i and more are now being grown by specialist farmers, but their best habitat is up in high, cool areas away from the sea. Some species are poisonous, as two of us confirmed by a mistake. If in doubt, be sure to make a spore print as additional identification. The mushroom that kayakers are most likely to find, and that is clearly identifiable, grows on the underside of rotten logs in wet jungles, even near the shore. In Hawaiian it is *pepeiao* or *pepeiao-akua;* in English it's tree-fungus or ghost's ear; in Japanese *kikurage;* in Chinese *muerh;* and in the Latin of a mycologist, it's *Auricularia polytricha.* By whatever name it is highly prized in Chinese cuisine and in mine for the ability to retain its crisp texture and to take on the flavor of a sauce. If you mistrust your abillity to find or identify this one, look for it dried in the oriental section of the large local markets. A few minutes of soaking will rehydrate it. Save and use the broth.

Some years back, returning from a January hiking trip along Nā Pali coast, four of us were stranded on the far side of Hanakāpīʻai Stream. It had rained 34 inches in 24 hours, and both the seas and the stream were impassable. Our food supply was down to one clove of garlic, but we rigged a tarp, made a fire, and survived nicely on foraged *pepeiao* and garlic soup until the stream was passable.

Pepeiao-akua, *or ghost's ear, growing on a dead stump. Edible and choice.*

The coconut tree was the most useful plant of all to the ancient Hawaiians for food, shelter, furniture, rope, and a hundred other uses. The young green nuts are the best for drinking, but you will need an agile climber to shinny up a tree and twist some off. Whack off one end of the husk with a machete until you get down to the nut, punch a hole, and if you want less mess, insert a straw. A slightly more mature nut will have soft meat lining the inside, about the texture of a stiff pudding. You can scoop out this "spoon meat" and mix it with fresh mango slices for a luscious dessert. Even better is to find someone with an ice cream freezer on your route. You provide mangoes and coconuts, they provide the freezer, ice, and salt, and you crank out the world's best ice "cream." No cream, no sugar, just angels singing, as Marjorie Kinnan Rawlings once wrote of a Florida dish. The other time-honored use of a spoon meat coconut is to drink half the liquid, fill it up with light rum, replug it, and refrigerate it overnight in your portable ice chest.

At the grating stage a coconut has a brown husk, but it still "shakes" with the liquid inside. Like most nuts, it has both an outer husk and an inner hard shell. To get the husk off, first sink the blunt end of a small pickax in the ground. If you did not bring a pickax, you can sharpen a hardwood stick (guava is good) and bury two feet of this stake, wedging and tamping it in place with rocks, and leaving about a foot and a half above ground. Now look at the nut. Three bulges surround the stem end. Jam the highest bulge down onto the pickax at a spot about one quarter of the nut down from the stem. Shift the nut one-eighth of the way around and poke another deep hole on the opposite side of the bulge. Hold the nut at both ends and pry off this first section of the husk on the point of the pickax. Then jam the nut down again about two inches from the edge of the torn off husk and wedge off the next section, and so on, all around. At first it will take 10 minutes or so, but with practice, and forearm strength, you can husk one in 10 seconds. Do not try putting the nut on the ground and whacking it with the pickax. When the nut rolls, it's very hard on the toes!

When the nut is husked, hold it in one hand and hit it sharply around the equator with a rock or hammer until it cracks open. The water is drinkable, but not as sweet and refreshing as that of the green nuts. This is not coconut milk or cream. Making that requires several

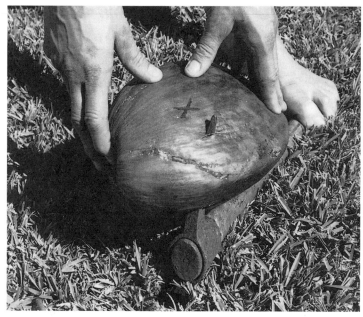

Husking a coconut. Step 1: Note toes gripping the pickax handle.

Step 2: Twisting the husk off the nut

Step 3: Whacking the nut around the equator.

Step 4: The opened coconut, ready to eat or grate.

more steps. Now you have two half-shells of thick, white coconut meat ready for grating, drying, or for prying out in chunks to eat on the spot. Don't try to pry it out with your fillet knife—a sure way to snap the blade. Use a screwdriver or a heavy sheath knife. Combine grated coconut with the heated coconut water and squeeze it through several layers of cheesecloth or strong sheeting to get coconut cream, a wonderful sauce for dipping or cooking fish. Tahitian raw fish (*poisson cru*) is made by soaking tuna chunks in lime juice until the acid of the lime "cooks" the fish (about an hour), draining off the extra lime juice, then stirring in thick coconut cream and chopped green onions. New research shows more possibility of parasites in raw fish, which are

Grating fresh coconut.

Grating coconut, showing the teeth of the grater.

Squeezing coconut milk out of the grated meat. Save and use the shells as bowls.

probably not destroyed by the lime juice. Further research is needed.

If you find a coconut on the ground that has sprouted three leaves and a root, trying to grow into a new tree, rejoice! When you husk this one, the inner meat will have changed into a crispy ball with the texture of an apple, but the flavor of coconut.

The fruits of Hawai'i are the real joy of eating in the wild. Start with avocados, whether you call them a fruit or nut. You can forage these en route to the put-in place better than you can along the shoreline because they grow best at higher elevations, but do include them in the menu. Hawaiian avocados are huge, with enough different species to be available in every month, and they sell in the stores for half the price of the small California ones. Along remote roadsides winding down the slopes to the put-in, some of us can spot an avo tree half a mile away. Fallen avos are tree ripened; even if they are part rotten, they can be salvaged for guacamole. The first course of the five course dinner mentioned in chapter 2 consisted of a nutty, buttery avocado half, filled with chilled sour cream and topped with red salmon caviar. Kayakers in Alaska would have to import the avo but get the caviar fresh from the salmon. We do the opposite. The green richness of the avo, combined with the tang of sour cream and climaxed with the little orange bursts of salty caviar, is a memorable sensuality.

Along the wet coastlines you can find two kinds of guavas. Strawberry guavas grow a bit inland, up the streams, but lemon guavas hang right over the sea. Both have twice the vitamin C of oranges and can be used in every way you use apples—raw or cooked, in pies, jelly, jam, juice, and more. Take a lemon guava, cut it in half lengthwise, scoop out the seeds, fill it with wild red thimbleberries, and droozle it with Grand Marnier. Served on a green leaf, it's a dessert to establish you as a wilderness chef. Be careful where you drop the seeds; guavas are already a pest plant. Books about the fruits of Hawai'i, listed under "Further Reading," have photos of guavas and dozens of recipes.

Sometimes you can find wild bananas growing in the jungle. They like water, so look along the stream banks. To be sure of a supply for a flamboyant dessert, take along some green ones to ripen en route. Plan to produce Bananas Flambées after dark for the full effect. Put half a cube of butter or margarine and half a cup of honey in a fry pan or pie pan. Lay in six peeled, whole or halved or chunked bananas. Simmer the mixture slowly until the fruit is translucent. Remove the pan from the heat. Warm a large spoonful or quarter-cupful of 151 proof rum, light it and pour the flaming blue liquid over the bananas. Take care not to spill that high-proof rum or you could have Fingers Flambées. Let the flames die down before you serve the dish. For the ultimate in decadence, top it all with whipped cream from a pressurized can that you carry in the ice chest.

You don't really need to go to such lengths. Mountain apples, passion fruit, soursop, lychee, papaya, and Java plum can all be found at various seasons around the islands, either growing wild or at the site of a former village, and they are all great au naturel or with a bit of sweetening.

Foraging in a Market

Just walking down the aisles of a supermarket in Hawai'i can give you menu ideas. Linda Daniel, author of *Kayak Cookery* (see "Further Reading"), was delighted with all the international items available here. Freeze-dried dinners from a camping store are fine for a quickie meal when you are tired, but grocery stores have prefab meals at half the price that require very little cooking. Look in the sections for rice, instant potatoes, soup, pasta, and Mexican foods to find side-dish or main-dish packets.

Fruit leathers are great to take along for lunches. You can buy expensive, commercially made fruit rolls, or you can buy the local tropical fruits and make your own. These thin slabs of flexible, dried fruit purée are made by combining pulp and juice in a blender, pouring the mix out onto plastic wrap on a cookie sheet, and dehydrating it in a 140 degree F oven until it is leathery. Crack open the oven door with a wooden spoon so the moisture can escape. Try passion-papaya rolls or passion-banana leather. If these both sound too erotic, just call them tropical fruit slabs, or make a more prosaic apple-strawberry roll. The passion fruit, *liliko'i*, grows wild on vines in the hills, but in the market you will find only the sweetened frozen juice to mix with pulpy fruits. If you are a visitor to the islands, you can make them up in a friend's kitchen to dry overnight just before a trip. If you live on the mainland, you can make up half your food before you arrive. If you live in Hawai'i you can make menus up way ahead and freeze them until time to go. The difficulty is trying to still have some fruit rolls left in the freezer the morning of take-off.

Another dish to establish your reputation as a chef is *sushi*, dried sheets of *nori* seaweed spread with cooked rice (local sticky rice, not long grain) and rolled up around a center of fish or crispy vegetables. Ingredients are easy to carry, easy to combine, and it's a good group project. Each paddler can create a few rolls to suit individual taste, using centers of gourd, mushrooms, raw fish, flaked shrimp (*ebi* in the store's oriental section), avocado, cucumber, green onion, or a dozen other ingredients. In Alaska I use thin strips of bull kelp plus salmon caviar and beach asparagus. In Hawai'i, if all we are carrying is *nori* and rice, we look for pickleweed, urchin eggs, lobster (cut into strips), and *wāwae'iole* seaweed.

Nori, the Japanese name, is a genus of seaweed well known from the imported dried sheets that are available in grocery stores at about two dollars for a pack of ten sheets. *Nori* contains 30 percent protein on a dry weight basis, more than even soybeans. Look also for the packets of crispy, hot or mild, teriyaki-flavored *nori*, good as a lunch snack in place of jerky or nuts.

Drying Food

To prepare ahead, save money, save fuel, save on-site prep time, and have a great variety in your menus, drying food is a simple skill that really pays off. A commercial freeze-dried menu of main dish and dessert for four people can cost up to 40 dollars. One freeze-dried main dish or dessert makes two cups of food, which is supposed to serve two people, but usually serves one hungry kayaker. You or I can make up the same quantity for eight dollars or less. Multiply that saving of 32 dollars by meals for a month and you've paid your plane fare to Hawai'i. Here's a sample menu, Speedy Spaghetti and Apple Cobbler.

Speedy Spaghetti: Make your own spaghetti sauce at home using olive oil, garlic, onions, green pepper, tomato paste, canned tomatoes, red wine, and whatever else goes into your favorite sauce. I usually omit any meat at this point. Dry the sauce by pouring it onto plastic wrap on a cookie sheet and drying it in the oven as described for fruit leather, or else use a commercial dehydrator such as American Harvest. (If you buy a dehydrator make sure it has a motorized fan. With-

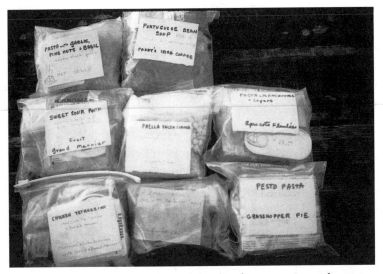

To save money and eat better, dry and package your own meals.

out it, drying will take two to three times longer.) Roll up the sauce leather in the plastic wrap. At dinner time, tear the sauce into pieces and drop it into the pot of boiling water along with the pasta and sausage or TVP (texturized vegetable protein, available at health food store, which resembles hamburger). Try to estimate the amount of water to have enough for sauce and cooking the pasta without needing to drain any off. Too much water, soupy pasta. Too little, add more. Serve, and pass among the diners a chunk of Romano cheese and a grater (much better than the pre-grated in those round boxes).

Apple Cobbler: Simmer one cup of dried apple slices with two cups of water and a mix of one-half cup sugar and two tablespoons of cornstarch (carry these two in a ziplock bag). Dish up into a bowl or individual cups. Crumble one crisp cinnamon granola bar onto each serving.

The total cost for this meal for four is about four dollars. Total cost of the equivalent in commercial freeze-dried packets would be about 30 dollars. More about drying is in "Further Reading."

Philosophy of the Kayaking Cook

The basic idea on any kayaking trip is to decide what you like to eat and then figure a way to take it along, whether fresh, frozen, foraged, resupplied en route, or dried and packaged far in advance. From one extreme of a helicopter drop of fresh steaks to the other of a can of chili beans, it is just a matter of planning and using ingenuity to eat what you like. Bulk, not weight, determines what you can pack in your kayak. I can carry food for three weeks in my 13-foot boat and include cioppino, sushi, stroganoff, corn fritters, pasta Alfredo, fresh fruit, and chilled wine.

Our five course dinner for 12 paddlers on Nā Pali coast of Kaua'i started with the stuffed avocado and chilled aquavit and continued with a green salad, mixed and served in a doubled, rolled-down garbage bag. The main course was wine pot roast, made at home and reheated, with loaves of home-made bread and three California Zinfandels. Coal-roasted, foil-wrapped onions accompanied it, and dessert was Bananas Flambées followed by Ficklin's Port and cheeses. (This took place before Nā Pali became a state park; in county and state parks drinking alcohol is illegal.)

Two of us shared the planning and carrying the load for that first night extravaganza, with plastic bagged boxes up to our eyebrows; we were lightweight for the rest of the trip. Assigning couples for each meal works well, and you get far more variety of styles and tastes than from a central commissary.

Whatever you serve, do it with flair. Just sitting on a rock with a plate of glop is not nearly as much fun as unrolling a beach mat, spreading out banana or *ape* leaves, or using a *pareu* as a tablecloth. Candlelight, a driftwood centerpiece, coconut shell bowls—imagination and panache take little space in your boat.

While you weave fern leis for each other, the bouillabaisse simmers, wafting a scent of herbs and wine. You shower under the waterfall, using fresh blossoms of shampoo ginger for soap, and you both laugh at how this tropical idyll, which would seem like purple prose in a tourist guide, can come true for kayakers.

6

₩

Planning, Packing, and Paddling
Making It All Happen

Planning

What time of year you can go on an expedition and for how long will determine where you go. If you can get away only in November or December, and you want to plan a two-week, long-distance paddle, then seasonal wind and surf conditions pretty well limit you to the Kona coast on the Big Island. If on the other hand you definitely want to paddle Nā Pali coast on Kaua'i, then you will need to schedule your vacation between the middle of May and the first of September, to have the best chance of avoiding big surf and rough seas and to meet landing and camping regulations. The information in "Where To" will help you decide when and where. The Planning Sheet below can help you organize and will serve as a checklist for each trip. Feel free to reproduce it for each of your trips.

Limiting your group to no more than four people has many advantages. More than four makes the crowd that you go paddling to get away from. More than four greatly impacts an isolated area. Four or fewer will be welcomed or at least tolerated by most local residents. Larger groups can seem like an invasion to shore fishermen, to a family on a beach, or in front of a residential area, especially doing what every kayaker does first after several hours at sea. One purpose of this book is to encourage paddlers to go on their own as a small group of friends rather than as a huge club or commercial tour. Another reason to limit size is cost. Commercial tours cost from 60 to 200 dollars a day. This is reasonable, considering that tour operators provide boat, paddle, safety gear, food, guides, local knowledge, permits, rescue and first aid capability, plus years of experience. If you are new to an area, have limited time to do research, don't have boat or gear or even kayaking skills, then you're certainly wise to carefully select a local commercial tour trip. A few of them are listed in "Sources." John Dowd's *Sea Kayaking*, listed under "Further Reading," has good advice about selection in his chapter entitled "Tours, Lessons, Clubs and Rentals." If you do have gear and experience, having invested time, money, research, and practice over many years, then you can go solo or with other qualified paddlers for a tenth of the cost of a commercial trip.

Another option is to join one of the local kayak clubs. An example is *Hui Waʻa Kaukāhi* ("club of one person canoes") on Oʻahu. Their annual membership fee of $16 entitles you to the newsletter listing weekly trips on Oʻahu and several each year on other islands, plus club meetings with speakers and discussion. You also get a 10 percent discount at Go Bananas, the largest kayak store in the islands, which carries gear and rents boats. On trips you are responsible for your own safety. (See "Sources" for address.)

After you have selected a route and have your maps, use the *Hawaiian Dictionary* or *Place Names of Hawaii* to look up the definitions of the names on the topos and pencil them in on your maps. This will give you clues to the legends, the topography, even the sea conditions. Some of the most vivid definitions are included in the trip descriptions in the following chapters.

Once you have answered all the questions on the planning sheet except 6.i., and have amassed the essential gear from the list in chapter 2, it's time to put your boat on the floor of your living room or garage and do a sample packing.

Your boat, its stability, and its type will determine packing procedures. Hardshell boats need the weight amidships in order to have buoyancy in bow and stern to lift over head seas or following seas. Wide, beamy, open-top boats can have some gear on deck without losing stability. Narrow boats are tippy enough without adding a high deck load. An open deck boat may or may not have interior compartments with waterproof hatches. Pack the heaviest gear lowest. Women have an advantage in that center of gravity question. Big-shouldered men are more top heavy.

Planning Sheet

1. When can you go? _____

2. For how long? _____

3. a. Where do you want to go? _____

   b. Is it advisable at the season and in the amount of time you have?
   _____

4. Why? What is your purpose? (a race for distance, an exploration cruise, day trips from a base camp, a teaching cruise for children or newcomers, photography, snorkeling, land hikes?) _____
   _____

5. How many miles a day can you go with the paddlers on this trip?

   _____

6. What advance information do you need: _____
   a. What is the put-in place? _____
   b. How will you get there with boats, gear, and crew? _____
   c. What maps will you need? _____
   d. Do you need a resupply point? _____
   e. What are the emergency access or exit points? _____
   f. Which way does the wind blow? _____
   g. What is your take-out place? _____
   *h. What are your alternate plans? _____
   i. What is the marine weather forecast? _____

**7. When and where will you have your shakedown cruise? _____
   _____

*For example: if high surf on the Kona coast delays your paddle for three days, are you prepared to shift to a Hawai'i Volcanoes National Park or a Kona coast Nā Ala Hele hiking trip until the surf goes down?
**A shakedown cruise should take place if you, your boat and gear, and the other paddlers have not all had experience together. Try to simulate the conditions you'll have on the trip, and have each person do at least one capsize and reentry in deep water. You may need to wash someone out of the trip rather than endanger the group.

Inflatable boats need the heaviest gear at each end to offset your weight in the center and to achieve an even waterline. If all the heavy weight including you is in the center, the boat will sag in the middle, lift up on the ends, track abominably, and pivot in the wind. If you plan a day paddle with no camping gear, at least put a gallon jug of water or a sack of rocks at each end. Also make sure to pump the bottom air compartment until it is hard, three pounds per square inch in the Sevylor Tahiti, four psi in the Grabner, Jumbo, and Aire.

Packing

In Hawai'i if you really want some of your food or drink chilled, you cannot just stuff it in the bow as I do in Alaska. Putting the food on the bottom of the kayak to be cooled by the water does not work here where the sea temperature is in the seventies instead of the Alaskan forties. Here a hardshell or folding boat with an enclosed top deck acts as a greenhouse in the midday sun, heating the interior to well above 100 degrees F.

Which items will you need to get at while paddling? Probably your water bottle, lunch, sunscreen, maps, binoculars, gloves, adhesive tape, knife, camera, hat, dark glasses, and shirt to cover up against sunburn. You'll need some kind of bag that attaches to the deck in front of you and is easily accessible. You will also need to keep your emergency gear at hand. It's best to have your signaling equipment attached to your life jacket in a waterproof pocket or bag. In the cockpit just behind me, I keep a small waterproof bag of emergency gear that I can grab if everything else disappears. It contains a plastic sheet for shelter, fire starter, lighter, extra flares, the VHF radio, my wallet, and the journal. Each of those items is packed in its own sealed plastic bag.

If the journey is to be a long trip along the coast or around the perimeter of one of the larger islands, you may want to mail a package ahead to friends or to yourself at general delivery at a post office on the route for later pickup.

When you have decided what is actually going to fit into your boat, you may have to repack it all for the plane trip if you're going to another island, keeping the carry-on luggage separate, then pack it into

A Scupper Pro rigged for safety with paddle line, thigh straps, and deck bag with emergency gear. (Photo courtesy of Rick Warshauer)

the rental car and again into the boat when you get to the launch site. If you are going to carry frozen food or an ice chest, you need to stick notes all over the house and on the car windshield, reminding you to "Get the Stuff out of the Freezer."

Just before launching, have a conference, if only with yourself. How far are you going, how fast, at what site will you stop for any readjustments? Go through the safety what-ifs. If you are paddling with a group, set a rendezvous in case of separation. Make a last-minute pit stop—to pee at sea is difficult. Go through a few minutes of stretching and limbering up to avoid the first half-hour's stiffness. Once in the boat the first step is to put your life line over your shoulder and under one arm and check that it is clipped amidship to the boat.

Paddling

After you are under way, you need to pause at the end of a mile or so, whether you are solo or in a group. Land if it is easy to do it. Otherwise, just float. Is your paddle clipped on so it won't float off? Take a drink, check the base of your thumbs for hot spots that indicate the start of a blister. Check your rudder system or have someone who knows what to look for check it. How's your seat? Is it high enough that your elbows don't scrape the sides of the boat? Check the first-time paddlers. Any problems? Is the pace okay? If someone keeps falling behind, put that person in the lead to set the pace. Put the strongest paddler at the rear sweep position to keep an eye on the whole scene. Keep tabs on your progress. With a group, you probably can't make more than two miles in an hour, unless you're all using surf skis. Solo, with no headwind, you can usually average three miles an hour or more. Ten to fifteen miles a day is a good rate for intermediate paddlers, five for beginners or if you want to do any exploring or snorkeling along the way. If it gets too hot, you can roll over the side and cool off. Remember to regoop with sunscreen if yours is not waterproof.

Are you going to make it to your planned campsite? You should plan to stop by 4 P.M. if you want to set up camp and eat by dark. Darkness comes at 6 P.M. in winter, at 7:30 in summer. Of course it is wonderful to paddle by moonlight, but the most enjoyable way to do that is to get up in the dark, paddle with a three-quarter-full moon, see it set golden and lopsided into the sea or behind the mountain, and then watch the sun rise.

If all the preparation paid off, you can now enjoy the scenery. Botanists, bird watchers, geologists, and marine biologists all need to be kayakers as well. It's such a good observation post.

What wildlife can paddlers expect to see along Hawaiian shores? Land and marine mammals, birds and insects. The only two mammals here before the Polynesian people came were the hoary bat and the monk seal, now rarely seen except in the islands to the northwest, from French Frigate Shoals to Kure. One mammal that is frequently seen on shores and sea cliffs is the wild goat. Both feral goats and feral pigs tear up the native forests. Few people will mourn if you substitute young kid for lamb in your menus. Check with the State Division of Fish and Game and the Department of Health for hunting regulations and for information on infectious diseases such as trichinosis in wild goats and pigs.

While on a paddling trip you are not likely to see many of the endemic plants or birds, those that occur in Hawai'i and nowhere else.

A rare and endangered monk seal.

Most of them are found today only in the back of deep vallys, on steep cliffs, and on mountain ridges and peaks. The land route out of Wailau Valley on Moloka'i is one place to find such plants, but you need a guide to avoid endangering yourself and the plants. Some of what you will see along the way is described in each trip in the "Where To" section.

The islands are home to several reptiles, including the little lizard-like gecko, whose cheerful, chirping castanet is heard each evening in my rafters. Since they eat mosquitoes, welcome them in your camp. Only one land snake lives in Hawai'i, a tiny, black, nonpoisonous charmer whom I've seen only once in my 45 years in the islands.

The sea birds of Hawai'i will surely be noticed by paddlers. Along sea cliffs a sea kayaker will hear the harsh "skark" of the noddy tern, and the fork-tailed frigate bird, or 'iwa, may soar overhead. Only once have I seen the ethereal fairy tern. Birdwatchers can build dozens of kayak expeditions around their hobby, and the little Audubon Society guide, *Hawai'i's Birds*, is easy to carry on deck along with your maps in plastic bags.

What about insects? Are those nonmalarial mosquitoes a problem? Strangely, many suburban areas have more than the wilder shores.

They seem to be regional, and in a few places you must either use a bug repellent or burn mosquito coils. In others you can sleep outside your tent all night with nary a whine.

Marine plants and animals are great attractions for paddlers, both as food and as scenery. Dangerous ones are mentioned in chapter 3, "Safety," and edible ones in chapter 5, "Food." Many fall into neither category, but like porpoises, whales, turtles, manta rays, flying fish, nudibranchs, and flowers, they are simply parts of the constant live show.

Underwater, possibly 80 percent of the fish you will see on the reef fall into one of six families: butterfly fish, wrasses, parrot fish, goatfish, surgeonfish, and triggerfish. Once you learn the general characteristics of each family, you can burble through your snorkel, "Oh, you must be a surgeonfish," and feel like old friends.

You may want to learn the Hawaiian names of the fish, which are often aptly descriptive. *Humuhumunukunukuāpuaʻa* means the trigger fish with a snout like a pig *(puaʻa)*. Yes, it's pronounceable—"hoo moo hoo moo noo koo noo koo ah poo ah ah."

The state fish, humuhumunukunukuāpuaʻa.

Part II

WHERE TO

7

≋

The Voyages
Using This Guidebook to Plan Trips

What is it really like to paddle in Hawai'i? It can be a luncheon picnic out to a small island with a sand beach, or a month-long expedition with rough seas and remote valleys. The variety is great. The choice is yours.

This "Where To" section describes trips that show the specialties of each island, from Kaua'i in the northwest to the Big Island of Hawai'i in the southeast. You can take parts of a trip, combine trips, or find new places on your own.

As far as I know, only Alan Ziegler, now retired from the faculty of the University of Hawai'i, has circumnavigated each of the islands solo in an inflatable kayak, and only Greg Blanchette of Vancouver, B.C., has made a kayak solo the length of the Hawaiian chain from the Big Island to Kaua'i and Ni'ihau, crossing all the channels in between and circumnavigating each island. Hawaiians voyaged between all the islands in their canoes before and after Captain Cook "discovered" the islands.

Some of the trips listed I've paddled many times, sometimes solo, sometimes as on of a pair or in part of a group. Several of them I've done as solo swimming trips, towing a small pack. Each trip is described in the direction of the prevailing wind. However, some kayakers here in Hawai'i prefer to go upwind, partly because of the difficulty of steering in rough seas with a tail wind, and partly because they can always go back, downwind, if they don't reach the planned destination.

Ni'ihau and Kaho'olawe are the two smallest of the eight major islands and are under private control. No provisions have yet been made for kayak trips around their shores.

The route descriptions indicate if the land is controlled by federal, state, or county agencies and parks, and if advance permits are required. For further information about "public lands" check with the federal, state, and county offices on each island for their expertise as well as for brochures they may have. Regulations change frequently. It's your responsibility to keep up to date. See "Sources" for addresses and phone numbers. If government is not mentioned, the land is privately owned. The best way to get permission to camp on private land is to check ownership through the State Department of Taxation maps of the respective islands, or through the *Real Estate Atlas* at one of the Hawai'i State Libraries, and then to make your request to the owners.

Some owners are very hospitable in person but do not want to be committed in writing. Some have learned through sad experience about vandalism and legal liability. Local residents or campers on the spot can often give advice about what is customary in their area. By law you have the right to land on and traverse any beach in Hawai'i. Beaches are public land up to the line of high water during normal wave action. Boat and passenger landings are restricted along Nā Pali State Park on Kaua'i). It is, of course, inadvisable to argue with any large, angry owner or caretaker. Ask his advice about other areas, express regret that his experience with trespassers has changed his natural hospitality, and then leave. In the ten years since the first edition of this book, Hawai'i has had major changes. Now there are a hundred thousand more people and ten times more boats. The pressures and the regulations have increased.

In many areas which are heavily used, if you are touring in a group the only responsible action is to carry your own toilet. Just as many rivers on the mainland have a policy of Pack It All Out, many areas here without public toilets need the same system, whether by regulation or by individual choice. Campmor Catalog of Saddle River, N.J., sells several simple systems which are packable in a kayak. An excellent source of information, with product evaluations, is *How to Shit in the Woods* by Kathleen Meyer, *absolute* required reading for all campers as well as for those who make the regulations and administer the parks and campsites. Chapter 3 of the 1994 edition lists names and addresses of fifteen companies who make portable disposal systems. This book has 300,000 copies in print; obviously it's filling a need.

The trip rating list below uses a classification system similar to the one developed for white-water rivers in other parts of the world. It is designed to help you plan a trip within your capabilities. On mainland rivers, conditions such as storms, melting snow, rain, dam water releases, and landslides can drastically change a river rapid rating within a few hours. On the ocean the changes are just as rapid; only the causes are different, and you don't have a shore within a few feet where you can get out. This list is for Hawai'i. A listing for other areas would have different definitions.

In the following chapters, trips for each of the six islands are grouped as shoreline paddles from the north coast clockwise around the island; as river paddles if there are navigable rivers on that island; and as paddles to offshore islands if that is an option. I have listed and described some of the places that I have found. I admit to being ecstatic about waterfalls I can bathe under, calm seas, warm sun, and isolation. I also think that billows of black *pāhoehoe* lava are beautiful, that caves are inviting, that night paddling by moonlight can be magic, and that tiny offshore islands are fairy tales come true. I hope you find new places and new marvels.

Trip Ratings

A knot is one nautical mile per hour, equivalent to 1.15 land miles per hour. Seas are measured in height of waves above normal flat water. Distances are in land miles, not nautical miles, since we're using Geological Survey land maps, not NOAA charts, for all paddles but one.

Class I	Rivers and bays. Easy paddling or swimming. Quiet water, little wind or current. Easy put-in and take-out. Short paddles of 1 to 5 miles.
Class II	Protected ocean area. Wind 0 to 10 knots and seas 1 to 3 feet. Sheltered put-in and take-out sites so you can make a short or long trip. Less than 1 mile between possible landings.

Class III	Moderate open ocean. Wind 5 to 15 knots and seas 2 to 5 feet. Often more than 2 miles between landings. Some rocky shores and surf during take-off and landing. There is access to roads and phones in the first three trip classes.
Class IV	Exposed open ocean. Prevailing winds 10 to 25 knots and seas 2 to 10 feet. Some sandy beaches to cushion the landings. No phones or towns. May be 5 miles or more between road access. Steady shore break.
Class V	Dangerous open ocean. You might get a quiet day, but this area often has winds of 15 to 30 knots, choppy seas up to 15 feet. Breaking surf on rocky shores, few or no sand beaches. Cliffs drop sheer into the sea. Experience, skill, and judgment required. No roads. 10 to 30 miles between phones. Difficult and dangerous.
Class VI	Winds to 60 knots, seas to 20 feet, surf to 30 feet. *Stay ashore*.

In Hawai'i in some areas and some seasons, a Class III rating can become a Class VI in two hours. Ratings for the areas described in the following chapters have been averaged for the best time of the year to paddle. The worst times of the year, bringing surf, wind, and rain, have not been averaged into the total. *There are no guarantees*.

8

Kaua'i

Shorelines and Rivers

The special places for paddlers on Kaua'i are the north coast (Nā Pali), the seas of the south coast from Nāwiliwili Harbor to Poi'pū, and the many river trips. Nā Pali is one of three spectacular sea-cliff coastlines in Hawai'i; the other two are on Moloka'i and the Big Island. In winter time when Nā Pali and the Hanalei area are closed out by seasonal surf, the kayaker can paddle the south coast and the rivers.

Geologically, Kaua'i is the oldest of the eight main islands of Hawai'i. According to the tectonic plate theory (and it's astonishing to realize that only thirty years ago it was regarded as a rather outlandish theory), a long series of eruptions about 6,000,000 years ago built Kaua'i as that plate passed in a northwest direction over a hot spot deep within the earth. That spot is now beneath the Big Island of Hawai'i and its active volcanoes. Having had more time to erode, Kaua'i has more plains and rivers than the other islands.

Kaua'i also has the greatest range of rainfall, from 10 inches a year at the southwest corner to more than 450 inches in the world's wettest (measured) area, the mountain top of Wai'ale'ale. The fourth largest island, Kaua'i measures 30 miles east to west and 25 north to south, with a population of about 44,000. Many people think it the most beautiful of all the islands, and that the view from the end of the Waimea Canyon down into Kalalau Valley is unsurpassed in all the world.

Tourism, agriculture, and government services are the main sources of employment. Tourist centers are located in Hanalei and Princeville on the north shore, Kapa'a on the east, around the county seat of Līhu'e in the southeast area, and Po'ipū on the South coast. Access to Kaua'i is through the main airport near Līhu'e. A smaller airport with

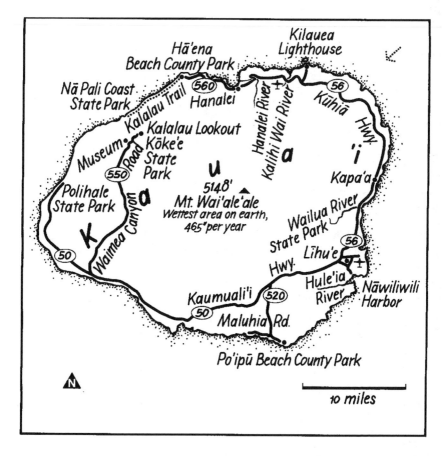

unscheduled flights is at Princeville near the north coast. The barge for shipping your rigid craft comes in at Nāwiliwili Harbor, two miles south of Līhuʻe.

Shorelines

Nā Pali Coast: Hāʻena Beach County Park to Polihale State Park

Rating: Class IV
Quad maps: Hāʻena, Mākaha, Kekaha
Total length and time: 15 miles, 1 to 5 days
Put-in: Hāʻena Beach County Park or Camp Naue YMCA

Take-out: Polihale State Park
Hazards: Surf landings, cliffs, rough seas, reef areas, commercial boats, changing regulations
Best time of year: June through August

Planning and permits are essential on this coast, the most popular paddle and hike in the state. Regulations change frequently, so double-check far in advance of your trip and again just before you go. The translation of *nā pali* is "the cliffs." The ancient trail into Kalalau Valley from the end of the road near Hā'ena has been a favorite of hikers for years. For them it is eleven miles of up and down, in and out of the valleys. For you, by sea, it is also up and down—on the waves—

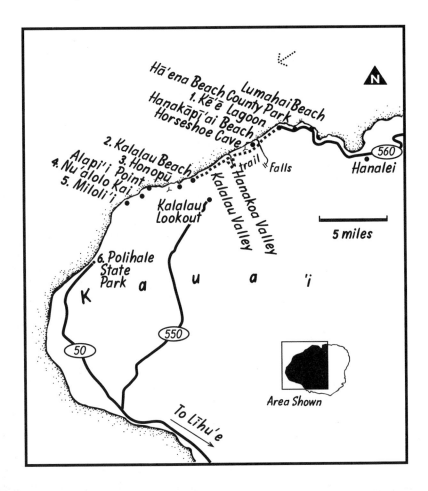

but it's only one mile from the end of the road to the first valley, five more to Kalalau. No roads go through the area. Kūhiō Highway, the north coast road, stops at Kē'ē Lagoon, less than two miles past Hā'ena Beach County Park.

You have several ways to preview the coast. One is on a boat or helicopter tour. A second is a sea-level view. Walk eastward along the beach from the end of the road at Kē'ē Lagoon. After about a hundred yards you'll be out on a small point of sand beach, where you can look down the long range of cliffs and sea to Alapi'i Point. That point is two miles past Kalalau and a bit more than half your total route. A third way to preview is to drive up the Waimea Canyon road from the south coast to the 4,000-foot level. At the end of this road, you can look down at the vast amphitheater of Kalalau, at the dozens of waterfalls, and hear the sea breaking on shore far below. Mornings are the best time for this view; clouds often roll in and obscure the valley in the afternoon. You can be down there, looking up from the sand beach in a day or two.

The length of time you take for the trip will depend on how much time you want to use exploring. You could do the complete 15-mile voyage in one day, but you'd miss the essence. Five days is almost a minimum if you want to see more than just the view from the sea, and do any land exploring. Eroded cliffs of fantasy-castle shapes alternate with lush valleys. Some of the streams meander to the ocean across a sand beach; others, in hanging valleys, plunge over a cliff into the sea. Still others foam and splash down a rocky bed and blend into the surf at the water's edge. Many streams have pools and waterfalls where you can bathe in the fresh water after a day of paddling through encrusting salt spray.

For people who have limited time, minimum skills, or can't get camping permits, the kayak outfitters on Kaua'i offer a trip twice a week throughout the summer that covers the whole route in one glorious, adventurous day.

The trip starts in tropical jungle country. As you move west and south you travel away from the windward coast, where the trade winds bring rain, and around to the drier area past Alapi'i Point. The monthly rainfall in summer at Hā'ena Beach Park is about seven inches; at Polihale at the end of your trip, it is not quite a half-inch. The temperature is the standard one at sea level, about 70 to 85 F.

The first seven miles of Nā Pali coast in winter surf.

Fresh water will be available from the streams or from rainfall or from the water tank at Miloli'i. It is mandatory to treat stream water before drinking it, because goats, pigs, and people upstream can pollute it.

For the current regulations, permits, and information, check with the State Parks Office in Līhu'e by mail or in person well in advance of your trip. For some permits you need to apply in person. State and county offices are open only during business hours on weekdays, so allow enough time. Inquire by mail or phone six months in advance. Sometimes all the permits for out-of-state use are gone months ahead. The enormous increase in public use of this area has made rules necessary. For example there are now 12 motorized and two kayak commercial boat trips going down the coast, plus 10 or more helicopter tours. Individuals and clubs need to let their desires be known to the agencies who make the decisions; certainly the commercial power boat companies will do so. There need to be some areas in Hawai'i open only to non-motorized, non-commercial boaters and hikers, but it's unlikely that Nā Pali will ever be one of them.

You may wish to get an early start on the trip by staying overnight in the Hā'ena area. You can camp at Hā'ena County Beach Park by permit, stay at the YMCA's Camp Naue (phone 246-9090), or rent a place from a choice of hotels or bed-and-breakfast houses. The hostel in Kapa'a is clean, has good information on island facilities, a fully equipped kitchen, and is just across from the beachfront park. To get to the north shore from either the Līhu'e or Princeville Airport you'll need a rental car or commercial shuttle. Check the Yellow Pages and phone for comparative rates. If you are renting a kayak, the kayak company can shuttle you to the put-in and meet you at the take-out. Watch as you drive north from Līhu'e for rivers that you may want to paddle later. In the towns of Līhu'e, Kapa'a, Kīlauea, Princeville, or Hanalei you can pick up last-minute groceries, ice, and fuel for your camp stove.

A highly recommended side trip is the two-mile drive out to the Kīlauea Lighthouse, where so many of the seabirds of all the islands can be seen. The high cliffs, the surf below, the close-up view of the birds, and the small museum will give you another fine preview of your trip. Check the opening hours in advance. This locale would also give you a preview of the first section of the other north shore paddle listed, from Kīlauea Stream to Hā'ena Beach Park. By car you could visit several other spots to look at the route.

Out at Hā'ena, take time to walk or drive to the end of the road, exploring en route the two caves, which filled with brackish water after the lava flowed out. Years ago two of us scuba dived in the cave closest to the road, an eerie experience after one of us touched the silty rocks with a fin, stirring up such a cloud of fine mud that we couldn't tell up from down. No buoyancy compensators in those days. A large, dry cave is at the base of the cliff just *mauka* (toward the mountains) from the beach park. If you snorkel at Kē'ē Lagoon, you can wash off in a fresh water shower near the lagoon or in the roadside pool of Limahuli Stream on the way back.

Look up at the jagged peaks so close to the sea. From those heights ancient warriors would throw burning brands of lightweight *hau* wood, lighting up the dark nights with a continuous firefall. Here, too, is the scene of old legends wherein Pele, the goddess of the volcanoes, fell in love with Lohi'au, the chief of this area. Later Pele sent her younger sister, Hi'iaka, to bring him back to her on the Big Island, with many more adventures on their travels.

Keep checking the surf conditions and listening to reports on your weather radio. You can also phone the National Weather Service (see "Sources"). Heavy surf is the rule from November to March. In April

Waikanaloa wet cave. Ha'ena area. Rip current at top center might provide a route out through the surf.

and May, September and October, you have a fifty-fifty chance of surf over eight feet, and a shore break of three to eight feet is not uncommon even during the summer. The park office may restrict Kalalau landings after the first of September, and camping permits for kayakers are issued only for after the middle of May. If you have to wait for the weather, spend a day at Limahuli Botanical Gardens, where they are doing an excellent job of cultivating native Hawaiian plants. Once under way you'll likely be paddling on wind-blown and choppy seas until you get around the half-way mark of Alapiʻi Point past Kalalau. Try to get an early start each morning. The more miles you can get in before 9:00 A.M., the better. After nine the wind usually starts picking up, and more commercial boats will be out there later in the day.

Since permits limit your stay to five days within Nā Pali State Park, you might spend three at Kalalau and two at Miloliʻi. Possible landing sites are numbered from east to the southwest side of Kauaʻi from Hā ʻena Beach County Park and are pinpointed on the map. Some of the more vivid meanings of the Hawaiian names are given in parentheses.

1. *Kēʻē Lagoon* (2 miles). No landing at the lagoon. Land at the point 100 yards east, surf permitting. Otherwise, see the lagoon and snorkel there from shore before your paddle trip. This small lagoon has a golden sand beach and a reef that extends east to the point where you get your view down the coast. Coconut palms and ironwood trees shade the edge of the shore, and colorful fish swim lazily in the clear turquoise sea.

Goatfish stir up the sand with their whisker-like barbels, and the official state fish, the *humuhumunukunukuāpuaʻa*, dives into a crevice, erecting his dorsal spine so you cannot pull him out. He is a member of the trigger fish family. That erect dorsal can be unlocked and lowered if you press a smaller spine just behind it.

In the first edition of this book, our first night's camp was at Hanakāpī ʻai, only a three-mile paddle from Hāʻena, but now kayaks are forbidden to land there. For more information about the Kalalau trail and valley, see "Further Reading," especially the books by John Clark and Kathy Valier.

Paddling On: A mile after you pass Hanakāpī ʻai, watch for the mystical sea cave that you paddle into through the waterfall of Hoʻolulu. Half a mile farther is Waiahuakua, the tunnel that the commercial

Kē'ē Lagoon from the trail.

boat people call Horseshoe Cave. It's wise to station a kayak at one
entrance as a lookout since power boats may enter full blast for
the U-turn and not see you in the dark. Going solo, you should hug
the walls, and perhaps wear your head lamp, pointed backward. The
cave narrows and seas are shallow at the rear, so waves often break inside the cave even when the surf is small. Enter only in very calm conditions. At the right time of day the waterfall inside the tunnel is lit by
a brilliant shaft of sunlight. Continuing on, you'll pass the hanging
valley of Hanakoa and its waterfall over the cliff. Soon you will start to
see tiny beaches at the base of the cliffs and finally a long beach ahead.

2. *Kalalau* (8 miles). The wide golden sands of Kalalau begin past the
rocky mouth of the valley's stream. No doubt, there will be campers
here. There is even a host, a Kaua'i-born park ambassador who knows
the valley well, and shares and protects its special beauty.

A waterfall for a shower is half a mile west of the main stream, and
before and beyond it are caves in the cliff. Far up the valley are orange
trees, fresh-water pools for bathing, and many places where you might
sit and read Jack London's story *Ko'olau, the Leper*. It tells of the tragic
clash in 1893 between the forces of law and a Hawaiian afflicted with
leprosy, who fled to this remote valley with his wife and child rather

Nā Pali coast between Hanakapiʻai and Kalalau.

Kayak camping at Kalalau. (Photo by Joseph Hu)

than be sent into permanent exile at the Kalaupapa leper colony on
Moloka'i.

3. *Honopū* (9 miles). Here is the most awesome beach in Hawai'i.
The cliff rises 1,200 feet in a single vertical wall back of shore, a giant
rock arch spans the Honopū Stream from waterfall to sea, and brilliant
green beach morning glory curves over the sand dunes. No overnight
camping or landing is allowed at Honopū, but you may anchor out and
swim ashore or else swim the quarter-mile to the beach from Kalalau.
Paddling On: A mile past Honopū, watch for the fallen lava tube cave.
You paddle in through an arch and around an island formed by the
roof when it fell in. The surge against the cliffs may give you the feeling of kayaking a white-water river before you paddle back out. It is an
eerie place, and some trick of light refraction gives a greater intensity
to the blue color of the swirling sea.

4. *Nu'alolo Kai* (11 miles). Along Nā Pali, fringing reefs are found at
Kē'ē, here, and at Miloli'i. The State Parks Office brochure describes
the sea life and the settlement remains of Nu'alolo Kai. People who
lived here used the reef for fishing and traveled by ladders and a nar-

*Maghna Zettle fishes on Nā Pali coast. Note a cooler attached to back deck with
bungee cords. (Photo by Joseph Hu)*

Entrance to the roofless cave.

row trail back around the eastern precipice of Alapi'i Point to
Nu'alolo 'Aina, the deep stream valley, where they grew taro, bananas, and other land crops requiring irrigation. Two of us once left
our kayaks at Nu'alolo Kai and swam back, wearing fins and with
shoes tucked into bathing suits, to explore Nu'alolo 'Aina. There is no
camping either place. Current regulations forbid even landing, but as

at Honopū, you could anchor out and swim in. The life of the coral reef is fragile, and to keep it alive you must not walk on it, land your kayak on it, or even touch it.

Now you are in drier country and in calmer seas, an amazing change in so short a distance.

5. *Miloli'i* (13 miles). Coming in you will see channel markers to align for the entry through the reef to the long sand beach. At high tide when enough water covers the reef, then body, board, or kayak surfing is possible. Beyond the beach to the west is the narrow valley of Miloli'i, with steep rocky sides, a stream, and a waterfall at the head. Several people have suggested hard hats for exploring here. Currently you can land without a permit at Miloli'i, but not camp.

When you leave for Polihale, prepare your boat and gear for a surf landing because it often will be required.

6. *Polihale State Park* (16 miles). Picnicking, tent camping, and car camping are all popular with local families here at the end of the south coast road. It is a hot dry area, but island surfers like it because the waves break almost continuously on the extensive sand bar.

When I came in here from Nā Pali the first time, at the end of May, eight-foot surf was breaking, with no channel. After paddling back and forth outside the surf line, looking for any kind of calmer route, I finally aimed through the smallest set of waves and rode a shoulder all the way to shallow water, only to dump and roll in a final two-foot wave onto the sand. On a second trip in August the surf was only a foot high all the way in. This is spilling surf, not plunging, and if you have practiced surf landings, it is not difficult. Occasionally there is a rip current channel at the north end of the beach where the sand ends. Heavy rains can cut other gulches and channels from the shore.

Other North Coast: Kīlauea River to Hā'ena Beach Park

Rating: Class IV
Quad Maps: Anahola, Hanalei, Hā'ena
Total length and time: 14 to 16 miles, 1 or 2 days
Put-in: Mouth of Kīlauea Bay

Take-out: Hā'ena Beach County Park or Kalihi Wai River mouth
Hazards: Turbulent water, cliffs, reefs, surf
Best time of year: June through August

Some people find this paddle even more enjoyable than the highly publicized and commercialized Nā Pali coast. It starts tough, ends easier, and requires scouting and careful evaluation of conditions and your own ability. Reefs, a tunnel, surge bouncing back from the cliffs—all can give an exciting or disastrous trip. The road down to the shore at the west side of Kīlauea Bay is steep and rough, and requires a 4WD vehicle or walking part way. The best preview is from the lighthouse at Kīlauea, though you can't see either put-in from there. If the first section around Kīlauea Point looks too rough, you could start from the mouth of Kalihi Wai, or you could change the whole plan and go up the river there. For this trip, you will almost certainly need a small bilge pump if you are paddling an open boat that isn't self-bailing.

If you plan to camp at 'Anini Beach Park, you will need a county permit. Water and showers are available there. Even if conditions

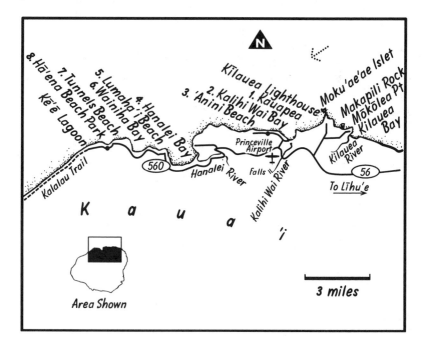

looked okay from the lighthouse, as you get down to Kīlauea Bay, the shore break may change your plans from a sea trip to a brief paddle up Kīlauea Stream. Even out at Mōkōlea Point it is not too late to turn back. Half a mile ahead is Makapili Rock with a sea tunnel you may be able to paddle through. Exciting stuff, but be sure to evaluate the conditions carefully before you commit to it; 500-foot cliffs mean you are not going to make any emergency landings. You will find another rough channel between Kīlauea Point and the sheer rock islet of Moku'ae'ae. Beyond it you will have a bit of a lee and quieter water.

Possible landing sites are numbered east to west from Kīlauea Bay and are pinpointed on the map. The distance from the put-in is shown in parentheses for each landing.

1. *Kauapea* (pronunciation and meaning uncertain) (2 1/2 miles). Also known as Secret Beach. It isn't a secret, but it is a lovely, long sandy shore, backed by a cliff with a steep trail up to private property. Before you head for shore, evaluate the surf to make sure you can get back out.

2. *Kalihi Wai Bay* (4 miles). Depending on the sand bar, you may be able to paddle up into the stream before stepping out. The beach areas on both sides of the stream are used for picnics by local families; the one to the west has more shade and fewer close houses. This is also the beginning of one of the river trips, if you decide the surf is a problem and would prefer a quieter continuation.

3. *'Anini Beach Park* (5 1/2 miles). Depending on the tide you may be able to stay inside the reef all the way down the two-mile length of 'Anini Beach. Wind surfers go in and out through the few reef channels, children play in the shallows, and the aquamarine sea makes you think of Mo'orea or Tahiti. The county beach park is half a mile down the beach, and other access trails lead from shore to the small road. This whole area is also called Kalihikai beach.
Paddling On: At the end of the beach road you can go out the reef channel or stay inside. Cliffs on your left mean no good landings, except one tiny one at the foot of a Princeville condominium area, until you get all the way around into Hanalei Bay. Condos and hotels cover the slopes.

4. *Hanalei Bay* (10 miles). This north coast center for tourism is rather appalling to those who remember it only 20 years ago, but it is still lovely, and they may say the same thing 20 years from now. The old mission houses still have palm-shaded expanses of green grass, and you can still sit out on the pier at sunset and watch the waterfalls from the peaks. The pier adjoins Black Pot County Park, where camping may be permitted.

5. *Lumahaʻi Beach* (12 miles). With the exception of Waikīkī, this may be the most photographed beach in all Hawaiʻi. No roads lead to it; only a dirt trail leads down through the jungle of *hala* trees. The tourist literature calls it "Nurse's Beach." Here the scene was filmed for the movie "South Pacific" in which nurse Nellie Forbush decides to "wash that man right out of my hair." Often it is not a safe landing beach—too steep, with strong swirling currents and a crunching shore break for much of the year. Last time I was there, a shama thrush sat on my shoulder. Despite being an import, this bird endears itself with a whole orchestra of warbles and trills.

6. *Wainiha Bay* (unfriendly water) (14 miles). At the west end of this dark, sandy beach is the mouth of the stream, and ironwood trees provide shade. This would be a good place to take out if it looks too rough ahead.
Paddling On: From Wainiha Bay, even in summer, it is usually better to stay outside the reef until you reach Kanahā Channel, which is not marked on the topo map but is between Lae o Kaonohi and Hāʻena Point. Board sailors are a good indication of the route.

7. *Tunnels Beach* (15 miles). This popular sandy beach is not marked on the topo map but is located at Hāʻena Point and is well known locally. Some commercial trips down Nā Pali coast put in here. Surf conditions will determine whether to stay inside or outside the reef for the next mile. Tunnels is often too congested with cars and boats to recommend it.

8. *Hāʻena Beach County Park* ("red hot," a sexual reference to Chief Lohiʻau) (16 miles). Beach cottages line the coast, but the sand beach

at the park allows easy landings. Camping permits must be arranged in advance. If you've arranged to stay at the YMCA area, check their beach area for landing.

South Coast: Nāwiliwili Harbor to Kukui'ula Bay

Rating: Class IV
Quad maps: Līhu'e, Koloa
Total length and time: 15 miles, 1 day
Put-in: Nāwiliwili Harbor
Take-out: Kukui'ula Small Boat Harbor
Hazards: Surf, wind, rough seas
Best time of year: All year, except during strong winds and heavy south swell

This trip offers many alternatives. You put in at Nāwiliwili, the main shipping port of Kaua'i. Scout out the large harbor area by car or on foot to see just where you want to put in. If you have shipped your kayak by barge from O'ahu, you pick it up here, carry it over to your chosen put-in, pack up, and go. The harbor has enclosed, quiet water surrounded by mountains and greenery. In the harbor area are a variety of accommodations, ranging from a small hotel to a grand resort. If you poke your kayak's bow out of the harbor and find the conditions too rough, you can turn around and take a trip up Hule'ia River (see the Rivers section later in this chapter). Once you do start down the coast, it will be about 10 miles before you get into the calmer seas beyond Makahū'ena Point with only two fair landings and no roads in between. If that prospect is daunting, you might leapfrog to Po'ipū by car and put in there. The trip is made frequently by Outfitters Kaua'i with a group of people. For the best guidance or to go with them, contact Rick Haviland. See "Sources" for address and phone. From the take-out point at Kukui'ula Harbor, you could go on another sixteen miles, with overnight camping possible by permit at Salt Pond County Beach Park near Hanapepe or at Lucy Wright County Beach Park near Waimea. The scenery along the way used to be just long views of sugar cane, but now the view includes 4,000 acres of coffee plants, producing 2.5 million pounds last year, which is half of the state's total. Along the route are three wonderful spots, all under private ownership: Lāwa'i Bay, Nomilu Pond, and Wahiawa Beach.

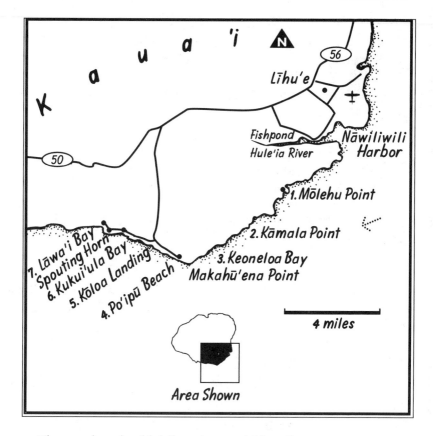

The weather should follow the usual Hawai'i pattern: more rain and occasional storms from November to March, steady trade winds in summer. Rainfall averages 50 inches a year at Nāwiliwili, 20 at Waimea. Along this coast you may be able to fly your airfoil kite and compete with the sea birds as you both glide along without flapping or paddling.

Water for drinking and showers will be available from the parks en route. In the tourist area of Po'ipū, several hotels, condos, or bed-and-breakfasts front on sand beaches. A registered guest can simply pull up a kayak, leave it in the care of the management, and walk to a deluxe room. This is not the free/find/forage philosophy of nomad travel that I prefer, but it is an option. You might try it as just a lunch stop. Phone ahead.

Possible landing sites are numbered from east to west from Nāwili-wili Harbor and are pinpointed on the map. Mileage from the put-in is indicated in parentheses for each landing.

1. *Mōlehu* ("twilight") (5 miles). Once past the breakwater and around the 500-foot cliff of Kawai Point, you can see the sand beaches ahead. You can come in on the lee (west) side of Mōlehu Point and get a sheltered landing on a sand beach. For anything more than a brief stop at tide line, you will need advance permission from the Kipu Kai Ranch management. A jeep road comes down to the shore from the ranch but without public access.

2. *Kāmala Point* (7 1/2 miles). Go a mile past the cliff of Kawelikoa ("the terror of the warriors") Point, and watch the landings. The channel to the sandy beach of Kawailoa is not always a calm route. A shallow reef at the mouth of the bay causes a shifting wave pattern. Use your binoculars and watch the waves wash up on the sand before committing yourself. A public dirt road close to shore as indicated on the topo map allows gated access; the gate is locked from 6 P.M. to 6 A.M. This is also the general area described as Mahaulepu Beach in John Clark's *Secret Beaches*.

3. *Keoneloa Bay* (10 miles). Hyatt Regency Kaua'i Resort and Spa is here, and you might call them to ask about public access and public parking, which all hotels in Hawai'i are required to provide. Then it could be an alternate take-out, a lunch stop, or just a pleasant mid-day break, a system I first used at the hotels on the north Kona coast of the Big Island.

4. *Po'ipū Beach* (11 miles). This is not intended as a landing place; it's given only for identification. Land your boat a quarter-mile west, and preferably scout the beach ahead of time. The area was devastated in 1982 by Hurricane Iwa and damaged even further in 1992 in the worse Hurricane Iniki. Planning and restoration are under way for the beach and the park.

5. *Kōloa Landing* (12 miles). It is a natural cove, cut into the shore by Waikomo Stream, located at the western end of Ho'onani Road. John

Clark in *Beaches of Kaua'i and Ni'ihau* says, "The landing is a popular site for patrons of commercial diving tours who enjoy exploring the bottom features, including tunnels and caves, and watching the wide variety of fish. Water conditions are excellent throughout the year except during periods of high surf and *kona*, or southerly storms." This was written before hurricane Iniki, so check with Outfitters Kaua'i for recent information about the underwater scene. Above water, it is rocky and uninviting but not usually crowded.

6. *Kukui'ula Bay* (13 miles). The small boat harbor and boat ramp here make it a good take-out place, but first paddle on west a half-mile to see if Spouting Horn is spouting. Waves enter an underwater tunnel there and force the water upward into a geyserlike blow hole. Air pressure causes the mythical giant lizard to moan and roar.

7. *Lāwa'i Bay* (14 miles). This is a small private sand beach and bay, a part of the Pacific Tropical Botanical Garden. Road access is locked off, so head back to Kukui'ula for take-out. A land tour of the garden is one of the highlights of any visit to Kaua'i.

Spouting Horn on the south coast of Kaua'i.

Rivers

Paddling up a river makes a great beginner's trip or a delightful way to check out all your systems before heading out on a more difficult ocean voyage. On most Kaua'i rivers you will be paddling through tropical jungle. You half expect the *African Queen* with Bogart and Hepburn aboard to come around the bend or Tarzan to swing down from a vine. You can carry an elegant picnic lunch with a styrofoam or padded, insulated nylon ice chest, and a nylon hammock to string between a pair of pandanus trees. Often you can pick fruit from trees hanging over the water. Some rivers have a waterfall upstream where you can indulge in that tropical dream we all have of bathing in a cascade.

None of the rivers is navigable for more than three miles, but you can have an enjoyable day on any of these. They are listed from the north, clockwise around the island.

Hanalei River

Rating: Class I
Quad map: Hanalei
Total length and time: 5 miles round trip
Put-in: River mouth, near the pier in Hanalei Bay
Take-out: same
Hazards: Commercial boats at river mouth, flash floods during storms, leptospirosis (see Department of Health booklet)
Time of year: All year, more rain from November to March

It used to be that you could go only as far as the highway bridge: now it's permitted to paddle, but not land, well past the bridge into the wildlife refuge. Get a preview from the marked viewpoint beside the road east of the bridge as you travel from Kīlauea to Hanalei.

Kalihi Wai River

Rating: Class I
Quad map: Hanalei
Total length and time: round trip 2 miles, half a day
Put-in: River mouth, west of Kīlauea town

Take-out: same
Hazards: Falling rocks in the waterfall area, flash floods, leptospirosis
Best time of year: All year; more rain from November to March

As you drive a mile and a half west past Kīlauea town toward Hanalei, you will see a paved lookout just before a long curving bridge. Park here and walk out along the bridge and you can see your route down the river and upstream to the waterfall. A third of a mile past the bridge is a side road *makai* (toward the sea). Down it a quarter-mile, the road forks, the left one leading to 'Anini Beach, the right one to Kalihi Wai. Head right and when you see the ocean, bear left for a quiet place to launch away from houses.

No landing sites are listed because the total distance is only a mile; then you run out of paddling depth. Follow a trail and slosh across a stream to the base of the falls. A steep trail leads to an upper pool. Be wary of falling rocks. Some of this is private land, so check with the kayak companies about access.

When you come back downstream, check the surf conditions. You may want to continue around the western corner of the bay and paddle along 'Anini Beach to its park for take-out.

Wailua River

Rating: Class I
Quad map: Kapa'a
Total length and time: 4 miles, 1 day
Put-in: Wailua State Park
Take-out: Same
Hazards: Power boats, water skiers, flash floods

This is the route up to the famed tourist spot, the Fern Grotto. Rarely does anyone but a kayaker go beyond, but you can go another half-mile through a jungle and out to an open area where lemon guava trees grow beside the stream. The weather is usually clear in summer; in winter take a rain jacket. However, remember that showers often last only an hour in Hawai'i, and then the sun is out again. Carry your own drinking water; don't drink from the river. Plans are afoot to require kayakers to purchase a Wailua River sticker from the Depart-

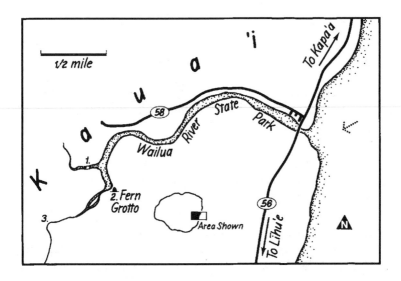

ment of Land and Natural Resources (DLNR) for $5 a year. Check in advance.

If you go early you'll have less traffic. Increasingly heavy use by all kinds of craft may result in regulations by the time this book is printed. After 10 A.M. the big motor barges from the landing across from your put-in depart twice each hour with tourists and blaring music. Keep to the side of the channel going upstream and on that same side (left) coming back, keeping within 30 feet of the bank until you get up past the Fern Grotto. Even then, watch for smaller size boat traffic.

To get to the put-in, drive north from Līhu'e five miles, cross the Wailua River bridge, and turn left toward the mountains on Kuamo'o Road. The Coco Palms Hotel (closed since Hurricane Iniki) will be on your right. Turn left again at the second drive and proceed to the parking area by the river in Wailua State Park.

Possible landing sites are numbered from the put-in and are pinpointed on the map. The distance from the put-in is indicated in parentheses for each landing.

1. *Small island* (1 mile). The river's north fork splits off before the Fern Grotto, and the island is just before the fork narrows to a rocky,

swift current. This would make a pleasant lunch site on a hot day, but more mosquitoes are here in the jungle than out in the open. Carry repellent. Look for a trail on the left (as you face upstream) and follow it one mile to a tributary stream on the left flowing from a narrow valley with steep sides. Follow that stream left toward its source for 150 yards to a high waterfall with a swimming hole at its base. The topographic map helps.

2. *Fern Grotto* (1 1/2 miles). Don't tie up at the landing here. It is provided for the commercial boat companies, and you risk having your kayak mashed. Try beyond the far end of the dock and tie to a tree. A walkway leads up to the natural cave, where dripping water irrigates the growth of hanging ferns. Plantings of ginger and other tropical flowers have made it a lovely spot, especially in early morning or at evening after the crowds leave. The whole area is a state park and a management plan calls for a kayak landing to be built.
Paddling On: Between the Fern Grotto and the next clearing is a Java plum tree with rope swings over a deep water pool. Big fun for big and little kids.

3. *Clearing beyond the grotto* (2 miles). Huge old mango trees, grassy knolls, and streamside guavas make this a peaceful place to spend a few hours or to have lunch. The river is usually too shallow and rocky to paddle beyond, but you could walk upstream a mile to the pool below Wailua Falls. Stay well out from the falls because of tumbling rocks.

Huleia River

Rating: Class I
Quad map: Līhu'e
Total length and time: 5 miles, 1 day
Put-in: Niumalu Park
Take-out: Same
Hazards: None
Best time of year: All year

To get to the put-in, follow the road around Nāwiliwili Harbor past the Matson docks to Niumalu Park. If you don't have your own boat, a

Kaua'i   149

commercial company here, Island Adventures, (808) 245–9662, has
been leading trips up the river for 20 years. You will not need landing
sites on this short paddle. Half a mile upstream you come to the
Menehune Fish Pond; a 900-foot-long stone wall cuts off an old bend
in the river to make the pond. It is said to have been built by a race of
small people who predated the Polynesian migrations and miracu-
lously built massive stone structures in a single night. You can probably find an equally impressive, more scientific account. The rock wall
is overgrown with mangrove now, and in a few places the wall is broken down enough to allow the tidal flow to move through.

Farther upstream, guava trees hang yellow fruit over the water, and
Java plum trees meet overhead to drop purple-staining olive-size
plums on your shirt, especially in their fruiting season of October and
November. Java plums make a wonderful wine-rich jelly. Recipes are
in "Further Reading" for chapter 5. When the stream becomes too
shallow to paddle, a trail leads to a dirt road. Rather than shuttle back,
it's easier to drift and paddle back to the harbor.

Check with Outfitters Kaua'i for information on other areas to
paddle.

Offshore Islands

This book does not include the island of Ni'ihau, 15 miles west of
Kaua'i. It is privately owned, and boats other than those of owners and
residents are not allowed to land. It would be a long and dangerous
paddle just to get a closer view from the sea. Helicopter tours are now
scheduled by the owners. No other islands are within paddling range
of Kaua'i. The Northwest Chain, extending out to Midway and Kure
islands, is under the control of the U.S. Fish and Wildlife Service, and
landing is strictly controlled. The closest of these, Nihoa, is 150 miles
away. Midway Island is accepting tours, mostly for fishing, through a
private company. A more rewarding way to visit Midway is to work as
a volunteer on turtle or monk seal or dolphin projects there and at
French Frigate Shoal through U.S. Fish and Wildlife, or through an
Elderhostel program if you meet the age minimum of 55.

9

~~~

O'ahu
Shorelines, Rivers, Offshore Islets

What can you say about an island with the best surf, wonderful restaurants, the most sand beaches, a variety of museums, and more than a dozen offshore islets? Only that it has too many people, and that's why it's great to get offshore in a kayak. While paddling inside the reef from Kaupō Beach Park to Kailua Beach Park on the southeast side of O'ahu just as the sun lifts out of the sea, the views of the pali on one side and the small islands on the other can make your heart soar. The light burnishes the greens and blues of the mountains and ocean and intensifies the shadows of the crenelated ridges. Those 800,000 residents of O'ahu seem very far away.

Geologically, O'ahu is made up of two volcanoes whose lava flowed together to make a single island with two mountain ranges, on the east the Ko'olau, and on the west the Wai'anae. Later volcanic eruptions formed the craters of Diamond Head, Punchbowl, Koko Head, and others. The highest mountain is Ka'ala (4,000 feet); the most famous beach is Waikīkī with its 25-story hotels and thousands of tourists. Yet, 15 miles away, the only footprints on the sand will be your own in the early morning on a Waimanalo beach. Back in Waikīkī be sure to visit the aquarium, only one block east of the zoo along the shore. There you can see films about sharks and see them swimming, see the rare and endangered monk seal, and watch most of the other underwater fauna close up while staying dry, before you go out snorkeling. The information from the docents is authentic, not just as entertainment. I usually plan to go there for an hour and stagger out four hours later, not sure that I'm really on land and human.

If you like day paddles followed by a warm shower, clean clothes, and elegant dining, then O'ahu is your island. With kayaking on your mind, you can ride around most of the island on the #52 bus for $1.00 and scout out the north and east half of the coastline. Since it is a four-hour ride, you'll probably want to stop somewhere en route. The bus does make a rest stop at the Turtle Bay Hilton Hotel, out on the northeast corner of the island. From the bus stop it would be a short carry to put your small inflatable into the water for a paddle west during the summer months. A bus route map would show several places where you could come ashore, with a short carry back to the bus. A second trip on the #51 Mākaha bus will take you out along the western or leeward coast, and a third trip on the #57 Kailua–Sea Life Park bus will take you around the southeast section of O'ahu. No buses and no roads go around the northwest corner, but you can walk the shoreline trail through the Ka'ena Point Natural Area Reserve, where endangered plants are struggling to make a comeback. Most newsstands and bookstores have bus guides to help you plan, or you can phone The Bus. See "Sources."

O'ahu is the place to contact kayak designers, watch outrigger canoe and kayak races (as on all islands), see the greatest variety of boats, rent an assortment of them, go on a paddling trip with the largest kayak club in the islands, get gear before taking off for another island, and make advance transportation plans.

Kayak trips on O'ahu can be of three types: shoreline, river, and offshore islet. Only on O'ahu can you do all three. You can, of course, combine two or three of them, or make a circumnavigation lasting a week or two, stopping at posh hotels or camping in beach parks.

All of the shoreline paddles described, except one, are accessible on The Bus for that $1.00 fare, if you have a small inflatable kayak that you can carry on your lap. The key is to avoid travel during rush hour traffic. Bus regulations read: "Baggage that can be stored under passenger's seat or on passenger's lap that will not protrude to another seat or otherwise interfere with other passengers will be admitted at no charge." With my folded-up nine-foot inflatable, the four-part paddle, and a small pump all in a bag marked Laundry, traveling during

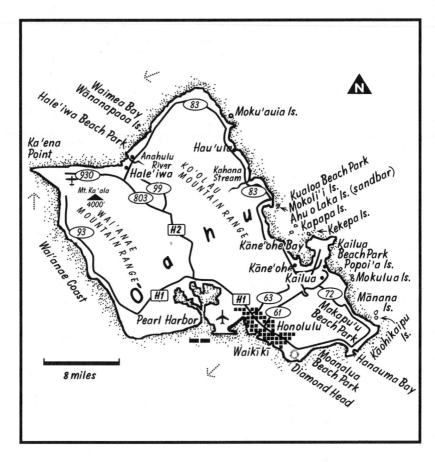

non-rush hours has never been a problem. I don't need to be concerned about parking or getting back to my car after take-out. While we're thinking "Go Light, Go Cheap," check out the two hostels run by Hostelling International on O'ahu, one near the University and one in Waikīkī See "Sources." The membership card gets you a 20 percent discount at Go Bananas Kayaks rentals plus other discounts that will more than cover your annual fee. A local hostel stay may be limited to out of state residents.

Only a few of the many possible trips on O'ahu are described in this book. Hui Wa'a Kaukāhi, the local kayaking group, does a paddle almost every weekend. Added up, they've gone all the way around the island. Address and phone for them are listed under "Sources."

Shorelines

North Coast: Waimea Bay to Hale'iwa Beach Park

Rating: Class III
Quad maps: Waimea, Hale'iwa (pronunciation: hah-lay-eeva)
Total length and time: 5 miles, 1 day
Put-in: Waimea Beach Park
Take-out: Hale'iwa Beach Park
Hazards: Surf
Best time of year: May to September

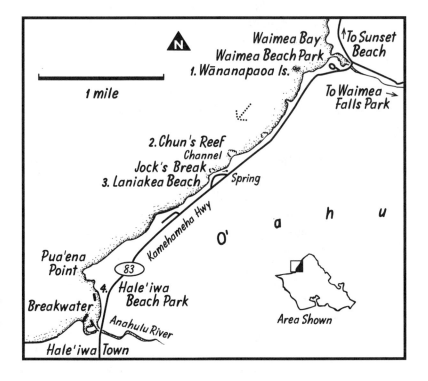

This area is home base for me. I've lived on the north shore for forty-three years, frequently swim home from Waimea, and know most of the rocks and reefs the hard way. It is also home territory for my sons Jock and James, surfers/kayakers/writers, who are quick to comment on my errors.

Get out to Waimea ("reddish water") Bay early on a weekday and you'll have a place to park and quiet seas. After 10 A.M. both will be more difficult. The best put-in is at the east end of the bay near the river mouth, which is sometimes open and flowing, other times closed by a sandbar. Watch the surf and judge where the flattest area is. Waimea, of course, is world famous for some of the biggest rideable surf in the world. In "vintage" years it has many days of 25-footers between October and April. Above 30 feet it closes out, with surf breaking across the whole bay and no open channel for surfers to paddle out. Kayakers do *not* go out. Waimea does not peak into rideable surf until it gets at least 18 feet high. Even when the outer surf is down, the shore break can dump you headfirst into the sand. All this is in winter season; for almost five months in summer it is flat, with just a gentle swoosh of wave wash on the sand.

As you carry gear down to the beach, pause a moment at the rock shrine at the edge of the grass and pay tribute to Eddie Aikau, a former lifeguard here at Waimea, a big wave surfer and a brave man, who was lost at sea in an attempt to paddle his surfboard to get help for the swamped double-hull canoe Hōkūle'a, on one of her early voyages.

Plan ahead so that before paddling, or when you come back to get your car, you visit Waimea Falls Park, just up the valley from the bay. It's a lovely place with both the history of the valley and its many Hawaiian and exotic plants, carefully identified and described. If you have a special interest in Hawaiian flora, history, or dancing, ask about their programs.

Possible landing sites are numbered from east to west and are pinpointed on the map. Mileage from the put-in is indicated in parentheses for each landing.

1. *Wānanapaoa* ("unsuccessful prophecy") *Islets* (1/2 mile). As you paddle out, you will see two rock isles directly out from the western headland of the bay. Paddle between them and around to the lee side of the outer one. It will probably be calm enough there to anchor or to

Waimea Bay in summer calm. Wānanapaoa Islets are in the distance.

tie a line to a rocky knob while you snorkel. The water is crystal clear, but the rocks on the bottom are black basalt so the sea color is a deep jade instead of the pale aqua color that you find over a sand bottom.

Stay awhile here (for brunch?) and look back to the mountain top at the east side of the bay, the site of Puʻu o Mahuka, the largest heiau (place of worship) on Oʻahu. The Hawaiian name of the islets seems to indicate a connection between them and the heiau. On the larger isle is a flat couch, which looks like a sacrificial altar. Did the priests from the heiau come out here in their canoes for special ceremonies? Captain George Vancouver's supply ship, the *Daedalus*, stopped at Waimea Bay in January 1794 to get water for his ships. The captain and two of the crew were killed in the valley, even though they had been warned by Hawaiians on board not to go ashore. It must have been a rare, calm January day for any of the crew to land through the surf.

Paddling On: The long sand beach west of Waimea Bay has many spots where you could land. Watch for rocky outcrops, which make a slightly sheltered spot in the shore break. Even better, just pause now and then to look around. Or roll overboard, clip your life line to the bow of the boat, and tow it along as you snorkel. This is a fine area for underwater shelves, some of them only ten feet below the surface, but with caves underneath where you can find a school of *'ala'ihi* (red squirrel fish). Remember to carry one of the laminated, waterproof fish guides and read as you snorkel. That would make a fine photo.

2. *Chun's Reef* (2 miles). You'll see this spot ahead as you paddle; there's an almost constant group of surfers. Chun's has rideable surf year round, whether it's two or ten feet high. It's the first surfing reef on your route that extends seaward, so you have to go out around it. Just past it is a channel leading in to shore. Watch the landing; rocks are underwater, so you may want to swim your boat ashore to take the weight out and to see the rocks through your mask. This sandy shore is a good place to watch surfing, to bathe in the fresh water spring at the west end of the beach, which may be covered with sand, and to re-goop with sunscreen.

Paddling On: As you leave shore, go back out the same channel and seaward of Jocko's surf break and around the next quarter mile of intermittent surf and rocks. Jocko's often has 15-foot lefts in winter, but usually only small waves breaking over its reef in summer. A "left" is a wave that you ride heading to your left as you face the shore. Since a surfer can see what a wave is doing better if he's facing it, a left is ridden to best advantage with the right foot forward, a stance called "goofy foot," the equivalent of being left-handed.

3. *Laniakea* ("wide sky") (2 1/2 miles). The channel here is narrow and hugs the rocks just past the big two-story house. In winter this is another famous surfing break, but it's calm in summer.

Paddling On: Enjoy the 360 degree view. Ka'ala, the highest peak on this island, rises 4,000 feet ahead, and the farthest point beyond is Ka'ena, the northwest corner of O'ahu. You cannot quite see Kaua'i, 70 miles to the northwest; even on a clear day you have to be higher than sea level. Past the next section of beach houses, you will paddle a mile of empty beach, the former site of the Hale'iwa air strip, active during World War II.

4. *Hale'iwa* ("house of the frigate bird") *Beach Park* (5 miles). You come around Pua'ena Point and see the bay and the breakwater ahead. Channel buoys and a range marker make it easy to see the route for small boats, or you may want to cut in left and follow the shoreline around. Here at the edge of the sand is a good place to forage in springtime for New Zealand spinach. If you haven't had enough paddling for the day, you can continue up the Anahulu River under the arches of the landmark highway bridge (see the Rivers section later in this chapter). The outrigger canoes of the Hale'iwa Canoe Club are stored at the club's shelter on shore east of the river mouth.

A few years ago my grandson Matt and I were paddling in the bay and offered to swap places with two of a canoe crew, since they were curious about our inflatable kayak. After the swap, as we swung into the cadence of the stroke, 14 on the right, 14 on the left, Matt and I were proud when the captain yelled, "Eh, da boy and da granny, dey strong. We no like change back!"

If you prefer looking at sail and fishing boats, paddle over to the small boat harbor inside the rock breakwater. For your own picnic lunch, veer east toward the low buildings and the rock groin of the beach park. Put on your shoes or tabi before landing, since the shore area has rough coral chunks.

From the park or the harbor you may want to meander around Hale'iwa town. It's only a short walk to Stanley Matsumoto's shave ice store, and around town with its art galleries, small shops, and restaurants. Fujioka Grocery Store has one of the best wine selections of the whole island. Ask Lyle for recommendations.

From Hale'iwa, one person could take The Bus back to Waimea Bay for your car. Or, you could start from Hale'iwa, paddle up to Waimea Bay and back, doubling the distance and doing the upwind part first before the wind comes up.

East Coast: Kahana Bay to Kualoa Beach Park

Rating: Class II
Quad map: Kahana
Total length and time: 4 miles, 1 day
Put-in: Kahana Bay State Park
Take-out: Kualoa Beach Park
Hazards: Reef and coral, small surf
Best time of year: All year except for occasional storms and high winds

This trip is inside the reef all the way and should be quite calm on most days. The wind will be onshore, a beam (side) wind, but unless it is above 15 knots will not be a problem. You will be passing residential beach houses all the way and will be in water only three to 10 feet deep, fine for snorkeling. The beauty of this trip is having the Koʻolau range of mountains so close to shore, just beyond Kamehameha Highway, which circles the island and parallels your route. Landing sites are not listed because you can stop wherever you wish or not at all on this short paddle. You may want to combine it with the Kahana River trip, and you could reverse the direction along shore since head or tail winds are not usually a factor. Note on the map where the reef off shore stops and patches of rocks close to shore may cause local surf off Kaʻaʻawa ("the wrasse fish") Valley.

At Kahana Bay you may wonder if you're really in Hawaiʻi and not in Samoa or Tahiti. The palm trees and the ironwoods wave in the wind, the mountains are high and jagged, and the small surf rolls in across a shallow beach. A boat ramp on the north side of the bay makes an easy put-in.

Out around the south corner of the bay look for the Crouching Lion, a rock formation about 100 feet above the beach; it really does look like one if you get the right angle. Farther on, as you pass Swanzy Beach Park, you can look up a steep gulch to an intermittent waterfall. The small beach park in Kaʻaʻawa makes a good stop. Newcomers to the islands delight in stuttering through the three a's in a row in that name. You may see a fisherman wading in the shallows, peering through a wooden look-box for octopus (see chapter 5, Food). From here on, keep watch up the valley for the *puka* (hole) in the pali back on the south side of the steep range of mountains. Ahead you will

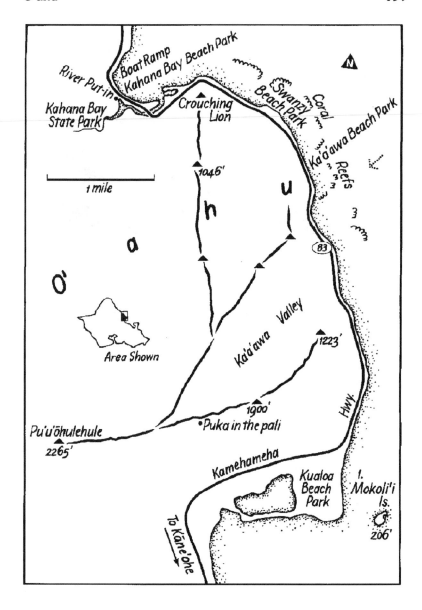

soon see Mokoli'i Island, whose distinctive shape earned it the nick-
name of "Chinaman's hat."

1. *Kualoa* ("long back") *Beach Park* (4 miles). This park, which curves
around a point to a camping area, has showers, restrooms, and lots of

Kahana Bay, looking south.

space. The trees along the day-use section have not yet grown big enough to provide much shade, but if you rig a tarp you'll have your own. The park is large enough to rarely seem crowded, and you can get permits to camp. Stop and take out here or extend your trip to Mokoli'i Island (see Offshore Islets at the end of this chapter). Like the Mokulua islets, Mokoli'i is often visited. You can make a rocky

Searching for octopus with a look box. (Photo by Heather Fortner)

landing on the north side, or go around the flat east side to a tiny cove where there is more surge but also a sand beach. A trail leads to the 206-foot summit.

Southeast Coast: Kaupō Beach Park to Kailua Beach Park

Rating: Class II
Quad maps: Koko Head, Mōkapu
Total length and time: 7 miles, 1 day
Put-in: Kaupō Beach Park
Take-out: Kailua Beach Park
Hazards: Surf, coral
Best time of year: All year except for occasional stormy days

This trip is recommended for sunrise, but if you're just not up for that, go later. If you push off the beach half an hour before sunrise, you can see the sky turn pink and then gold. Watch the shadowed thousand-foot pali just across the highway behind you change to giant pillars. Is there a green flash in the instant before the rim of the sun comes up, as there is sometimes just after sunset? Yes, but it's hard to be watching in exactly the spot where the rim of the sun will first appear. Five islands are offshore and three are ahead on your route (see Offshore Islets below). You'll be inside a reef most of the way, so big surf will not be a problem. The wind is usually onshore, a beam wind for you.

Landing sites of interest are listed, though you could land almost anywhere. Most of the first part of the route is past a continuous stretch of beach parks, and it is easy to see the residential areas, all of which have the required beach right-of-ways for access to the road.

The Kaupō Beach Park put-in is not clearly designated, but once you spot the Makai Pier half a mile north of Sea Life Park, you can see a slight cove just north of the pier. Paddling out from here, you will

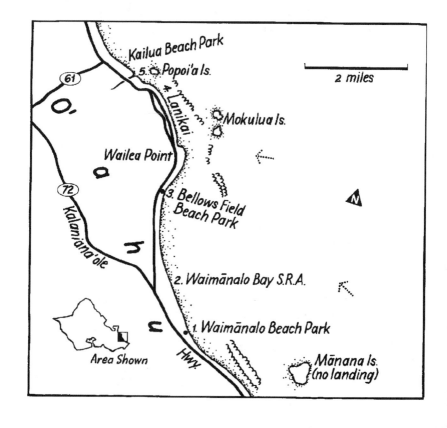

see the sharp outline of Mānana ("rabbit") Island offshore. Landing there is not permitted because it is a seabird sanctuary. South of it is Kāohikaipu Island, which you will want to save for the next shoreline trip described.

The following possible landings, which are pinpointed on the map, are numbered from Kaupō ("landing of canoes at night") Park. The distance in miles from the put-in is indicated in parentheses for each landing.

1. *Waimanālo* ("potable water") *County Beach Park* (2 miles). Twenty-five years ago this was a great place to find glass ball fishing floats washed here by currents from the north Pacific. A friend found 21 of them one morning between three and five A.M. Alas, plastic has replaced glass, and today they are very rare.

2. *Waimanālo Bay State Recreation Area* (3 miles). Past the residential area is this ironwood tree area that used to be called Sherwood Forest. Richard McMahon, author of *Camping Hawai'i*, names this as one of his favorite campsites in the state, and you could make this a base for day trips up and down the coast. It would be a fine place for breakfast, and sometimes there are small waves to practice surf landings. Only 12 campsites keep the place from being overcrowded.

Jean Ehrhorn, ready for a paddle from Kaupō Beach Park. (Photo by Joseph Hu)

3. *Bellows Field Beach Park* (4 miles). The north end with the cottages is reserved as a military recreation area. The rest is open to the public on weekends with about fifty campsites under the jurisdiction of the City Department of Parks and Recreation.

Paddling On: Ahead is Wailea (the name of a fish god that stands here) Point. You can hug the point or aim out to Mokulua ("two islands"). The surf and seas beyond Mokulua can get rough enough to turn that part of this Class II paddle into a Class IV. Inside the northern islet is a small sand beach that is usually crowded on weekends and holidays.

4. *Lanikai* (5 miles). This mile-and-a-half long beach is in a residential area. In places the sand has eroded so that you would be very close to a residence if you landed. In others, it is a wide sand beach. Several right-of-way paths lead from the beach to the road. In May of 1996, Lanikai was named the best beach in the United States by Stephen Leatherman, a University of Maryland coastal geologist, who has rated beaches nationally since 1991. "Dr. Beach" chose Lanikai because of its clean white sand and turquoise water, but he warned the beach will soon be gone because seawalls are causing erosion.

5. *Kailua Beach Park* (7 miles). Just around the point from Lanikai is the boat ramp for this long park. Kayaks of all kinds, sailboards, sailboats, powerboats—nearly every kind of craft can be found here, especially on weekends and holidays. Kayaks are not as fast or visible as some of these. One kayaker attaches the rod and flag from his motor scooter to make himself more conspicuous in the weekend traffic. Popoi'a, the flat, three-acre islet just offshore, is a bird refuge. Kailua was ranked as the second best beach in the nation by Dr. Leatherman.

Kaupō Beach Park to Maunalua Bay Beach Park

Rating: Class IV
Quad map: Koko Head
Total length and time: 9 miles, 1 day
Put-in: Kaupō Beach Park
Take-out: Maunalua Bay Beach Park
Hazards: Surf, rough seas, cliffs
Best time of year: June through August

Shena Sandler, taking off for the Mokulua Islets. A Twogood surf ski is offshore.

   This is the toughest short paddle on O'ahu. It is even harder if you go the other way, against the wind. It is a good test of your judgment and your ability. The local kayak club, Hui Wa'a Kaukāhi ("club of single person canoes"), calls this the "Weed Out the Wimps Paddle." You put in on the windward side of O'ahu, paddle out into a head-wind, paddle in the nasty troughs of a beam wind around the cliffs of

Makapuʻu Point, where you cannot come ashore, come around past Sandy Beach, where even good body surfers sometimes break their necks, paddle past more cliffs and a blowhole, and come into Maunalua Bay into semi-calm seas—with boat traffic. People who drive the parallel route every day say there are calm days. I have never seen one. Many days you should not try it at all. Before launching check with the lifeguards at Makapuʻu Beach Park, a quarter of a mile away from the put-in. Their advice is good; they haul people out every day. Do get the marine weather forecast on the morning of your planned paddling day, and cancel if the wind prediction is more than 20 knots.

Possible landings and their advisability are listed with mileage from Kaupō Beach. See the previous paddle for finding the put-in.

1. *Kāohikaipu Islet* (1 mile). You usually can land on the tiny, rocky beach closest to shore. A Laysan albatross project, begun three years ago, is trying to restore the island as a nesting site, by luring new birds with decoys and with CDs playing albatross mating songs. If it is cur-

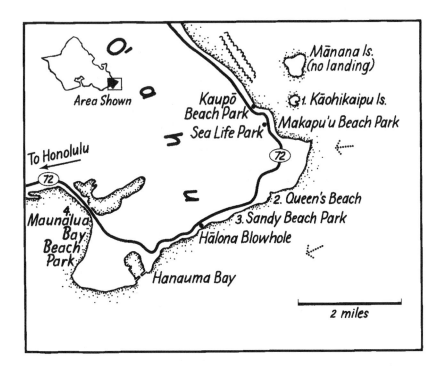

rently a seabird nesting season, no landing is allowed, and signs will be posted. If no signs are there, walk up to the summit (83 feet) and scan the route ahead with binoculars. Is it within your capability? How about an hour from now, when you will be paddling around the cliffs with the seas hitting you broadside?

2. *Queen's Beach* (3 miles). This shore has rocks and sand but less surf than Sandy Beach ahead. Ease of landing is greatly dependent on wind and surf. If it's calm, two landings are possible, one at a small breakwater at the southwest end of the sea cliffs, and another at the mouth of the intermittent Kalama Stream.

3. *Sandy Beach Park* (4 miles). This is listed only as an emergency landing. It has dumping, plunging surf filled with body surfers, and your kayak would be very dangerous among them. You and kayak could also shatter in a nose dive on the sand. The east end that fronts the life guard tower is not a body surfing site and is less crowded with smaller surf if you *have* to land.
Paddling On: After Sandy Beach you pass the Hālona blowhole and a series of cliffs. If you paddle too close, you'll get practice in rebound waves, which first hit you from the open sea, then bounce off the cliffs to hit you from the other side. Three miles from Sandy you pass the entrance to Hanauma Bay. No landing is allowed there now, but you could paddle in between the arms of the bay to rest briefly, out of the wind-blown seas.

4. *Maunalua* ("two mountains") *Bay Beach Park* (9 miles). You finally come around the cliffs of Koko Head and into the comparative calm of Maunalua Bay. Calm winds but frequent small surf is likely. Watch ahead and back over your shoulder. Look ahead to the bridge that marks the entrance to the Koko Marina. Some of us still remember when it was a peaceful fish pond area with a few roads and single-story cottages. To the left of the bridge is the Maunalua Beach Park with facilities and parking.

Southwest Coast: Waikīkī Beach

Rating: Class II
Quad map: Honolulu

Total length and time: 3 miles, half day
Put-in: Sans Souci State Recreation Area
Take-out: ʻĀinamoana State Recreation Area (Magic Island)
Hazards: Offshore winds, surf, canoes
Best time of year: All year; more surf in summer

See the world-famous beach from a different viewpoint. Those high-rise hotels are in a better perspective against the majesty of Diamond Head and the mountains in back of the city. If you haven't yet visited the Waikīkī Aquarium, now is the time. If you start your day before they open, begin your paddle at the other end and make it the finale. Waikīkī is also only four blocks from the Go Bananas Kayaks shop, if you are trying out rental kayaks before selection for a longer trip.

Possible landings are not listed since the distance is short. Also, you should be cautious about coming ashore along this beach, because you risk injuring some swimmer or tangling with a surfer or an outrigger canoe full of tourists. Even beyond the surf, watch for swimmers, who practice out here for competitive, long-distance, rough-water swimming events. If you are paddling an inflatable, be especially wary here of offshore winds. See chapter 4.

You could extend your trip by cruising past the boats in the Ala Wai Yacht Harbor and on up the two-mile-long Ala Wai Canal, where people practice with many types of paddling craft. It is a dead-end canal, with no exit by water except the way you came.

West Coast: Yokohama to Kaʻena Point

Rating: II to III
Quad maps: Kaʻena
Total length and time: 5 miles, 3 hours
Put-in: Yokohama Bay Beach Park, near the lifeguard stand
Take-out: Same, a loop trip
Hazards: Choppy seas and nasty currents at Kaʻena Point
Best time of year: All year unless surf is wrapping around Kaʻena Point

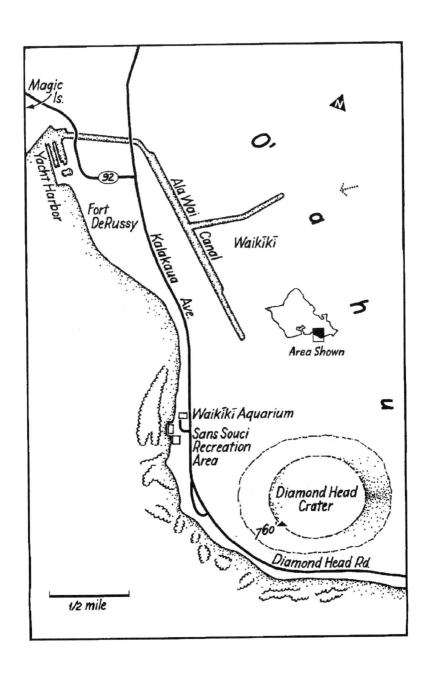

Magic Is.

Yacht Harbor

Fort DeRussy

92

Ala Wai Canal

Kalakaua Ave.

Waikīkī

O'

a

h

u

N

Area Shown

Waikīkī Aquarium

Sans Souci Recreation Area

Diamond Head Crater

760

Diamond Head Rd.

1/2 mile

This is the leeward side of O'ahu, the Wai'anae coast, and many short loop paddles are possible, or you can connect them into one long trip with a shuttle pick-up. The paddle described is not accessible by The Bus, though others are, as far north as Mākaha. This one is beyond towns and traffic. Do remember that this is a leeward coast. Close to shore, you will be protected by the Wai'anae range of mountains. Half a mile out, you risk being blown out to sea. The next large land mass to the west is China. At any time of year the winds and currents meeting at Ka'ena Point, plus occasional huge winter surf there, may make you decide to turn back before the point. All of the shore land here is under the jurisdiction of the Makua-Ka'ena State Park. A brochure issued by the park office describes the many endangered species of plants you can see along the trail to the point.

A slight tail wind blows up the coast, giving you a chance to try out a kite or a sail. Then you have a good workout coming back against it.

Check with the lifeguards before setting out, to get their advice for the day.

Rivers

Oʻahu rivers are shorter and narrower than those on Kauaʻi, and only three are possible for paddling. Two of them tie in with shoreline paddles described in this book, and the third could be a make-your-own combination. On the Hawaiian islands farther south there are no rivers to paddle. The first two rivers listed combine well with other north shore paddles, but don't have great scenery. Only Kahana is really worth a trip by itself, and it also combines nicely.

Anahulu River

Rating: Class I
Quad map: Haleʻiwa
Total length and time: 3 miles, half day
Put-in: Haleʻiwa Beach Park
Take-out: Same
Hazards: Muddy water; sand bar at the mouth
Best time of year: All year, except after major rainstorms

Two of us once did a Sunday morning spoof of a fancy hotel brunch by taking two ice chests, sterling silver, a stove, an omelet pan, eggs, fresh strawberries, chilled champagne, and fluted glasses, all in two kayaks, up the Anahulu. Next time we'll add a folding table and chairs, and an FM radio for the KHPR classical music. Maybe croissants, too.

Get off the #52 bus—naaah, not with all that gear. Leave your car at Haleʻiwa Beach Park, load up on shore, and head west toward the small-boat harbor. Turn upriver, hug the rocks of the breakwater to avoid the sand bar, and pass under the arches of the highway bridge. Divebombing kids and fishermen with hooks used to be a hazard, but both are forbidden now.

Upstream are small docks, huge monkeypod trees that hang over the river, and small-farm taro patches. Now you also go under the highway bridge of the Haleʻiwa Bypass road. You can only go a mile before the stream becomes too shallow and rocky to paddle. Tie up your boats and walk under the cane-road bridge to find a small, shady picnic spot, or return downriver and lunch at the park or in one of the restaurants of Haleʻiwa, from the Aloha Joe's Seafood Grill through a complete range to the small China Chop Suey across from the bank. Try the latter's Sour Soup or Pork Eggplant, or wander on another quarter-mile to the Coffee Gallery for an eclectic menu.

Paukauila ("the lightning ceases") Stream

Rating: Class I
Quad map: Haleʻiwa
Total length and time: 2 to 3 miles, round trip, one day
Put-in: Kaiaka State Recreation Area
Take-out: Same
Hazards: Muddy water, hidden branches
Best time of year: All year

This is a great trip for kids. Most of them are intrigued by frogs and mud. They love looking up into trees that they can climb or swing from into the water. From the quad map you can pick your choice of two river branches to explore. To find the put-in, go west from the half-arched bridge intersection on Haleʻiwa Road; pass Aliʻi Beach Park; continue on another mile. Across from the Fire Station is the entrance to the Park; follow its road all the way to the shore. The put-in and the route up through Kaiaka Bay change with shifting sandbars. Branches of the river lead off to the right. Four bridges go over the route, and the *mauka* one is the largest, the new highway bypass. By now you've come to the end. I keep evaluating the big banyan trees just ahead as possible tree house sites. Which paddler is the child?

Kahana Stream

Rating: Class I
Quad map: Kahana
Total length and time: 2 miles, half day
Put-in: Kahana Valley State Park

Take-out: Same
Hazards: Hau tree branches growing out in the stream
Best time of year: All year

Kahana County Beach Park is on the *makai* side of the highway; Kahana State Park is on the *mauka* side. Driving, you turn into the state park entrance, park to the right, and put in across the grass to the left.

Since the distance is so short, landing sites are not listed. There's a pleasant picnic clearing about a quarter-mile upstream on the left, with hala trees to string a hammock. The total distance is only about a mile; then a thicket of hau trees blocks further progress. Hau in my back yard is a twenty-foot shade tree, but in the wild, as here, it becomes an impenetrable thicket. The leaves are heart-shaped and make a flat dish for a dessert of guavas and other fruit. The blossoms open in the morning as bright yellow cups, change to a tawny orange by afternoon, and, when they fall in the evening, resemble windblown mahogany-red butterflies. A handful of yellow blossoms sprinkled over a green salad add color, and taste like mild lettuce. The light, tough wood was used for the outriggers of canoes. The inner and outer bark woven together made a strong rope.

My most memorable cruise on this river was with Bea Krauss, when she had a mere 89 years of wisdom about Hawaiian ethnobotany (see "Further Reading"). Bea sat in the bow with a pair of loppers, cutting the hau branches out of the way of our passage. She will forever be a heroine for many of us, for her integrity, knowledge, and enthusiasm.

Coming back down the stream to where it widens, you could bear right, go under the highway bridge, and paddle out to the reef offshore for some fishing or diving. You might want to make a full day of it by combining this trip with the Kahana Bay to Kualoa Regional Park shoreline trip and the Mokoli'i Island trip.

Offshore Islets

The little offshore islands are described in a table since they have similar conditions. None is more than a mile offshore. They are listed clockwise around O'ahu from Hale'iwa, on the north side of the

Bea Krauss and author on Kahana River. (Photo by Sheila Laffey)

island. On all of the islets it is "illegal to disturb birds, to possess any weapons, to introduce or land any plant or animal, to camp, to start any fires, to trespass into any posted area," according to the regulations of the Department of Land and Natural Resources. The rules exist for a good reason—to protect the nesting habitat of many of Hawai'i's sea birds.

Keeping in mind all the rules, and following them, I still find something lovely about landing alone on an island with a bit of food and a map, walking its shores, beachcombing, maybe rigging a tiny hammock if there is a scrubby pair of trees and if no signs about bird habitats prohibit leaving the beach. Even if the island is only a few square feet of rock, it is special. While they were all under 12 years old, my children named a rock islet on the north shore Magic Island because they could wade out to it and crawl through a tunnel to come out on its summit. It is not listed in the table, since it is only 50 feet from shore.

No landing at all is permitted on Mokumanu (off Mōkapu Peninsula on east O'ahu) or on Mānana (Rabbit Island) off southeast O'ahu, because of nesting birds.

Offshore Islet Trips

Island	Quad map	Summer Rating	Winter Rating	Put-in and Take-out
Wānanapaoa	Waimea Bay	II	VI	Waimea Bay Beach Park
Mokuʻauia	Kahuku	II	IV	Mālaekahana State Area
Mokoliʻi	Kahana	II	III	Kualoa Regional Park
Kapapa	Kāneʻohe	II	IV	Kāneʻohe Fishing Pier (Heʻeia)
Ahu o Laka	Kāneʻohe	II	II	Same
Kekepa	Kāneʻohe	II	III	Same
Mokulua	Mōkapu	III	IV	Kailua Beach Park or Lanikai via access paths
Kāohikaipu	Koko Head	III	V	Kaupō Beach Park

An afternoon picnic moves out as the tide comes in at Ahu o Laka sandbar in Kāneʻohe Bay.

The quad maps give adequate information, but for the three islands in the Kāneʻohe Bay area, you'll find that NOAA chart, #19359 is of much more use. It shows the numerous channels, marker buoys, and sandbars, which nautical charts mark, and land maps do not.

Class ratings are averaged. There might be surf large enough in summer to change a classification, and there might be flat, calm days during the winter season. Help the DLNR and your fellow paddlers by carrying garbage bags with you for clean-up.

Mālaekahana and Kualoa Parks both have good camping facilities, the first through the State Parks Office, the second through the County Parks Office. See "Sources" for addresses.

By now you have discovered that Oʻahu is far more than Waikīkī and the downtown business district of Honolulu. You may also get curious about all of those spectacular mountains. If you park your kayak, you could go with the Hawaiʻi Trail and Mountain Club or the Sierra Club to some wonderful mountain waterfalls and wild swimming pools. See "Sources" for addresses.

10

≈

Moloka'i
The Northeast Coast
and a South Coast Possibility

Moloka'i is the fifth island in size, with a population of about 6,000—and an amazing variety of terrain. The west end has rolling hills and plateaus, sandy beaches, including the longest one on any Hawaiian island, and is dry and windy. The south coast has shallow reefs, mud flats, and walled fish ponds, a few of them being restored for use in aquaculture. The east end has rugged mountains nearly 5,000 feet high, deep-cut valleys, and heavy rainfall on the north side. There, the rain, wind, and surf have aided in cutting the highest sea cliff in the world, 3,400 feet at its highest point, but the steady erosion was not the primary cause. Recent research has shown that the cliffs, like Nā Pali on Kaua'i and the northeast coast of the Big Island, were sheared off by a series of giant underwater landslides. Don't be concerned; it happened several hundred thousand years ago.

Three volcanoes formed the island, the last small one creating the peninsula that is the site of a leper colony, now Kalaupapa National Historical Park. To learn some of the history of Kalaupapa, read the books by O. A. Bushnell and by Gavan Daws listed in "Further Reading."

Moloka'i is a special place with no freeways, no high-rises, no elevators, no traffic jams and no tourist mobs. Residents have strong family values and have a protective feeling for their island home, feelings shared by many of us from other places. Of the six major islands that you can paddle, Moloka'i is the most like old Hawai'i. Since the closure of the pineapple acreage, new crops are being planted, including many vegetables that we hope will replace the picked-green, no-flavor ones that we ship in now from the mainland. This morning I had one cup each of Malulani and Muleskinner coffee. And yes, the famous mule ride down the switchback cliff trail to Kalaupapa is open again. For general tourism information call the Moloka'i Visitor Association. Phone from other islands is 800-553-0400.

Shorelines

Northeast Coast: Hālawa to Kalaupapa

Rating: Class V
Quad maps: Hālawa, Kamalō, Kaunakakai
Total length and time: 14 to 20 miles, 3 to 10 days
Put-in: Hālawa Valley, east end of Moloka'i
Take-out: Kalawao area or Kalaupapa Settlement, each by advance permission
Hazards: Cliffs, heavy shore break on rocks, rough seas
Best time of year: June to August. Sometimes 15-foot seas and 35-knot winds in July

This coast is a unique, magnificent place that deserves to remain wilderness for all time. It is not easy country. It rains more than 100 inches a year, and it seems very cold when you are wet in the wind. The greatest danger is being smashed with your kayak onto the boulders in the shore break. Unlike Kaua'i with its sand beaches, or O'ahu with its sloping shores and outlying reefs, northeast Moloka'i has only one beach with sand and one with small rocks. Ninety-five percent of the shore is boulder, or sheer cliff that drops straight into the sea.

The wind blows almost constantly from the northeast, usually 10 to 25 knots. This means you will have onshore wind and surf against you as you put in at Hālawa, a beam wind for the first mile where you're paddling in troughs, then a tail wind down the coast. Steering with a following sea whose crests are breaking off, as they do when the wind gets up to 15 or 20 knots, is difficult.

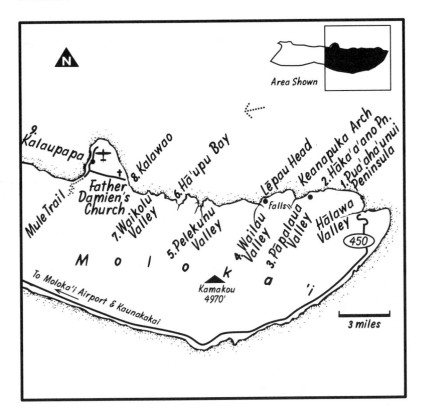

You'll have no shortage of fresh water along the coast, in streams and rainfall. Many streams have pools and waterfalls for bathing. Use your own catchment rain water for drinking.

You can walk up three of the deep valleys that indent the coast: Pāpalaua, Wailau, and Pelekunu. Access into the fourth valley of Waikolu is forbidden because it is a watershed for the drinking water of Kalaupapa Settlement. Only Wailau has a trail out to the south shore. In Pāpalaua and Pelekunu you simply walk and scramble up the boulder beds of the streams to get to the headwall at the back of the valleys. To explore Pelekunu, get permission from the Nature Conservancy.

Many private owners have land along the coast. Overall conservation jurisdiction is by the State Department of Land and Natural Resources as far west as the boundary of the Kalaupapa National Historical Park.

Why has this coastline appealed to me so much that I have made eighteen trips from Hālawa to Kalaupapa? The first two were by swimming the distance, towing a small pack, and camping in the valleys. A quote from the dust jacket of a book I wrote after eight solo trips explains a bit. "This Hawaiian place was special: lonely, threatening, beautiful, beckoning." See "Further Reading." And yes, Moloka'i has more visitors now, but it is not commercialized as much as any of the five other islands where paddling can be done.

Several take-out sites are possible for the trip. By prior arrangement, you can end at Kalawao on the east side of the Kalaupapa Peninsula. Again by prior permission, you can paddle around to the settlement on the west side and take out there. Exit from Kalaupapa is by plane, mule, or foot; no roads lead into the area. If you're paddling a rigid craft, you'll need to go on to Mo'omomi Beach (access by permission) or all the way to the west end to take out near the Kaluako'i resort. The Kalaupapa barge, which could ship your rigid craft directly out of the settlement, comes only once a year. Check also with Polynesian Air which may be able to fly out your hardshell kayak (up to 12 feet long) as cargo only and no passengers. (See "Sources.")

Before going to Moloka'i you must apply to the Department of Health in Honolulu for a permit to enter Kalaupapa, even if you will be there only long enough to get on a plane. Richard Marks, a Kalaupapa resident, can arrange a permit and pick you up as part of his Damien Tours (808-567-6171), a fascinating way to see the area and learn its history.

Before you start paddling you'll also need to arrange a flight out from the Kalaupapa airport, as planes land there only by advance reservation. To start the trip you fly to the main airport of Moloka'i in the west central plateau from any of the other five major islands. Rental cars are available but scarce, so reserve one well ahead of making your plane reservation. If you plan to pick up your harshell boat from the dock, you'll need to bring or arrange for car-top racks and a car with gutters that will accept racks. You would need one nonpaddling driver to bring the car back from Hālawa or else arrange with one of the transport companies (try Kukui Tours and Taxi) to take you to the put-in.

If you ship your kayak, by barge, to Moloka'i it will arrive at the dock in Kaunakakai on the south shore, nine miles from the main airport. You'll need to make advance arrangements to have your hard-shell boat shipped out of Kalaupapa, but don't miss the once-a-year schedule. Passenger planes that can land at the Kalaupapa airstrip are too small for hardshell boats. An inflatable will work fine. I'd be re-luctant to use a folding boat on this coast—too many boulder landings through surf. An inflatable will bounce-land on boulders and can be deflated and carried out by mule, backpack, or plane. A plastic hard-shell will survive the landing, but won't work for any of the other three. Yes, a mule could carry it, but the trail switchbacks are too tight!

Kaunakakai is the main town of the island. You can pick up last-minute supplies there and stay in a hotel or bed and breakfast in order to get a good night's sleep before take off. You might want to drive the 30 miles or arrange a ride out to the east end and camp there. It takes two hours to get up, eat, and pack your boat, and it's best to be under way by 7 A.M. on this coast. A later launch means rougher seas when the wind picks up.

As the road curves to drop into Hālawa Valley, you get a view of the small bay and the surf conditions of the moment. You should pause

Even in summer the surf often breaks across Hālawa Bay.

here and with binoculars check out the waves that often break across the entrance to the bay. In summer, small power boats are anchored in the bay and people are camped on the point on the north side. You can drive over to that side, sheltered somewhat by trees from the wind, to pack and launch.

Sometimes getting out of the bay is an easy, calm paddle, but more often you need to pick the smallest set of breaking waves to punch through. Then it's three miles of 1,000-foot cliffs before the first possible landing. En route you may see the red-tailed or white-tailed tropic birds who nest in the cliffs and soar overhead. I have rarely seen them on other islands.

The following possible landings, which are pinpointed on the map, are numbered from east to west from Hālawa Valley. The more vivid meanings of place names and the mileage from the put-in are indicated in parentheses.

1. *Puaʻahaʻunui* ("pig snorting much") *Peninsula* (3 miles). This is the first of five small peninsulas along the coast. It's a hard place to land, with large, rounded boulders on all sides, but there is a slight lee as the coast curves in on the west side. A 1,000 foot intermittent waterfall makes a small pool at its base, but the water then disappears underground and doesn't flow to the sea. It's a half-hour slog through brush to the pool. *Hala* (pandanus) is the dominant tree here, as it is along most of the wet coasts of Hawaiʻi. Its angular branches, aerial roots from the trunk, and pineapple-shaped fruit make it distinctive. To an islander away from Hawaiʻi, a photo of pandanus says home. The thorny leaves are used for weaving mats and baskets, for thatching roofs, and were even woven into sails for canoes in the old days. A few papaya trees are also there among the rock walls of a prehistoric Hawaiian population— pre-written history, that is. For nearly 2,000 years the Hawaiians had an oral history, carefully memorized by each generation.

From Puaʻahaʻunui you get a good view down the coast. The Kalaupapa lighthouse seems very far away (12 miles). If you camp here, you will have that reassuring flash every 10 seconds all night, but do not count on a Coast Guard crew there for help. All lights in Hawaiʻi are now automated—no more lighthouse keepers.

2. *Hākaʻaʻano Peninsula* (4 miles). A bamboo framework shelter with a tarp and sleeping area is on the west side. It is rebuilt annually and

maintained by local residents for their family's use. I would not use it without obtaining permission and knowing when they and their friends are coming. If the wind is strong, the trees a tenth of a mile east offer better shelter than the exposed shore. Carry water from the Pōhakuloa Stream waterfall, a few yards west. Look for papaya trees in the tangle of *hala* at the base of the fall.

3. *Pāpalaua Valley* ("rain fog place") (4 1/2 miles). You can get ashore here through surf onto boulders; you get back out with difficulty. Some of the wind and surf techniques mentioned in chapter 4 were learned here through nasty experience. Unless it is unusually calm, it is best to land at Hāka'a'ano and walk the half-mile to this valley. En route you will need to wade or swim under the stone arch of Keanapuka ("the cave hole"), where wave erosion scoured out the softer rock, leaving a 20-foot high arch. The water under the arch is deep enough to let you paddle your boat through for vivid photos of black rock and blue-green sea.

Pāpalaua Valley has campsites back among the hala trees, stream pools for bathing, and red shampoo ginger blossoms. A deep pool for swimming is the reward after a mile scramble upstream to the base of the 1,000-foot waterfall.

You are on your own here. Boats do not anchor in this exposed bay, and a rescue helicopter could not land in the swirling winds. Just past Pāpalaua Stream is a small cliff face that you have to swim around if you want to go on to the peninsula of Kikipua. There you can explore the rock remains of ancient Hawaiian houses and a heiau, said to have been a training place for priests of the polytheistic religion. What you also can find there are remains of an irrigation system—clearly defining taro terraces and the watercourses between them. The waterfall on the cliff above, Kahiwa, is reputed to be the highest in the state. I have often wondered, however, if that name was switched when the maps were made, with the next one west, which is called Waiaho'okalo, "water for making taro." That waterfall drops sheer into the sea; there's no possible space for growing taro. A drawing of its sea level base is an illustration in my *Paddling My Own Canoe* (see "Further Reading").

Paddling On: Between Pāpalaua and Wailau Valley is a three-mile coastline of 2,000-foot cliffs. Here you are likely to hear the harsh "skark" of terns flying overhead. Remembering that sound and the

You can paddle through the arch at Keanapuka.

rough grumble of the boulders rolling in the surf can bring an instant recall of Moloka'i to me, no matter how far away I may be.

4. *Wailau Valley* ("many waters") (7 1/2 miles). This valley, the largest on the coast, has a temporary anchorage for small powerboats in the lee of Lēpau Head. The best landing is on the boulder shore at the mouth of Wailau Stream. A sand beach is farther west, but since it is

A cool, pounding massage in Pāpalaua Stream.

beyond the lee of Lēpau Head, it always has surf and a plunging shore break. A few people live in the valley (one permanent house), and residents from the south shore establish a little village each summer at the mouth of the stream, using ingeniously rigged blue plastic tarps for shelter. Some are quite luxurious, with ice chests and food resupplied by boat. In the evening if you are camped to the west above the sandy

You may be swimming with the mythical giant mo'o.

beach, you can look back to the lights of gasoline lanterns and sometimes hear a local-style guitar concert. Residents here are a good source of information about the valley—where the mountain apples grow, where to find the deep swimming hole in the stream, and where to camp without intruding. You could spend months exploring just this one valley.

An ancient seven-mile trail, restored by the Hawai'i Chapter of the Sierra Club over several summers, leads back along the valley floor, up a steep pali where you cling to root hand holds, and then down to the south shore. Unless your boat is a very lightweight deflatable kayak or you are swimming the coast, you would not choose this exit from shore. The trail is often overgrown and hard to follow.

Paddling On: Between Wailau and Pelekunu valleys is another small peninsula, Waiehu. Just beyond it is the highest sea cliff in the world, 3,450 feet, according to *The Guiness Book of Records.* It is not a sheer drop; the cliff leans back at a 70 degree slope, and down the face tumble waterfalls, leaping and misting in the steady winds. Sometimes their heights are hidden in clouds. In very dry years they may not flow at all; in heavy rains they double in number. You will never forget them.

Ahead expect washing machine turbulence as you enter the passage between Mōkoholā Rock and the two points of Kaholaiki Bay. You could make a landing in this bay, but it is not good for camping, and you could return to it as a day trip from Pelekunu.

5. *Pelekunu* ("smelly from lack of sunshine") *Valley* (10 miles). Four streams pour into this U-shaped bay. The main one is Pelekunu Stream, at the east side of the rocky beach. Near the stream mouth a small area of black sand comes and goes. It may make landing easier, but while still afloat check out which section of the beach has the smallest shore break.

It is hard to write about Pelekunu; my experience there during 16 years of brief visits was so intense. Others have lived there much longer in the old pre-Captain Cook days and more recently, and have felt its power. The Nature Conservancy recently bought the valley—good news for all of us who have a special reverence for this place. Call the Nature Conservancy for permission to go above the shoreline. They have offices on both O'ahu and Moloka'i.

Do not climb on the rock cliffs near shore. One person who tried shattered an elbow when the crumbly rock gave way. The helicopter medevac was costly.

Paddling On: When you leave Pelekunu you thread between the 100-foot seastack of Mokumanu and the sheer cliff at the base of Hā'upu ("crooked hill") Peak. You will need all your balancing skills here, as

The waterfalls of Wailele reach 3,000 feet into the clouds.

the seas bounce back and forth between them. Ahead is Kapahu Point ("the drum" or "coffin"). Around it you will be in quieter water again.

6. *Hā'upu Bay* (11 miles). Keawanui, a cliff-locked cove on the east side of the bay, is the only anchorage for larger boats on the north coast, and even it is precarious. A hard-working Moloka'i family has built a permanent home here on a sloping cliff above the sea. With

Joseph Hu fishes off north Moloka'i on a rare calm morning. Hā'upu Peak in the distance.

the increase of boats and people along the coast, they have more drop-in visitors than even their kind hospitality can handle. Don't intrude up their trail unless you have been invited. Under that slope, a lava tube leads 100 feet into the cliff. You can paddle in and listen to the echoing boom as the surge pounds against the back wall.

The only landings are on the ledge near the cave or on the boulder shore by the waterfall a quarter-mile farther. If you camp on those boulders you surely will want an air mattress. Camp well out from the cliff or tucked back under. That boulder beach came from above.

Paddling On: A half-mile west of Hā'upu Bay, marked on the topo map as Kapailoa ("the long lift"), but referred to in other literature as Ana-puhi ("cave of the eel"), is another lava tube tunnel which you can paddle through when wave surge does not close off the entrance. The best time to enter is about 10 A.M.—good timing if you were at Pelekunu the night before and got an early start. The morning light shines down through the sea just outside the cave and reflects back up to you floating just inside, creating the brilliant acetylene-torch blue that made the Grotto of Capri famous. I once left my boat floating, with a tethered paddle and a bag hung overboard to slow its drift, and

Displacing the ʻoʻopu in a Pelekunu Stream.

dove to the sandy bottom to see if the blue went all the way down. It's a lovely feeling to spiral back up through the watercolor.

Paddle on out the other end and around the rough-water point of Kūkaʻiwaʻa. Ahead is a 200-foot rock, the sea stack called Huelo. On its top is a thatch of Pritchardia palms, *loʻulu,* with their large fan-shaped leaves. Legend says that the Hawaiians gathered these and

At sunset the shadow of Hāuʻpu Peak falls across Pelekunu Bay.

Leaving Pelekunu Bay on a calm July day. (Photo by Noelle Sutherland)

Turbulence around the 100-foot rock stack of Mokumanu.

The rock stack of Huelo is capped with rare lo'ulu palms.

used them as wings to leap from that cliff ahead where the winds blowing down the coast made an updraft for soaring. Perhaps Hawaiians invented hang-gliding. Now you are within the boundaries of the National Historical Park of Kalaupapa. Check with the park in advance for information and any restrictions. See "Sources."

Beyond is the inverted cone island of 'Ōkala ("bristling"), and farther out is Mōkapu, sometimes called Bread Loaf Island for its shape.

Neither has any place to land. Next trip I'll check out at low tide a ru-
mored underwater cave on ʻŌkala.

7. *Waikolu* ("three waters") *Valley* (14 miles). The sudden calm
around Leina o Papio ("Papio's leap") is wonderful. It is the easiest
landing of the four valleys. Stay on shore here. Trespass notices are
posted against walking into the watershed area. That "grass" on the
slope just above the rocks is mostly a pest plant called beggar's lice,
whose seeds stick like glue to your shoes, socks, and pants. The only
way to avoid them is zori, bare legs, and short shorts, or staying on the
rocks.

You can bathe in the stream below the little spillway—and how
welcome it is. From here you could walk the mile-long boulder shore
and up the steep slope to Kalawao Park on the east side of the Kalaupapa Peninsula, but carrying a hardshell kayak that mile would be
very difficult. Since you probably plan to continue in your hardshell
beyond Kalaupapa, skip to #9. With my 24-pound inflatable rolled
into a backpack, and making two trips, I had little trouble. Certainly
you need to be wary of rocks falling off the cliffs.

8. *Kalawao Area* (15 miles). This eastern, inside corner of the peninsula is closer to the end of the road that ends at Kalawao Park, so it is
easier to carry your gear to the park from here than from Waikolu. The
trade-off is a rough landing, through almost constant shore break. Permission to land here will be required in advance from the National
Park. If you plan to have Richard Marks meet you here for his tour and
for transportation to the airfield, that will also require advance
arrangement. It is three miles from here across the peninsula. After a
steep climb up the hill, the trail meanders. Keep veering toward the
sea, down through a small gulch. You can rest at the pavilion of the
park, where fresh tap water is available for drinking. Before you leave
the Kalawao area, stop at Father Damien's church, itself a monument
to his sainthood and to his long years of work here at Kalaupapa. On
the trip you should carry Gavan Daws' *Holy Man*; finish the final
chapter here in the most fitting place.

9. *Kalaupapa Settlement* (20 miles). If you elect to paddle around the
peninsula to the settlement dock or to the little pavilion closer to the
airstrip, be wary of the wind, which will try to mash you against the
jagged cliff on the east side of Kalaupapa peninsula before you can get

Noelle digs in her heels and grimly holds the boat in the backwash at Kalawao.

far enough out at sea to clear the outside of Kahi‘u Point. If you landed at Waikolu, paddle all the way out to Mōkapu Island and beyond before aiming for the point. You need the sea room to outmaneuver that strong onshore wind. This is a place for which the sailor's expression "Beware a lee shore" was meant; a crunch into those sharp rocks would not be just bruising, but almost certainly fatal.

At Kalaupapa Settlement (by advance arrangement), you can make a tour of the area, then catch the plane out, or take the mule ride up the trail to see more of "topside" Moloka‘i.

A Southside Possibility

As I flew low and close along the south side of Moloka‘i recently, I saw good snorkeling country was out there a quarter-mile off shore, beyond the mud flats. It was clear water, about ten feet deep, with rocks for fish and sand flats in between. You'd need to be wary of the wind, which parallels the shore, and keep lined up with shore markers. Or you could start a mile or two east of town and drift back. Local knowledge here can help you decide the best place to anchor and explore. Call Mike Holmes at Fun Hogs (see "Sources") for advice and information about other south shore paddles.

11

♏

Maui

Four Coastlines

Maui has one long, almost wilderness shoreline paddle beginning in Hāna at the east end of the island and going west to Kahului town. It starts in green jungles and waterfalls, and ends in a drier, urban area. You could split up the long voyage into sections, since there is road access to shore at several points along the main route. For most of its distance, the Hāna "highway," which parallels the coast, is far enough inland to let you feel isolated. In addition to this long one, several moderately easy day trips are possible along the way.

Three other shoreline paddles are described. Two islands, Molokini and Lānaʻi, could be reached by kayak, but both trips can be hazardous because of strong winds and currents, and both have access by commercial tours and transportation. Lānaʻi is discussed in chapter 12.

Maui is the second largest island in the state of Hawaiʻi, the third most populated, and is second only to Oʻahu in number of tourists. With a population of about 110,000, and 44,000 tourists on any day, nearly half the people you see will be visitors. Two volcanoes formed the island. The older one, in West Maui, has a high point of nearly 6,000 feet, an annual rainfall of 400 inches, and deeply eroded canyons. The other, Haleakalā ("house by the sun"), is 10,023 feet, high enough that the residents can sometimes go up for snowball fights in the winter. It was the second national park in Hawaiʻi; the first was the Hawaiʻi Volcanoes National Park on the Big Island (chapter 13). What appears to be an eight-mile long crater at Haleakalā summit is actually the intersecting heads of two eroded valleys. The last eruption was in 1790, when lava on the southwest flank flowed into the sea, changing the bay where the French explorer La Pérouse had landed.

The main population center is in the adjoining windward towns of Kahului and Wailuku, the seat for Maui County. Kahului is now world-famous among kayakers as the place where Ed Gillet completed his epic 63-day, 2,100-nautical-mile, solo paddle from California in August of 1987.

Maui has three airports. The largest is at Kahului for jet planes; two smaller ones at Hāna and at Kapalua–West Maui are for small prop planes. The only barge port for shipping your kayak is Kahului.

Maui County includes the islands of Maui, Molokaʻi, Lānaʻi, and Kahoolawe. The main tourist centers are on the leeward coasts at Lahaina, Kīhei, and Wailea. Both sugar cane and pineapples are grown on the island, as are crops of interest to oenophiles. Wine grapes are crushed, fermented, and the wine bottled at the ʻUlupalakua Ranch, on the southwest slope of Haleakalā. If you want to add real local flavor to your kayak trip, include a bottle of their Tedeschi champagne. Two microbreweries have added some different flavors to the local menus.

Of all the islands, be most aware of winds on all Maui paddles. Many days I would look out and judge it as 20 knots by 10 A.M. Resident kayakers on Maui generally plan to complete their day's voyage by 11 A.M. Maui lies between two notoriously rough channels and has an isthmus between two high mountain areas. It's going to get the result—wind-tunnel winds.

Maui offers the possibility of imaginative trip combinations. For instance, you could organize a crater-to-kayak expedition in which you would hike the trail into Haleakalā Crater and spend the night at Hōlua cabin, which you've reserved far in advance through the headquarters of the Haleakalā National Park (see "Sources"). The warmth of the wood stove is welcome at this altitude. If you didn't win the cabin lottery, you could bring your tent, tarp, and a warm sleeping bag and camp out. The next day you could wind around the colorful cinder cones, nibbling ʻōhelo berries. You would spend the night at Palikū ("standing cliff") at the foot of the eastern wall of the crater. At sunset you might sit in the door of the cabin, or at your tent site, watching the nēnē, the endemic Hawaiian geese, feeding there in the grassland. The next day you could trek down the long slope, out of the

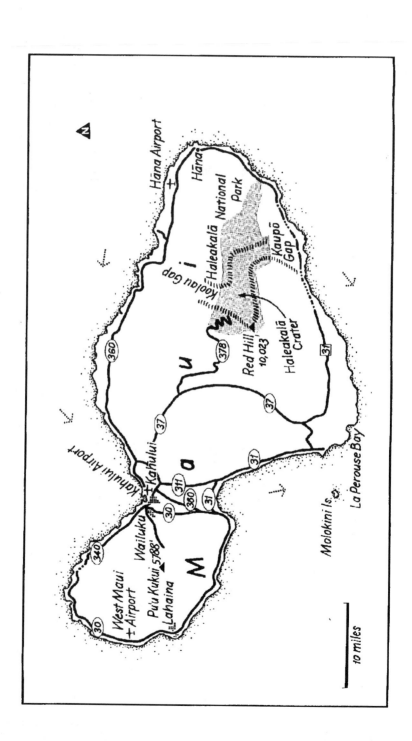

national park, down to the sea at Kaupō, where you would have arranged to exchange your backpacks for kayaks. Then you would have a choice of paddling upwind to Hāna or downwind and around the southwest corner to Kīhei.

Before driving to Kaupō or to Hāna, inquire about road conditions. Floods sometimes wash out some of the bridges to Hāna, and the south coast road between Kaupō and Kīpahulu is often under repair, though all but four miles of it is now paved. The road along the north coast to Hāna is famous for curves, for 54 bridges, many of them one-lane, and for general lack of improvement. Most residents want it that way. People who do not understand that the whole trip is the experience, not just the small town of Hāna, or the Seven Pools area, should not go. Carry Angela Kay Kepler's *Guide to the Hāna Highway* as a knowledgeable companion. A cassette tape describing the trip is available at the Shell gas station in Kahului, one mile before the airport.

Shorelines

Northeast Maui: Hāna to Kahului, the Waterfall Coast

Rating: Class IV
Quad maps: Hāna, Nāhiku, Keʻanae, Haikū, Pāʻia
Total length and time: 42 miles, 4 to 8 days
Put-in: Hāna County Beach Park
Take-out: Kanahā County Beach Park
Hazards: Wind, rocky shores, surf, sunburn
Best time of year: June through August

Here is a windward coast with the northeasterly wind splitting at the Hāna end of the island and blowing west along both the north and south shores of Maui. The seas are likely to be four to eight feet in summer and especially rough around Keʻanae Point.

For your put-in, the beach park in Hāna Bay is sheltered and quiet. The small town of Hāna has one or two grocery stores for last-minute supplies. For take-out, the coast road comes down to the sea in five places if you decide to shorten the voyage. East to west they are Nāhiku, Wailua, Keʻanae, Honomanu, and Māliko. The last one even has a boat ramp. It would be the preferred take-out, unless you need to get to the airport or to the harbor for shipping your kayak. You could also go on to the Hoʻokipa or Baldwin County Beach Parks, though you would have to find your way in through reefs, surf, and sailboards. The take-out closest to the airport is at Kanahā County Beach Park, which also has week-end camping by permit. If you plan to ship your kayak out from Maui on the barge, paddle on around the breakwater and into the Kahului barge dock. Arrange ahead for this and get a map from Young Brothers barge service.

Water is available from streams or rain or from the four parks en route: the first stop, Waiʻānapanapa, is a state park. The others, Hāna where you start, Hoʻokipa, Baldwin, and Kanahā, are county parks. Camping is by permit at Waiʻānapanapa. Apply at the Maui State Parks office in Wailuku. This park also has housekeeping cabins; as of 1997, they rent for $45 a night for one to four people. They are very popular with Hawaiʻi residents, so apply months in advance. We don't

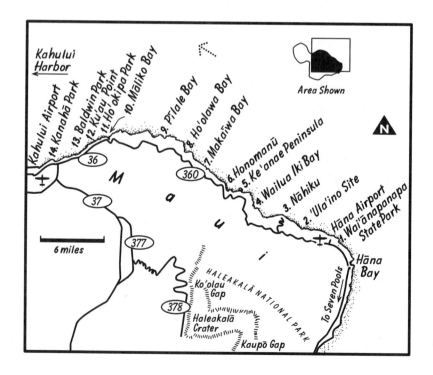

recommend camping at Baldwin; it's a long carry from shore and you pitch your tent in a fenced cage with no shade.

The terrain along this coast is small cliffs, jungles, tiny islands, and waterfalls upstream. On one trip we counted over 30 streams coming down to the shore. You'll delight in those pools with cascade showers along the first half of the route. "But isn't the water cold?" About 70 degrees F—just right on a hot day, exhilarating on a cool one.

The following possible landings, which are pinpointed on the map, are numbered from east to west from Hāna County Beach Park. The mileage from the put-in is indicated in parentheses for each landing.

1. *Wai'ānapanapa* ("glistening water") *State Park* (3 miles). Contorted black *a'ā* lava, *hala* trees, jungle vines, a black sand beach with crashing white surf, fresh water caves—this is spectacular country. The caretaker who lives here knows the area well. Check in with her with your permit before setting up camp. A short trail leads from shore up to the office and to the camping area. The caves also figure in Hawaiian legend. In one story, a chief's unfaithful wife took refuge from his wrath by hiding in one of the caves. He saw her reflection in the water, entered the cave, and killed her. The water is said to run red with her blood every April. It may be the annual spawning of red shrimp, *'ōpae*, that stains the water. If it is low water, at the left side of the pool you can see a hole in the rock wall where you could swim through to another cave. The first time I did it I was solo, so I tied a line to a big rock in the first pool and tied the other end around my waist. Then, with mask and fins on, the extra line looped in my left hand, and a waterproof flashlight in my right, I went exploring. If your light goes out, you'll learn what total darkness is. Carry two.

2. *'Ula'ino* ("stormy red") *Site* (7 miles). Just past 'Ula'ino on the topo map, Helele'ike'ōhā ("taro sprout falls") Stream has a deep pool with lacy waterfalls trickling in and others spilling out over the edge and down to your kayak on the rocky shore. Local people call it the Blue Pool. To photographers and nereids alike it is irresistible.

3. *Nāhiku* (10 miles). In these last three miles you've passed eight streams and 15 rock islets. Now you come around Ōpūhano Point, around some rock outcrops and into the large, protected bay of

The waterfall into the Blue Pool. (Photo courtesy of Go Bananas Kayak Shop)

Honolulu Nui. A tiny bathing pool where you can sit under a water-fall is under a ledge just ahead as you move in east to the rocky shore, 50 feet from the point where cars come down and park. For a less pop-ulated site (no road), paddle on half a mile to the edge of Hanawī tream with its boulder beach.

4. *Wailua Iki* (12 1/2 miles). Out at the entrance of the cove is the 80-foot-high islet of Makoloaka where you might stop to do some dive exploring. Ahead on shore are two streams. Aim for the one to your right, and if the shore break is small and the tide is high, you may be able to paddle right up the stream from the sea, an easy way to get your boat next to your meal site without carrying.

5. *Ke'anae Peninsula* (16 miles). The bounciest water of the trip will be these four miles as you go around Pauwalu Point with its rocky spires and caves. You can come ashore near an old boat landing on the west side of Ke'anae Point. A side road from the Hāna Highway comes

The bow of the boat, the peak of the wave, and the ridges of Haleakalā on Maui's north coast.

down to this community with its historic Congregational church that was built in 1860. The boat ramp is still a jagged edge, but boulder beaches make a possible landing. You could stay overnight at the YMCA's Camp Keʻanae (242-9007) but I'd choose to go on to the next bay.

6. *Honomanū* (17 1/2 miles). A deep bay and valley here have road access; the bay is a popular surfing spot. The stream flows into the sea across a rocky shore with some patches of black sand.

7. *Makaīwa* ("mother of pearl eyes"—as in an image) (21 miles). This deep inlet is usually calm even in a mid-size ocean swell. I have flown close to this coast en route to Hāna Airport, before paddling it back; with the topo maps on my lap, I made notes and comparisons. Coming into Makaīwa you can bounce pass inside of Keōpuka Rock, an islet of 1.7 acres and 120 feet elevation.
Paddling On: Just out of Makaīwa you'll pass Kapukaamaui Point where you can look for a sea cave. As you paddle into the dark, words like troglodytes and cavallas and nematodes (Captain Nemo's monster

Wailua Iki Bay at dawn.

amphibians?) whirl in your brain. If it's calm you can safely explore many cliffs and caves. If not, you'll just want to get to the next quiet landing. Waipi'o (curved water) Bay often has more surge than you'd choose for a stopping spot.

8. *Hoʻolawa Bay* (26 miles). Now you're getting into drier country. A grassy plateau is just east of the river mouth. As you leave this bay, steer between breakers on the reef that is marked on the topo map and those at Honopou Point.

9. *Pilale Bay* (28 miles). Halehaku Point usually creates a lee of calmer water in this bay. You may want to check in advance at the Bishop Museum in Honolulu for the archeological report on the heiau in the area. With the increase in awareness of the old ways and values, *nā heiau* (places of veneration or worship) have become a sensitive issue. Please observe and respect Hawaiian customs when visiting such sites throughout the islands.

10. *Māliko* ("budding") (34 miles). This sheltered bay and the privately owned boat ramp make a good take-out. The owners of the surrounding area usually do not mind if you make a quick, clean exit here. For anyone meeting you, the landmark is the small, well-used horse corral near the curve of the road.

11. *Hoʻokipa* ("hospitality") *County Beach Park* (36 miles). Don't let the translation lull you. This is wind surfing territory, and if the wind is up you'll have to go way out around these winged boards. They fly in a colorful oval pattern in and out from shore at a speed ten times yours. Some of Maui's biggest surfing waves are also found here in season.

12. *Kūʻau Point* (37 miles). The blue roof of Mama's Fish House is a landmark, a possible take-out, with a grassy lawn and nearby condos you could rent for a night.

13. *Baldwin County Beach Park* (38 miles). Camping by permit, but the fenced, shadeless tent area is a long carry from shore. We'd advise going on.

14. *Kanahā County Beach Park* (42 miles). A long, sandy beach and a pleasant park. Camping is by permit and, so far, on week-ends only. It is within half a mile of the airport, so if you have a folding or inflatable boat, roll it up and call a cab or hike on over if you're flying out this same day.

15. *Kahului Harbor* (43 miles). If you are shipping your hardshell out
by barge to another island, paddle around the breakwater and into the
Young Brothers Dock. Get instructions from them in advance.

Northwest Maui: The Tourist Coast

Rating: Class III
Quad maps: Honolua, Lahaina
Total length and time: 18 miles. One day or break it into several half
day picnics
Put-in: Honokōhau Bay
Take-out: Launiupoko State Wayside Park, or your choice
Hazards: Seasonal surf, off-shore winds, boats, swimmers
Best time of year: All year. If surf closes out the northern section,
move west and south

Except for the first three miles, this is a populated, touristy area,
and you could put in or take out at more than a dozen beaches along
the coast. I suggest Honokōhau as a put-in because it has a bit more
wildness to it than most of the coast, and because you can get your vehicle close to shore and don't need to park on the highway. Another
quieter trip would be to put in at Fleming Beach Park, paddle and
snorkel upwind to Honolua and then back to your car. It might be
safer here than at Honokōhau.

No camping parks are available along this coast, so unless you have
made the Lahaina-Nāpili-Kapalua area your hotel headquarters, you'll
need to paddle whatever route you've selected all in one day.

The wildest water will probably be the first two miles, the best snorkeling the next two. Remember that the fish live and the coral grows
where the rocks are. If it's a sandy beach with no rocks or reefs—then
no fish.

All along the route you get a fine view of three islands: Moloka'i to
the north, Lāna'i eight miles west, and Kaho'olawe to the southwest.
On the shore side you look up deep gulches to the misty summits of
the West Maui mountains. Nearing the end of the trip, you will be on
the edge of the whale-watching area, seasonal from November to
March.

Although resorts cover most of the coast, remember that all of
them have public access to and from the shore. In addition, four

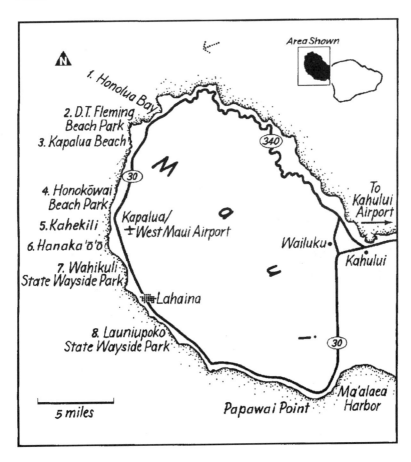

county beach parks and three state wayside parks have access, parking, and water. From the sea it is difficult to figure out just where you are along the coast. You may want to drive the route first, or you may decide to just play it by paddle and come ashore wherever it looks best. In addition to state and county park information, the "County Shoreline Access Guide," funded by Nā Ala Hele, Hawai'i Trail and Access System, and issued by Maui County, is very helpful as a countywide summary of beach access.

The following possible landings, which are pinpointed on the map, are numbered from north to south from Honokōhau. The mileage from the put-in is indicated in parentheses for each landing, and some of the more vivid meanings of place names are given.

1. *Honolua* ("two harbors") *Bay* (3 miles). En route from Honokōhau, you'll have two and a half miles of a tail wind (try a sail), lots of rocky islets, and one sandy beach without shade. Once you round Lipoa Point you'll be sheltered from the wind. Honolua is a Marine Life Conservation District that extends on to the next bay, Makuleia.

2. *D. T. Fleming Beach Park* (4 miles). A local favorite, this curved, scenic cove has complete facilities and paved, shaded parking. An alternate day trip would be to start here, where the parking is reasonably secure, paddle up to Honolua for lunch, then come back here, snorkeling most of the way.
Paddling On: Rocky points, condominiums, and sandy beaches for the next two miles.

3. *Kapalua Beach* (6 miles). A public right-of-way is at the south end of a sandy beach, which is usually safe for swimming and kayak landing. This used to be called Fleming's Beach—confusing.

4. *Honokōwai* (9 miles). Paved access, sandy beach, parking, restrooms, picnic tables, swimming. Erosion has removed some of this public beach park.

5. *Kahekili* (9 1/2 miles). The road entrance to this pleasant area is at the large Kā'anapali sign. The general landmark (just south) is Black Rock, site of the Sheraton Maui, the first major hotel in the "new" development of the whole area back in the 1960s. We admired the hotel then, built beside Black Rock, where kids made the long arching dive into the sea, as in Acapulco. Now the hotel has remodeled and rebuilt on top of the rock. The beach park is a good take-out site, has an excellent snorkeling reef, restrooms, showers, a picnic pavilion, and shaded parking.

6. *Hanaka'ō'ō* ("digging stick bay") (11 miles). This park is just past Black Rock. I remember when I could fly into the small landing strip here, carry my pack down to the end of the runway, inflate my boat, and be under way in less than an hour. Now the airstrip has moved to the mauka side of the highway and become much more complex.

7. *Wahikuli* ("noisy place") (14 miles). This popular park has showers, picnic tables, and restrooms. There are two small sandy beaches; along the rest of the shore is a rock wall.

Paddling On: For the next five miles you'll be cruising past the town of Lahaina, its small boat harbor, boats anchored offshore, and thousands of tourists. Do your research ahead, and you can find some great restaurant to pull into. Why else paddle in civilization?

8. *Launiupoko State Wayside Park* (18 miles). Occasional surfing waves offshore may give you a bit of fun. Showers, picnic facilities, and parking make it a good take-out place.

The Cave and Cliff Coast

Rating: Class III
Quad map: Māʻalaea
Total length and time: 5 miles, 1 day
Put-in: Pāpalaua Wayside Park
Take-out: Māʻalaea Small Boat Harbor
Hazards: Cliffs, rocks, power boats, whale regulations
Best time of year: November through March for whale watching

You might extend this paddle from the previous one by leapfrogging past some of the Tourist Coast landings by car with your boat on top. Then paddle the "cave coast" at the base of the cliff road where the highway curves in and out and through the only car tunnel on Maui. On this short paddle, landings depend on surf conditions.

1. *Papawai Point* (3 miles). Once past this point and past Manuʻōhule, you'll come to McGregor Point. John Clark's *Beaches of Maui County* describes the area: "To the east of McGregor Point, between the last shoreline houses at Māʻalaea and the lighthouse, are three small pockets of white sand. The offshore bottoms are shallow and a mixture of sand and rock—fine swimming areas for children on calm days. The lava shelves between these sandy areas contain many small tidal pools. To the west of McGregor Point are several similar beach areas, except that the shoreline is shingle and cobblestone, not sand, and the waters offshore tend to be a little deeper. All of these small beach

parks are excellent areas for snorkeling, fishing, and picnicking. They are completely unimproved and unmarked by signs."

Kayakers must stay aware of the Marine Mammal Protection Act. Basically, you do not approach a whale. If they approach you while you stay on your course, okay. Certainly whatever you do will be observed and photographed from shore or from the many whale-watching cruises. November to March is whale season, but all year you may see dolphins and turtles.

La Pérouse Bay to Makena Landing

Rating: Class III
Quad map: Mākena
Total length and time: 3 miles, 1 day (take time to snorkel)
Put-in: La Pérouse Bay
Take-out: Kanahena shore
Hazards: Wind, coral, rock landings
Best time of year: All year except in strong winds and south swell

This is the second shoreline area on Maui that is under special protection. The first was the Marine Life Conservation District of Honolua and Makuleia Bay on West Maui. This one contains the Natural Area Reserve System (2,045 acres) of 'Āhihi-Kīna'u, which includes three-quarters of this route.

To get to the put-in, follow the beach road south through Kīhei, past the last hotel, the Maui Prince. You'll run out of pavement, but the road is passable by ordinary passenger car to its end at La Pérouse Bay, next to the walled Carter Estate. The coral-lava rubble underfoot requires shoes. I suggest you wear lightweight tennies or felt-soled tabis that can be stuffed into a bathing suit or into a waist bag. That way, it's easy to change from shoes to fins and back again.

The shoreline has a number of small coves between lava points, each with its own population of colorful reef fish. Looking at the rather barren shores, you are doubly delighted by those pieces of rainbow under water. Some of the coves you won't see unless you keep looking back over your shoulder or exploring back into each inlet. One cove even has a small tree for shade and to hang your water bag while making lunch.

Paddling and snorkeling with South Pacific Kayaks out of La Perouse Bay.

'Alelele Stream on the south coast of Maui.

Once past Nukuʻele Point (about two miles), you can see your landing spot where the road runs next to the shore. If you've thought ahead you may have shuttled your car back to this spot after unloading at the put-in at La Pérouse Bay.

Depending on the force of the head wind and upon your shuttle, you could go on up to the Maui Prince Hotel or Mākena Landing for take-out. The landmark on all this coast is the 360-foot Puuōlaʻi, believed to be the tail of a moʻo (lizard) who angered Pele by becoming the wife of her lover, Lohiʻau. The tail became Molokini Islet, two miles offshore. It looks like an easy two miles, but at least four people in small craft have been lost in the treacherous winds and currents of these channels. Take a commercial trip if you want to visit the crowded diving sites of Molokini.

Like all the islands, Maui has possibilities that are not included in this book. Paddling from Hāna at the east end, you could go south and west, past the Seven Pools area of Haleakalā National Park, past the Kaupō Gap, which leads up into Haleakalā Crater, and on along the dry south coast to a take-out at La Pérouse Bay. The people at South Pacific Kayaks in Kīhei have done it often, and sometimes lead groups along this route.

While on Maui, you could check out the scheduled boat trips over to Lānaʻi, and include some diving or paddling days on that island.

12

≈

Lāna‘i
Day Trips

The title of your Lāna‘i journal could be "Paddling on a Tropical Island." The island even comes complete with a mile-long, isolated sandy beach, a coconut palm grove, and a coral reef, each in a different locale. It is not a lush-growth island because it is in the lee of Moloka‘i and Maui and therefore gets little rainfall.

Of all the islands, Lāna‘i has changed the most in the last ten years. It was once "the Pineapple Island" literally, with the fruit scent heavy in the air, teenagers expecting to grow up picking pine, and 90 percent of the people dependent on those 16,000 acres of spiny fruit. Now pineapples are down to 100 acres, grown only for the hotels and local residents. Two of the hotels are luxury class—the Mānele Bay Hotel on the south shore, and the Lodge at Kō‘ele in the cool uplands. You might believe from all the excellent reviews that the island has no other place to stay, but three bed-and-breakfasts are listed in the Hawai‘i Visitors Bureau Accommodations Guide, and the updated Hotel Lāna‘i, with moderate prices, has eleven rooms. Aloha Island Air and Hawaiian Airlines each fly in on daily schedules, and rental cars are available but expensive.

Basically, paddling on Lāna‘i means day trips only. If you don't intend to stay overnight, and make prior room reservations, then you'll need to check all the ferry and plane schedules to fly out at evening. On the whole island, only one area has public camping, and its three sites are tightly controlled. Lāna‘i is the smallest of the six islands you can paddle. It's 13 miles wide, 18 miles long, and 47 miles around, with the highest point at 3,400 feet. Hiking the trails in the cool uplands among Norfolk and Cook pines is a pleasant change from the summer heat at sea level. On the coast there are day paddles from a put-in at Kaumalapau Harbor on the west side, up to the snorkeling area of Nānāhoa Rocks, or south down to Kaunolū Bay. If you are a strong paddler, you could go from Kaumalapau up to Polihua Beach and back in a day. From the other put-in at Mānele Bay you could paddle to Club Lānaʻi and back, or out to Puʻu Pehe Cove and on to Kaunolū, then return. Each would be a reasonable day trip.

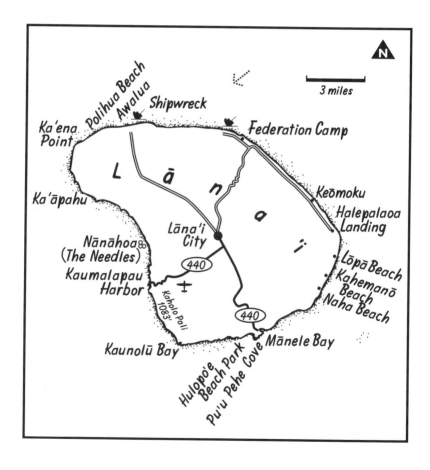

Shorelines

Rating: Class III
Quad map: Lānaʻi
Total length and time: Day paddles only
Put-in: Mānele Small Boat Harbor or Kaumalapau Harbor
Take-out: Same
Hazards: Wind, surf, heat, lack of water
Best time of year: All year; oppressively hot in summer if there is no breeze; occasional summer surf on the south and west shores; cooler but more wind in winter

Winds vary according to your position around the island. Trades blow onshore on the northeast side, wrap around the north and south sides, and often swirl or die on the west side. The seas are fairly calm inside the long reef on the northeast side, and calm on the south and west sides except in a summer swell coming up from the "roaring forties and furious fifties," the high latitudes of the far south Pacific, during the southern hemisphere's winter. Local Kona storms from the south also kick up a chop and local surf. The wind can be strong in the afternoon along Kealakahiki Channel to the south and Kalohi Channel to the north.

The 10-acre area of Mānele Harbor on the south shore is controlled by a harbormaster for the state Division of Harbors. Five round-trip ferries come daily from Lahaina, Maui. Much of the rest of the island is administered by the Kōʻele Corporation, a part of the larger Castle and Cooke Incorporated.

You can ship your hardshell kayak by Young Brothers barge to Kaumalapau Harbor and start your day paddles there. The harbor is also the closest put-in to the airport. Be aware that Hulopoʻe allows only Hawaiian canoes to land there, in keeping with traditions, so you would need to land your kayak at Mānele Harbor, make arrangements for its safekeeping, or else carry it over to your campsite.

Residents of the island are allowed to camp almost anywhere, so if you know people on the island you can camp with them. It is even possible to put in at Lahaina, and paddle the eight-mile downwind crossing of ʻAuʻau Channel, but I wouldn't try it or recommend it.

The winds are too unpredictable. You would be paddling the northern edge of the area between the four islands of Moloka'i, Maui, Lāna'i, and Kaho'olawe, where humpback whales come to mate and to give birth each winter. The whales are seen throughout the islands, but the greatest concentration is here. They start arriving in October, their numbers peak in mid-February, and by May nearly all have left for northern waters. Whales are protected by law from harassment, but if you simply keep paddling on your course they may come to see you.

Drinking water en route is very scarce. Carry your own. You'll need a minimum of three quarts per person per day.

The two following possible day trips, with landing sites which are pinpointed on the map, are numbered from Mānele Harbor first to the east and north, then back to Mānele and south. The mileage from the put-in is indicated in parentheses for each landing.

1. *Halepalaoa* ("whale house") *Landing* (9 miles each way). If you leave Mānele after 10 A.M. you will most likely have a head wind. Whether it wraps around from the northeast corner of the island or comes whipping across the isthmus of Maui, it will find you. The first few miles of your trip have a sheer cliff on your left, with no landing possible. Stops may be possible at Naha Beach, Kahemanō Beach, or Lōpā Beach along the way, depending on wind and surf. I preferred going on to the landing, where I knew a better channel for coming ashore. The Club Lāna'i has rebuilt the old pier there, and has added many recreation facilities. Boats come in daily from Maui with passengers, who can choose from a variety of activities before they leave in the afternoon. If you have a folding or inflatable boat you might arrange in advance to go back to Lahaina with them.

Going back to Mānele Bay, a round trip of 18 miles with half of it against the wind, would be a good workout.

2. *Pu'u Pehe Cove* (3 miles round trip). Tide pools on the west side and a sand beach on the east, with a tiny legendary islet, lure people out to explore this cinder cone, which separates Hulopo'e from Mānele. The pocket sand cove usually has fine snorkeling and swimming, but when I was there one October, the surf was too rough to land.

3. *Kaunolū Bay* (6 miles each way). When the sea is quiet you can land in the small U-shaped bay and walk inland to the site of an ancient fishing village, now a registered national historical landmark. The stone ruins are well preserved but take care: it is easy to damage an unmortared wall.

A second base of operations would be Kaumalapau Harbor. You could ship your hardshell kayak into here from any other island, and then paddle north or south.

Paddling north:
1. *Nānāhoa Islets (3 miles)*. Place Names of Hawaii says, "Of the four sea towers off west Lāna'i, the one farthest to sea is said to be female and the others males. . . . Nānāhoa was a legendary character and symbol of sexuality." Nānāhoa, Three Stone, The Needles—all are names for the soaring rock stacks here. The pinnacle closest to shore has a cave inside. Before the isles were designated as seabird sanctuaries, I was told that you could climb into it, but as I sat watching the cave from my kayak, a sudden surge leaped 30 feet high and scoured it out with a huge roar. When the seas are calm the snorkeling is excellent around the stacks.

Nānāhoa Islets on the west side of Lana'i.

2. *Polihua Beach* (9 miles each way). The largest sand beach on Lāna'i, Polihua is more than a mile long and is not often visited. The wind blasts the sand across the shore, the current is strong, and the beach drops off sharply, so landing and launching are difficult. When I was there, a swarm of bees were also inhospitable. I'd like to go back at a different time of day. As you round Ka'ena Point, you'll move into or out of windswept seas coming down the channel between Lāna'i and Moloka'i.

Paddling south from Kaumalapau:
1. *Kaunolū Bay* (4 miles). En route down to the southwest corner of Lāna'i you pass the 1,083-foot Kaholo Pali, the highest sea cliff on the island. It is mute evidence that storms and cliff-cutting surf can come from the south as well as the north.
Paddling On: The next five miles are along rocky cliffs and shore with no good landings, but it is fine fishing country and you may want to troll a line or snorkel. I well remember diving with huge schools of *nenue;* each school had one golden fish among all the gray ones. Probably both legend and science have an explanation.

2. *Hulopo'e Beach Park* (9 miles). This is the best swimming beach on Lāna'i, but landings may be *kapu* (taboo). Check in advance. It is also part of the Mānele-Hulopo'e Marine Life Conservation District and signs are posted showing the restrictions. If you can't land, go on to Mānele and walk back. A fascinating bit of geology is in this area. Evidence shows that about 100,000 years ago a submarine landslide, possibly from the cliff coast near Waipī'o on the Big Island, displaced sea water, forming a wave that rushed up onto island shores. It carried with it rock and reef debris to a height of 1,000 feet. This tremendous wave has been likened to the one in 1958 at Lituya Bay, Alaska, which reached 1,700 feet.

Hulopo'e has three campsites, each one limited to six persons. There is a $5 registration fee plus $5 per person per night. Write to Kō'ele Company, Box L, Lāna'i City, Hi 96763. Phone is (808) 565-7233.

13

⚞

Hawai'i, the Big Island
The Cliff Coast, North and South Kona

Of the six major islands, Hawai'i is my favorite. You could fit the land area of all the other islands onto the Big Island and have space left over. It has the greatest variety of terrain: the Ka'ū desert, one active and two dormant volcanoes, the highest mountains, the largest rain forest, and of course, the longest coastline for paddlers. The population is still small, about 140,000, so you can have a sense of space. I have often looked out from a shelter and murmured happily, "Miles and miles and nobody in it."

Three areas are especially good for paddling. The first is the northeast Waipi'o to Kēōkea cliff and waterfall coast, with its jungled valleys and no-road wilderness. Because of seasonal high surf, it can be planned only as a summer trip. The second and third are the North and the South Kona coasts. I treat them separately because the wind blows in opposite directions. These two coasts are jewels for paddlers. Clear water for snorkeling, small villages in the south, lonely beaches between plush hotels in the north, tiny coves, lava flows, ancient trails, petroglyphs, and calm seas most of the year make this 100-mile coast the best place for long beginner expeditions.

There is plenty to interest the veteran paddler as well. Inland explorations, paddling by moonlight, sea caves, fishing, scuba diving—there is always something new even though you have been to the route before. If you are a hard-core kayaker, you can find local experts to advise you on more Class IV and V trips on the Big Island.

What you will not find on the Big Island are the long stretches of white sandy beaches with coconut palms leaning out over the sea that are the South Pacific ideal in many people's imaginations. The island is too young, geologically, to have developed extensive coral reefs and to have had them erode into sand beaches. You'll need to visit Kaua'i and O'ahu to find more of those. Two large airports, Hilo on the eastern windward coast and Keāhole on the western Kona side, serve the two population centers. A smaller one is at Kamuela (Waimea) in the north central upland. Rental cars are available in Hilo and Kona. You can ship your hardshell kayak or canoe by barge from O'ahu to two ports, Hilo and Kawaihae; the latter is 30 miles north of the Keāhole-Kona airport.

Hilo, whose airport is closest to the Hawai'i Volcanoes National Park, is old-style Hawai'i, with rivers, waterfalls, orchids, lush growth, frequent rainfall, a University of Hawai'i campus, and a non-tourist atmosphere. Hilo has some scenic day paddles inside the breakwater and out around Coconut Island, or up the river into Waiākea Pond. A great place to see six-person and one-man outrigger canoes is along the Bayfront County Park. Come in after a women's team has just won a statewide race and share the exuberance. Coastlines beyond Hilo to the northwest or to the southeast have rough windward seas and few landings for paddlers.

You could fly into Hilo, paddle that area, then drive to Hawai'i Volcanoes National Park and explore some of it before driving across the southern part of the island to the Kona Side. The South Kona coast paddle described later in this chapter could be done in reverse or as a loop trip from the southern end, since the wind coming south down the coast is usually less than ten knots.

Kailua-Kona town on the west coast (the hyphenated name distinguishes it from Kailua town on O'ahu) is much more touristy and industrial than Hilo. It's hot in summer, famous for fishing and sunsets, and close to calmer paddling country. Since 1983, continuous eruptions in the Kīlauea area have created a volcanic haze, locally called vog, which sometimes blows over to the Kona side and sits there. A county-run public bus goes between Hilo and Kailua-Kona and to other island towns. You may be able to use it to return to your launching point to pick up your car and return for your kayak. See "Sources" for their address to get routes and schedules.

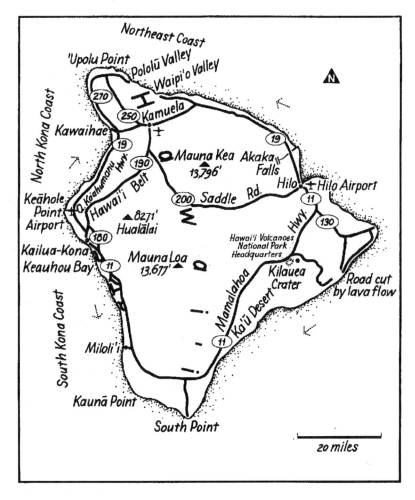

Shorelines

Northeast Coast: Waipi'o to Kēōkea

Rating: Class V
Quad maps: Kukuihaele, Honokāne, Hāwī
Total length and time: 16 miles, 1 to 6 days
Put-in: Waipi'o Valley
Take-out: Kēōkea County Beach Park
Hazards: Surf launchings and landings, rocks, cliffs, rough seas

Best time of year: Mid-May through mid-September. Frequent high surf in other months

This coast is a third version on the themes of Nā Pali on Kauaʻi and the north coast of Molokaʻi, with high cliffs, remote valleys, waterfalls, rock islets, and no roads. Nā Pali has several sand beaches to make landing easier; Molokaʻi has none. The northeast coast of Hawaiʻi has one long one at Pololū and a small one at Honokāne Iki. Recommended boats for here are inflatables or "plastic" hardshell open-top kayaks; both are better able to bounce-land on rocks than fiberglass or folding boats, but you could simply paddle the whole route in one day for the scenery. At least you would have a tail wind. Experienced, capable water rats could do the amphibious walk-swim method of travel described in chapter 1. Wind and current come up the coast from the southeast, and rainfall is the usual 100 to 200 inches a year.

Nine miles northwest of the town of Honokaʻa, Highway 240 ends at a small park overlooking the deep valley of Waipiʻo and the coast beyond. A thousand feet below you the surf curls onto the black sand beach, and at the far end of the shore, the first mile of the trail to the next valley of Waimanu switchbacks up the steep mountainside. For hikers it is 10 miles to Waimanu. For you, by sea, it is only four.

Standing at the lookout it is easy to visualize Waipiʻo as a center of politics and culture in the pre-European days, and as a place of legends. Taro and rice were grown here until the devastating tsunami of 1946. Taro farmers were prospering again when floods wiped out their crops and homes in November 1979. But they continue to work in the valley. Theirs is a hard way to make a living and they, like the farmers of Waiāhole Valley on Oʻahu, should be able to wield their opinion in the occasional conflicts between taro growers, transients, and tourists. We *need* taro, for its food value and its traditions.

Before you leave the lookout, study the shoreline for the best and quietest spot for launching. Sometimes there is a rip current flowing out in a channel where there is less surf, usually at the river mouth.

A mile back from the lookout, on the lower road, is the office of the Waipiʻo Valley Shuttle and the Waipiʻo Valley Artworks, where you can arrange a ride down to the shore if you have a folding or deflatable boat which will fit into their 4WD van (phone 775-2121). They also

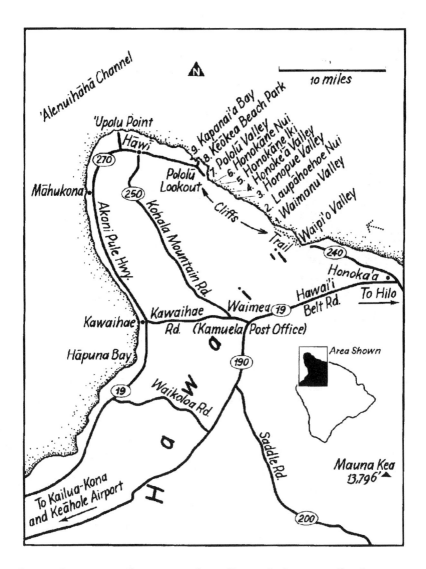

know about rooms for rent in the valley and about unofficial camp-sites. You now need a permit from Bishop Estate to camp on the southeast side of the river. An alternative to an arranged ride is to rent a 4WD from Harper's in Hilo, bring your own boat racks, and to have a non-paddler driver drop you off and then pick you up at Kēōkea at the other end. You need to get an early morning start from Waipi'o

Waipi'o Valley and Stream.

before the wind picks up a choppy sea. No, you can't drive your fancy little rental car down the three-mile road. Well, you could, but the 25 percent grade would prevent driving back up, and 4WD tow trucks are expensive.

Possible landing sites are numbered from southeast to northwest from Waipi'o and are pinpointed on the map. Permits are required for camping in Waimanu Valley (State Division of Forestry and Wildlife in Hilo) and at Kēōkea County Beach Park. The other sites have various owners, private, corporate, and state. The distance from the put-in at Waipi'o is indicated in parenthesis for each landing. Before you land, try to have some assurance that you can get back out. Conditions can change by the hour and overnight. I once waited six hours at Waimanu for the tide and the surf to let me through to the open sea. You may need to allow three days for conditions to change, even in summer.

Caution is also needed when crossing Waipi'o and Waimanu streams; both are swift flowing and subject to sudden rises in water level and to flash floods.

1. *Waimanu Valley* (4 miles). This whole area (5,900 acres) including the trail to get there by land is a National Estuarine Research Reserve. The bottom of the valley is flat, with a meandering, swampy stream, but the sides slope up steeply. The trail from Waipi'o winds down through Norfolk pines on the southeast side; a waterfall from a spring is about a quarter-mile in from shore on the northwest side. With your permit you'll be assigned a numbered campsite, and will receive information about the valley, its endangered species, and about drinking water hazards such as leptospirosis and hepatitis. Boil the water, use a .5 micron or finer filter, or use other reliable methods to purify it. See chapter 5, Food.

2. *Laupāhoehoe Nui* ("large leaf of *pāhoehoe* lava") (6 miles). This shallow peninsula, backed by thousand-foot cliffs and four high waterfalls, is a tangled garden spot. Bananas, mangoes, breadfruit, coconuts, taro, guavas, sweet potatoes, watercress, and more grow here, but landing in your kayak may be difficult through the surf onto a rocky shore. Try the northwest end, where there is a slight lee. Look for the row of lighter green kukui trees leading away from shore toward the cliff and waterfall. You cannot walk here from Waimanu;

An old photo of Waimanu Valley. Note the slight channel at the stream mouth.

A photo (ca. 1925) of the coast between Waimanu and Honopue Valleys.

sheer cliffs that drop into the sea block the way, but amphibians could walk and swim, and walk on to Honopue.

3. *Honopue Valley* (9 miles). The walls of this narrow gorge with its boulder shore become vertical as you scramble upstream. University of Hawai'i scientists made surveys here during the last decades, and, as has been true in most remote valleys, they found evidence of a centuries-long population. Do not try to climb out of the valley; the rock is crumbly and the plants on the cliff are shallow-rooted. Some of us have learned the hard way. Campsites are on both sides of the river.

4. *Honoke'ā Valley* (10 miles). The steep boulder shore and strong surge make this the least-visited beach in all Hawai'i. Recent floods have left the stream bed weedy and uninviting. The islets offshore are scenic but are sheer rock. Landing there is not feasible. One of them, Mokupuka, is named for a cave hole that pierces it high above sea level.

5. *Honokāne Iki* ("Kane's small bay") (11 miles). Rough seas bounce from one cliff side to the other in this bay, building a conflicting shore break and erratic currents. You come around Pau'ekolu ("death of

three") Point to get into the bay from the southeast. Do not make it
'*eha* ("four"). Usually there is a small sand beach in the lee corner of
the bay. Sometimes you find a cool stream for bathing; in drought
years you find only a dry stream bed. You may find luscious strawberry
guavas up the overgrown trail on the southeast side, especially in early
June. The cabin near shore has been restored by the owners, the
Sproat family from the Kohala area. Because of vandalism and other
problems, they are very protective of the Honokāne Iki and Honokāne Nui lands under their control. When I first paddled that coast in
my six-foot, 12-pound inflatable boat, I rolled it into a pack and
walked out from Honokāne Iki.

6. *Honokāne Nui* ("Kāne's big bay") (12 miles). It is the usual landing
in surf on boulders, and it can close out even in summer, but the lower
section of this big valley is worth exploring. An ironwood grove on
shore provides shelter; the intermittent stream has tide pool bathing
at its mouth, and farther inland are the remains of the old Hawaiian
irrigation system for growing taro. I have walked the boulder shore
from here to Pololuū, but to do so you need quiet seas, a low tide, and
the ability to time the wave sets so you don't get bashed.

7. *Pololū* ("long spear") *Valley* (13 miles). The road from the Kohala
area to this end of the cliff coastline stops at the lookout a half-mile
up a steep trail from the beach, so Pololū is one of three possible take-
out spots for your trip. Landing would be through a series of waves, but
at least you have the cushion of a sand beach. Up next to the lookout
once lived Bill Sproat, a great Kohala historian and a legend because
of his career from 1928 to 1968 as trail boss and mule skinner on the
40-mile Kohala Ditch Trail. The trail and tunnels of the ditch, built
in 1908, were an essential part of the irrigation system of the former
Kohala sugar cane plantation. The cane is gone now, but the water
system remains, and Bill is well remembered.

Around Akoakoa Point it is possible to tuck into Neue Bay and
land for a brief rest, but it is not a take-out point. It's a difficult climb
out and not feasible with kayak and gear.

8. *Kēōkea County Beach Park* ("sound of whitecaps") (16 miles).
Three roughwater miles take you non-stop from Pololū around two
cliff points to Kēōkea Bay and its popular park. The shore is rocky, but

Pau'ekolu (the death of three) Point.

The view southeast from Pololū Lookout.

the entry to the tiny, kayak-size, sheltered pool opens up as you hook in to your left. Time the swells, steer your best, and decide at the last moment whether to bash your boat or use your body as a cushion. A strong friend on shore to meet you would be helpful. Above all else, before you attempt to enter the pool make sure no little kids are swimming there. If so, make a U-turn and wait, or go on to the next landing. A short carry for your kayak and gear, showers, pavilions for packing up, and a paved road to the highway make Kēōkea the best of the three possible take-outs. The nearest public phones are at the Wo On Gallery or the Arakaki Store about four miles up the road, so make pick-up arrangements in advance.

9. *Kapanai'a Bay* (17 miles). This landing is usually quieter water than Kēōkea, but you have to walk up a steep quarter-mile trail to the dirt road with an unlocked gate, which leads out a mile to the highway.

Now you are in the special region of Kohala, the north end of the Big Island. It's worth several days of sightseeing in its own right, for its history, green hills, small towns, talented musicians, and magnificent views of the sea.

It's a tight landing at Kēōkea Beach Park.

Northwest Coast: North Kona, the Gold Coast

Rating: Class III
Quad maps: Kailua, Keāhole Point, Makalawena, Kīholo, ʻAnaehoʻo-
malu, Puʻu Hinaʻi, Kawaihae, Keawanui Bay, Māhukona
Total length and time: 55 miles, 5 to 10 days
Put-in: Kailua-Kona next to the pier
Take-out: Māhukona Harbor
Hazards: Surf, wind, sunburn, lava, coral
Best time of year: All year. Hotter in summer, more surf in winter

This "gold coast" is one of contrasts. It has several pieces of an ex-
panding state park, eight large resort hotels, and one residential area,
but it also has miles of rough, uninhabited shore line, mostly lava,
with a few isolated sandy beaches.

Here you could make a voyage entitled "The Elegant Paddler" (described below), staying at a different resort hotel each night. I well recall an article that Paul Theroux wrote about this coast for the *New
York Times Travel Magazine*. He spent $2,500 a day for one week at a
resort, then the next week lived on $2.50 a day at a solo campsite with

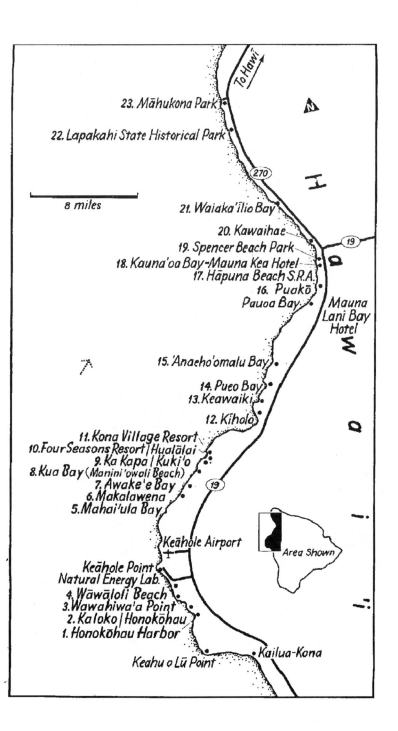

To Hawi

23. Māhukona Park

22. Lapakahi State Historical Park

270

8 miles

21. Waiaka'īlio Bay

20. Kawaihae

19. Spencer Beach Park

18. Kauna'oa Bay–Mauna Kea Hotel

17. Hāpuna Beach S.R.A.

16. Puakō

Pauoa Bay

Mauna Lani Bay Hotel

19

15. 'Anaeho'omalu Bay

14. Pueo Bay

13. Keawaiki

12. Kīholo

11. Kona Village Resort

10. Four Seasons Resort / Hualālai

9. Ka Kapa / Kuki'o

8. Kua Bay (Manini'owali Beach)

7. Awake'e Bay

6. Makalawena

5. Mahai'ula Bay

19

Keāhole Airport

Area Shown

Keāhole Point

Natural Energy Lab.

4. Wāwāloli Beach

3. Wawahiwa'a Point

2. Kaloko / Honokōhau

1. Honokōhau Harbor

Kailua-Kona

Keahu o Lū Point

an inflatable kayak. He enjoyed the second week more. You could paddle the whole coast, alternating expense systems, or paddle just day trips, or stay in one spot. The choice is yours.

This coast is not all flat water. The wind does blow and the seas can build into a chop, bounce back from low cliffs, or rise into breakers over the blue-green shallows, but there are coves every four miles or less where you can make a quiet landing.

North Kona is subject to tourist development, and where you found an isolated beach one year you might find a huge hotel two years later. I remember with nostalgia paddling this shoreline in October 1972 from Māhukona in the north to Kailua-Kona, before the Queen Ka'ahumanu Highway was built, back when the Mauna Kea and the Kona Village were the only resorts there. It was against the wind in a nine-foot inflatable canoe, with five nights camping and one night at the Kona Village Resort. The cost then was $36 including meals, which seemed enormous at that time, but prorating it for six nights made it reasonable.

A quiet cove on the Kona coast.

The highway is a mile or so inland for most of the route. It comes to the sea at Kailua-Kona town and at Kawaihae, but public side roads lead to the shore at Honokōhau Boat Harbor, the Natural Energy Laboratory of Hawai'i near the airport, Puakō Bay, Hāpuna Bay, Spencer Park, and Māhukona Harbor. Kayakers are now banned from landing at Hāpuna and Spencer Parks. All small-boaters, whether they be in canoes, kayaks, motorized skiffs, small sailboats, or on jet-skies or surfboards, need to be aware of the danger their craft can be and to work for designated landings that keep boaters and swimmers apart. Other roads come to the sea through hotel grounds, and by law, all resorts and subdivisions must provide public access to the beach. (See Table 3, page 239.)

More than any other paddling area in Hawai'i, the North and South Kona coasts are subject to orographic weather patterns—that is, the wind and weather are partly determined by the bulk and height of the two enormous volcanoes. Mauna Kea, at 13,796 feet above sea level, is the higher of the two, but Mauna Loa, at 13,677, is the world's largest active shield volcano and the tallest single mountain on earth. Geologists measure the height of a mountain from its base, and Mauna Loa rises 30,000 feet above its base on the sea floor. A third mountain, Hualālai, though a mere 8,000 feet high, is only eight miles from the Kona shore, so it and Kohala Mountain at the north end of the coast also churn up the wind.

The height of these mountains and the chilled night air of their summits plus the heat of the day's sun and the warmth at sea level form wind-weather patterns that take precedence over the usual trade winds (see the map on p. 221).

Two miles northwest of Kailua-Kona town is Keahu o Lū Point, where the daily onshore wind splits. From this point the prevailing daytime winds blow north to Kīholo Bay and south to Kaunā Point. South of town near shore, the wind usually does not exceed 10 knots. On the north Kona coast the prevailing daytime wind is five to 15 knots, but early morning and late evening winds usually reverse due to the cooling of the three mountain masses. Paddlers must be watchful of fast-changing wind conditions, keep within a quarter-mile of shore, and be prepared to paddle hard toward land. Asia is over 5,000 miles downwind. You'll need to watch ahead, not only for single waves breaking over isolated rocks, but also for a series of white caps, which may indicate the edge of a changing line of offshore winds. Surf on these Kona coasts, even in winter, is less frequent and smaller than on the north sides of the islands, but it does sometimes come in from a storm in the northwest Pacific or wrap around from the north shore.

A special delight along both the North and South Kona coasts is the presence of anchialine ponds (from the Greek *anchialos*, "near the sea"). These are shoreline pools without surface connection to the sea but with stratified salinity and showing tidal rhythms. Though brackish, these coastal ponds were important water sources for early Hawaiians, and some continue to be waterbird habitats. For paddlers, finding one of these pools after a hot, salty day can be wonderfully refreshing. Since many of them contain endangered species of plants and animals, it's best to simply dip your pot or bucket at the surface and pour the cool water over your head. Keep any soap or sunscreen well away from the pool. Many of them are indicated on the topographic maps, and you may find others as you explore, some deep within lava cracks. It is wise to carry at least a two-day supply of drinking water with you, since you may want to stay awhile in some delectable but waterless spot. Public water supplies are at Kailua town, at Spencer and Māhukona County Beach Parks, and at Hāpuna Beach State Recreation Area. If you ask caretakers or lifeguards at the hotel areas, they can direct you to a tap to refill your container. In addition, the boat harbors and ramps at Honokōhau, Puakō, and Kawaihae have a water supply.

Permits for the three Kona Coast county parks that allow camping are available at the county parks offices. Camping in the small A-frame cabins at Hāpuna can be arranged by advance reservation at the state parks offices. See "Sources" for addresses. You'll also want to know about Nā Ala Hele, the Hawai'i Trail and Access System, which is part of the state Department of Land and Natural Resources. On this North Kona coast the trail is the Ala Kahakai, with 14 access points; most of them are also listed here. Okay! Let's get on the water.

The following possible landings are numbered south to north from Kailua-Kona and are pinpointed on the map on page 231. The distance from the put-in by the Kailua pier is shown in parentheses for each landing. Alternate put-in or take-out points are indicated under appropriate landing sites. The first mile of your trip will be along the shore of the old Kona Airport, now a park and a Marine Life Conservation District.

Put-in for the north Kona coast is on the beach in front of the King Kamehameha Hotel.

1. *Honokōhau* ("bay drawing dew") (5 miles). A very busy small-boat harbor has been dredged out here. 'Alula Beach is a sandy cove just south of the entrance. Several boat ramps are within the harbor, but traffic is heavy, so stay alert and out of the way.

2. *Kaloko-Honokōhau National Historical Park* (5–6 miles). This park was established in 1978 and is still under careful research and restoration. Two ancient fish ponds and a fish trap make up nearly half the 1,160 acres, and hundreds of archeological features are reminders of a once-thriving settlement that harvested from the sea and fishponds, cultivated sweet potatoes and coconut, and raised dogs, chickens, and pigs. Because of rough lava flow shores, coral reefs, and a hot, dry climate, it is not yet an inviting spot for the casual paddler or commercial trip. In the future a landing place for canoes and kayaks may be in place for paddlers to park their craft while on a pre-arranged tour. Kaloko ponds are an excellent place to see endangered shore birds. (See "Sources" for address.)

3. *Wawahiwaʻa* ("canoe crusher") *Point* (7 miles). Note the meaning, and take care. The landmark is a high cluster of mangrove trees surrounding small brackish ponds inland from the rock and sand shore. Local surfers call it "Pine Trees," mistaking the mangroves for ironwood trees (which resemble pines but aren't). If the surf is up, you would have a tricky landing. A 4WD road connects north to the paved road of the Natural Energy Laboratory of Hawaiʻi (NELH) and out to the highway.

4. *Wāwāloli* (9 miles). A park here is maintained by the NELH, with showers and restrooms, just where the road from the highway turns north. The only landing is a tiny gravel beach about 50 yards south of the park restrooms. There is no camping. As you paddle on north and pass the buildings of NELH, be wary of the surge around Keāhole Point. You may be startled also by the low-flying planes landing or taking off at the airport.

5. *Mahaiʻula Bay* (13 miles). This sheltered, deep bay with sand and lava shores is now part of the Kekaha Kai State Park. The gated road from the highway is open from 8 A.M. to 5 P.M. Further development and marine education are planned. A kayak landing area has been designated in the small cove a few feet north of the lifeguard stand at the south side of the bay. One could hope for a designated tent camping area that is not open to automobile traffic, but only to boaters, bikers, and hikers.

6. *Makalawena* (14 miles). Clear, quiet water in summer and occasional surf in winter, tide pools, enough trees for shade—this is a special place. A large pond inshore is an important waterbird sanctuary. Kamehameha Schools/Bishop Estate is the owner, and a caretaker lives on the property. Camping is only by advance permission (see "Sources").

7. *Awakeʻe Bay* (15 miles). Here's a black pebble beach landing with some shade of kiawe trees, and with part of Nā Ala Hele, the shoreline trail, going across it. Just ahead is Puʻu Kuili, a 342-foot grassy hill and a conspicuous landmark.

8. *Kua Bay* (Manini'ōwali Beach) (16 miles). This is a dazzling, white sand beach with a turquoise sea. As of January 1997, no toilet facilities were in place. Be a responsible visitor: Bring your own and pack it out. See chapter 7 for further ideas. No landing area for canoes and kayaks has been established within the point-to-point area of the bay. South of the main beach are two small sand pockets with smaller surf.

9. *Kakapa/Kūki'o* (16 3/4 miles). This area has been recently sold, and its proximity to the new Four Seasons Resort Hualālai Resort has changed the ambience. The point of land with its seaward lava ledges and rocky pool belongs to the state. North of the point is a two-hundred yard sand beach with landings possible between rocks.

10. *Four Seasons Resort Hualālai* (17 miles). A paved path follows the shore from the hotel area south to the sand beach.

11. *Kona Village Resort* (18 miles). If price were no object, this would be my choice of all the resorts in Hawai'i. Each "room" is a separate thatched cottage in the style of one of the South Pacific island groups. Open-top kayaks are available for guests. If you are en route north, you may want to stop here for lunch or an early dinner. Advance reservations are required. (See Table 3 for hotel phone numbers.)
Paddling On: The mountain Hualālai, 8,271 feet in elevation and eight miles inland, last erupted in 1800. Two separate lava flows covered an area of about 17 square miles, one at the Keāhole airport area and the other in this area between the Kona Village Resort and Kīholo Bay. Local lore says Hualālai is due to erupt every 200 years. Geologists say only that Hualālai is dormant. Between Kona Village and Kīholo Bay are nearly four miles of the last flow. At a mile and a half and at three miles are small pockets of black pebble beach where it is usually possible to land. Others are near Waikukua Point around the edge of Kīholo Bay.

12. *Kīholo Bay* (24 miles). Between the pool of Luahinewai (privately owned) and the lagoon across the bay are several private homes and some state land. Be careful not to trespass. Read the history of Chiefs Keoua and Kamehameha for the poignancy of this area. John

Clark's book *Beaches of the Big Island* has more of the human and natural history.

13. *Keawaiki* (27 miles). The sandy beach is a good landing site. The private home and grounds are fenced off.

14. *Pueo* ("owl") *Bay* (27 1/2 miles). This small bay was formed by the 1859 lava flow from a vent at the 10,000-foot level of Mauna Loa, 30 miles away. Black lava and white coral pebbles make up the steep beach. A short trail leads inland to refreshing ponds and small trees.

15. *'Anaeho'omalu Bay* (30 miles). Many rocks and coral heads will keep you alert as you come into this deep bay. During winter swells, the channel in and out is along the north shore. In the center of the beach is a park with showers, restrooms, public access and parking, all maintained by Waikoloa Land Management. They've done a great job of allowing for multiple use by residents and visitors. This park would make a good alternate put-in or take-out place for the coast. Check for the closing time for the park gate. No camping is allowed in the park. A small frontage of state land in the southeast corner of the bay is sometimes used by one or two campers. See Table 3 for destinations in the ten miles north and south of 'Ana'eho'omalu.

16. *Puakō* (37 miles). This area has a two mile-long strip of privately owned beach houses, six rights of way from road to shore, and a state-maintained boat ramp at the north end, with water to hose off your boat and to shower. Geologists say this is where the lava flows of Mauna Loa and Mauna Kea "interfinger," a vivid image.

17. *Hāpuna Beach State Recreation Area* (39 miles). Here is the widest sand beach with the least rainfall on the Big Island. Only body surfing is allowed, no boards, and at present no kayak landing. Because of this and the danger of mixing body surfers, swimmers, and boats, we recommend you land elsewhere if you need only a short stop. If you plan to stay overnight and have reserved one of the A-frame shelters, then also check in advance with hotel lifeguards at the Hapuna Beach Prince Hotel about landing and leaving your kayak there. The shelters, which sleep four people and rent for $20 a night, including the use of a communal kitchen, are a quarter-mile inland from Hāpuna

Table 3

Access to Shore through Hotel Property

North Kona Coast. South to North.

The distances are from the public parking area to the water by way of the Public Beach Access. These routes are indicated by signs on the roads into the hotels. If you don't see them, ask at the entry gate or at the hotel lobby entrance. For day paddles, using access routes through hotel parking areas may be safer than leaving your car in a remote area.

Name	Phone	Distance	Comments
1. Four Seasons Hualālai	325-8000	100 yards	Follow entry road from highway to public access. Then board and paved walk to shower, restrooms, and beach.
2. Kona Village Resort	325-6787	1/4 mile	A long haul from public parking to a sand beach. Phone ahead for a lunch reservation to come by sea and park your boat on shore alongside the resort's guest kayaks.
3. Royal Waikoloan	885-6789	50 yards	ʻAnaehoʻomalu Bay. Sand beach. Excellent facilities. One of the two best access areas.
4. Hilton Waikoloa Village	885-1234	200 yards	Paved path. Coral and lava rubble beach. This ornate resort makes no use of the shore.
5. Mauna Lani Bay Hotel	885-6677	1/4 mile	Paved trail with tight turns for a long kayak. Historical signs along the route. Sand beach. Shaded car parking.
6. Orchid at Mauna Lani	885-2000	50 yards	Holoholokai Beach Park. The best of the eight. Shaded car parking, good restrooms, picnic

Table 3 (continued)

Name	Phone	Distance	Comments
			tables. A path (.7 mile) leads to a petroglyph field. The coral and lava rubble beach makes entry a bit difficult, so walk your kayak into the water.
7. Hāpuna Beach Prince	880-1111	200 yards	No car shade. Rough, dirt trail to shore. The Mauna Kea Beach Hotel, just north, is a better choice. The Prince resort is new and perhaps will improve.
8. Mauna Kea Beach Hotel	882-7222	100 yards	Use of sandy beach. Shaded parking. Tile showers. Get parking permit at gate. Paved path. Elegance.

Wheels for your kayak are recommended for distances of more than 50 yards. Try Peter Bukas (966-4999) on the Hilo side for wheels and other kayak gear. See Places For Boats and Gear under "Sources."

Beach State Recreation area. You need to reserve well in advance through a state parks office. Their board bunks are hard; bring some kind of mattress, a light blanket, and your own lantern. Water taps are available, but you may want your own water bag to hang in the shelter.

18. *Kauna'oa Bay* (40 miles). Site of the Mauna Kea Beach Hotel. This is the farthest hotel to the north, and a possible take-out point. Here you can shower at the public facilities at the south end of the beach, put on clean clothes, and by reservation attend the lavish buffet lunch. Flags on shore, visible from the sea indicate the surf conditions: green for go (mild), yellow for caution, and red for stop (dangerous). If you've paddled all the way from Kailua-Kona, you're well aware of what the sea is doing.

Racing canoes on the beach at ʻAnaehoʻomalu.

A state park A-frame cabin, a quarter mile from the sea at Hāpuna Beach.

19. *Spencer County Beach Park* (41 1/2 miles). This popular park has camping by permit, restrooms, tables, a pavilion, showers, grass and shade, and is usually crowded with local families. A sign forbids kayaks. It is a long beach with quiet water, so a canoe and kayak landing area could easily be designated near the parking lot. "No drinking" has been enforced and the park is much more pleasant than it was ten years ago.

You can walk up to visit the Pu'ukoholā Heiau National Historical Site on the hill above the park. This enormous rock platform, a place of worship of the ancient gods, was built in 1791 at the direction of Chief Kamehameha as part of his consolidation of power on the Big Island.

20. *Kawaihae* (43 miles). This shipping port for west Hawai'i is where your kayak comes in or goes out on the Young Brothers barge. It has a breakwater, docks, a small boat harbor with a boat ramp, and a sand beach at the north end with restroom and showers. The Kawaihae Canoe Club has a facility here, a good place to see six-man canoes, one-man canoes, and the new three-man sailing canoes. Here you

Pavilion at Spencer County Beach Park with calm December seas.

should talk to the local experts about *mumuku*, the strong wind that blows across the island saddle of Waimea and accelerates to a higher velocity between Mauna Kea and Kohala mountains. They can tell you, too, about other winds that build up on the east side of Kohala, spill over, and whop down suddenly on unsuspecting paddlers along shore (see chapter 4). Several small grocery stores and restaurants are nearby, and highways lead out to the north, east, and south.

Paddling On: Now you start a 12-mile stretch with some of the quietest open ocean in the state, and some of the best snorkeling. Fishermen occasionally walk or 4WD down from the highway, boats go by farther at sea, but the rocky, dry shores have no houses, and you will see few people.

21. *Waiaka'ilio* (46 miles). A small bay and a local campsite are here. From sea, watch for two painted rocks that mark the entry. Three miles farther check out Keawanui and Keawe'ula bays on your topo map. None of these are deep or large bays, but the farther you are from Kawaihae, the clearer the water.

22. *Lapakahi State Historical Park and Koai'e Cove Marine Life Conservation District (MLCD)* (54 miles). This restored fishing village and cove are part of a sea-to-mountain population center of old Hawai'i. The aim of MLCD (two miles long) is to protect fish and coral. Avoid walking or grounding your craft on any coral area. You may want to send for a pamphlet that describes these refuges on four islands from the DLNR (see "Sources"). The Division of Aquatics Resources personnel on each of the four islands are an excellent source of information to help you plan your trip. Ask for their office phone numbers.

23. *Māhukona Harbor and County Beach Park* (55 miles). Here there are permit camping, showers, restrooms, tables, and a dock with a rough boat ramp. The shear line for the wind coming around the north tip of the island is usually about one mile south of Māhukona, and the line between white-capped sea and lake-like calm is clearly visible. When there is no vog from an erupting volcano on the Big Island, you get a stunning view of the 10,000-foot dormant Haleakalā on Maui, 30 miles northwest across 'Alenuihāhā ("great billows smashing") Channel.

The Elegant Kayaker or the Posh Paddler on the North Kona Coast

Rating: Class III
Quad maps: Kailua, Keāhole Point, Makalawena, Kīholo, Anaehoʻo-malu, Puʻu Hinai, Kawaihae
Total length and time: 43 miles, 5 days
Put-in: Beach in front of the King Kamehameha Hotel in Kailua-Kona
Take-out: Kawaihae
Hazards: Surf, sunburn, rocks, lava, coral, overeating
Best time of year: All year; hotter in summer, more surf in winter

First night: The most deluxe kayak trip in all Hawaiʻi would start at Kailua-Kona on the sand beach in front of the King Kamehameha Hotel, where you would stay the night after your arrival in Kona. That evening you would have had a tour of the heiau near the beach.

Second day: After breakfast you head out. You carry only kayak safety gear, paddling clothes, lunch, dry dinner clothes, sunscreen, fins/mask/snorkel, waterproof camera, and a credit card. Landings and overnight stops are indicated with the mileage each day. Guide is provided.

Second night: A campsite near the mangrove trees at Wawahiwaʻa Point, camping gear and dinner catered (7 miles).

Third night: Kona Village Resort (11 miles). Dinner and breakfast. Lunch to go.

Fourth night: Royal Waikoloan Resort at ʻAnaehoʻomalu (12 miles). Dinner, breakfast, and petroglyph tour.

Fifth day: Lunch at the Mauna Lani Resort (4 miles).

Fifth night: Overnight at the Mauna Kea Resort Hotel (6 more miles). Dinner and breakfast.

Sixth day: Art tour of the Mauna Kea. Sailing, windsurfing, snorkeling. The famous buffet lunch. Paddle to Kawaihae Boat Harbor (3 miles). Take-out, showers, and pick-up are at Kawaihae.

Cost: $2,000 to $3,000 per person, depending on accommodations. I don't usually guide trips, but I might lead this one. You could cut the cost by organizing this on your own, camping some nights, and finding a bed and breakfast in the Puakō area.

Kona Village Resort with the New York Times—*for the posh paddler.*

Southwest Coast: South Kona

Rating: Class III
Quad maps: Kealakekua, Hōnaunau, Ka'uluoa, Miloli'i, Manukā
Total length and time: 55 miles, 5 to 10 days
Put-in: Keauhou Bay
Take-out: Miloli'i
Hazards: Surf, rocks, sunburn, lava, coral
Best time of year: All year; hotter in summer, more surf in winter.

Loop trips or just day paddles are great in this area.

With each paddle stroke you move back into history. An ancient place of refuge, the shore where Captain Cook was killed, a small village scarcely changed in 50 years, the best old Hawaiian trail, an unrestored heiau that is still in use—all are in this trip, plus the best underwater scenes in the state. This is where the technique of towing your kayak as you snorkel evolved.

The highway around the island is not close to this shoreline. South of Kailua-Kona, one road hugs the coast through five miles of wall-to-wall condominiums, beach cottages, and hotels, angles back at

Keauhou to climb 1,500 feet into the cooler coffee country, and continues south around the island. Four paved side roads curve down to the sea, so put-ins and take-outs may be planned for trips from half a day to a week or more.

The prevailing winds are from the north during the day. Near Miloli'i the wind often intensifies at about 5 P.M., lasts an hour, and then dies down. Rainfall is 30 to 40 inches a year. The terrain is lava, rock, and low cliffs, with a few sand beaches. Coconut trees are frequent; once planted, they propagate themselves. The most common tree is the kiawe. Local people had a big laugh when an earnest young California chef debated the relative merits of broiling steaks and fish over his desert mesquite or over this different new kiawe wood, imported from Hawai'i. Botanically, the two trees are nearly the same, both of the Mimosa subfamily that includes the koa (famous for its use in canoe building), kolū, monkeypod, wattle, koa haole, and many others in Hawai'i. Kiawe makes excellent cooking fires, the flowers produce a distinctive honey, and the pods are fodder for cattle. A high-protein flour can be ground from the pods and seeds. The tree's long, sharp thorns are painful for bare feet, lethal for air mattresses and inflatable boats. You might carry a small bamboo rake for clearing the campsite.

Potable water is at the state park of Kealakekua in Nāpo'opo'o and at the national park at Hōnaunau. Bring your own water elsewhere.

Keauhou Bay is an ideal put-in. A small park on the northeast side has water, restrooms, and a shady area for sorting and packing gear. There is no camping. To find the park, locate the Keauhou shopping center, then go toward the sea on Kamehameha III Road to the end. Even if the surf is breaking on the reefs outside the bay, you can usually put in here or at the boat ramp on the south side of the bay and go out through the channel. Then you quickly leave hotels and tourists behind as you paddle past the Kona Surf Hotel and around the 20-foot cliff. The best landing is seven miles ahead at Kealakekua, so resist the temptation to stop and snorkel here. Keep the topo maps handy so you'll know where you are, as you pass low cliffs and open, brushy hills, looking up to the misty slopes of coffee country. A ridge and a cloud layer at the 3,000-foot level hide the massive higher slopes of Mauna Loa, but you are paddling over its lower slopes, which are beneath sea level. Paddle too close in and you will get the rebound

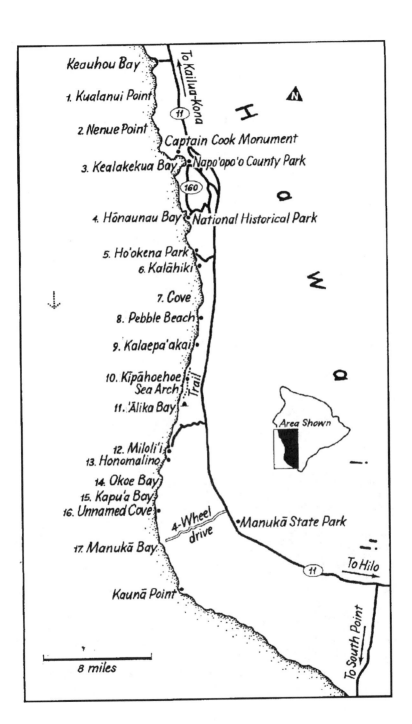

Keauhou Bay

1. Kualanui Point

To Kailua-Kona

11

2. Nenue Point

Captain Cook Monument

N

3. Kealakekua Bay

Napo'opo'o County Park

160

4. Hōnaunau Bay

National Historical Park

5. Ho'okena Park
6. Kalāhiki

7. Cove

8. Pebble Beach

9. Kalaepa'akai

10. Kīpāhoehoe
Sea Arch

Trail

11. 'Ālika Bay

Area Shown

12. Miloli'i
13. Honomalino

14. Okoe Bay
15. Kapu'a Bay
16. Unnamed Cove

4-Wheel drive

Manukā State Park

17. Manukā Bay

11

To Hilo

Kaunā Point

To South Point

8 miles

action of the waves bouncing back from the cliffs. Go too far out and you'll miss the color changes of the water—aqua and jade over sand bottom, deep blue-purple over lava.

Paved access roads for take-out are at Nāpoʻopoʻo (Kealakekua), Hōnaunau, Hoʻokena, and Miloliʻi. A very rough, unpaved 4WD road leads to Manukā. It is not recommended that you paddle past Kaunā Point. The wind turns strongly against you and there are only private roads until South Point, where the landing is exceptionally difficult.

On rare calm summer days you could start at South Point, paddle the 16 miles to Kaunā Point with a tail wind, and reverse the 16-point route described below. The winds wrap around South Point and blow west-northwest to Kaunā, where they meet the lesser wind coming down the coast. Kaunā is a "wind point," where they meet and swirl.

The following possible landings, which are pinpointed on the map on page 247 are numbered north to south from Keauhou Bay. The mileage from the put-in is indicated in parentheses for each landing.

1. *Kualanui Point* (2 miles). A 4WD road extends past the golf course to this point, but surge may prevent coming ashore. Depending on

Big Island lava flows are clearly seen on this relief map at Hawaiʻi Volcanoes National Park.

tide and surge and how much time you have, you may be able to explore sea caves in this area.

2. *Nenue Point* (3 miles). Just north of Pu'u Ohau (230 feet high) is
this possible landing. I camped there once years ago and found a *ko'a*,
a small fishing shrine, near the point.

3. *Kealakekua* ("the way of the gods") *Bay* (7 miles). When I was here
in 1996 the north side of the bay was cleaner than I had ever seen it.
Several kayakers I know carry garbage bags and clean up a bagful of
trash each place they land. Māhalo. Since this area has many visitors
and no toilet facilities, it is imperative to carry your own way of packing it all out. Digging "cat holes" in this rocky soil is not possible. See
chapter 2.

A gentle *pāhoehoe* lava shore for easy landing is 50 yards west of the
tall, white monument erected in memory of Captain James Cook.
Carry your kayak ashore; don't drag or anchor it, to avoid damage to
coral, rock, and kayak. Rock and sand above tideline are covered with
the leaves and thorns of the gnarly old kiawe trees. Wear shoes. A
brackish water spring and a waist-deep pool for a cool evening dip (no
soap, please) are east of the monument at the edge of the sea. An ancient stone-lined well is a few yards inland. This year, for the first time
in the 35 years I've been going there, clear water was seeping up in the
well. The more modern stone and cement structure in the area was
part of a missionary school built in the 1850s.

See Craig Chisholm's book ("Further Reading") for the land route
to this area by trail. Part way up that trail, and marked "Cook's Heiau"
on the topo map, is another site in the tragic Hawaiian chapter of the
story of the great navigator—the probable place where his body was
ceremonially dismembered. His death was a tragedy for Cook and his
crew, and also for the Hawaiian people, though it seems doubtful that
any meeting of this isolated Polynesian people with any European ex-
plorers or sailors would have had any better results.

Kealakekua has some of the best snorkeling in the islands. This is a
State Underwater Marine Life Conservation District and bans fishing,
spearing, or grabbing by hand. The regulations and the boundary lines
are posted at the outer corner of the district near the small lighthouse,
but they should also be posted near the monument, where people

Analu Richards in front of the Captain Cook monument.

come ashore. Tour boats come in and out of the bay daily. It used to be that they were only there between 10 A.M. and 3 P.M., but now motorized Zodiacs are there almost daily by 9 A.M.

You can replenish fresh water by paddling a mile across to the Nāpoʻopoʻo section of Kealakekua Bay State Historical Park, where you can also have an outdoor shower. While there, see the stone platform heiau and read the inscription. It was here that Cook made his second visit to the islands (the first was at Waimea on Kauaʻi a year earlier). Cook was welcomed with great ceremony and met the young chief Kamehameha. Here, too, Lieutenant James King, under the command of Cook, set up instruments for astronomical observations, one of the objectives of Cook's voyages.

Back at the monument area, walk west around Cook Point. Find an isolated place to hang your hammock and spend the day reading O. A. Bushnell's *The Return of Lono*, a novel of Cook's last voyage ("Further Reading"). Here at the site of the village where he died and of the beginning of great changes for the Hawaiian people, you have a deep sense of history. Near your landing is a foot-high marker, washed by the quiet waves, which shows the actual place of Cook's death.

An *Achilles tang and a school of* manini.

When you leave Kealakekua, you may be accompanied by spinner dolphins. Twice I have also seen whales here, the giant humpbacks with their long, seemingly lazy arch and dive and a grand finale of dripping black flukes. As on Maui, you are most likely to see them between December and March. It is illegal to approach whales or dolphins closer than 100 feet. If you sit still, they may come to you and swim under your boat.

Paddling On: As you leave the bay you'll pass the surfing area of Palemano Point. *Place Names of Hawaii* says that with the macron over the *o*, Palemanō means "shark defense." Without the macron it might mean "much defense," referring to the protection afforded by the point from the *ulumano* wind. The next three miles are dry scrub country, but try snorkeling. Above water you see only one or two lone fishermen atop the dark lava bluff.

You may notice that I've said nothing at all about hotels on this South Kona coast. There are none.

4. *Hōnaunau Bay* (11 miles). Check out the five-foot-high ledges on the north side of the bay, where local fishermen often camp. The bay may offer some delightful surprises. One December I was lucky to be swimming there with fins, mask, and snorkel when a giant manta ray came cruising into the bay. It dove under me and turned on its back to look up at this creature. I dove down and turned over to swim beside its 10-foot wing spread. It laughed, I'm sure of that, and spiraled up again to the surface. We played another 10 minutes, a ballet, each one astonished and curious, before it swam out to sea. They are rather shy creatures, plankton feeders, not man eaters. It is the only one I have seen in Hawai'i, though they sometimes come to feed near a hotel in North Kona.

On the south side of the bay, Pu'uhonua o Hōnaunau National Historical Park ("the place of refuge of Hōnaunau") is well worth a visit. No camping is allowed, and no boats on shore within the park, but a tiny sand beach is just to the right of the boat ramp as you come in to shore. You might ask permission from the personnel of the school at the right of the beach about parking your boat on the land between the boat ramp and the park. Since it is part of a heiau, the park requests that you wear clothing over your bathing suit to show respect. At the entry desk you can get a free brochure for a self-guided tour. An entry fee is now required for all national parks.

Paddling On: A mile south of Hōnaunau in Alahaka Bay, watch for a shallow cave in the cliff. Paddle in close and look up. The tunnel overhead has its entrance beside an ancient walled trail leading up from the left. (See Russ Apple's *Trails*, in "Further Reading.") The Hawaiians would call it a *kawa*, "leaping place." In another 2 1/2 miles, you will come around past Keālia Beach with some attractive homes and tall palm trees, but it is a rocky, reefy landing place.

5. *Ho'okena County Beach Park* (15 miles). Often there is more surge than you'd like for landing here, but at least it's a sandy beach. A spreading *kamani* almond tree provides shade, and you may want to laboriously extract some almonds as you sit under the colorful red and green leaves. See Euell Gibbons' *Beachcomber's Handbook* for more

A *fishing canoe and a racing canoe at* Hōnaunau *National Historical Park.*

about these almonds. Camping permits, restrooms, and showers may currently not be available because of lack of water. Check with county.

6. *Kalāhiki* ("the sunrise") (16 miles). This area is privately owned and has no road access. Landing is through a narrow passage two-thirds of the distance south along the beach, seaward of the most southern coconut trees. You may need to swim your boat in to lighten its weight over the ledges, or perhaps you can swing your hula hips (and rudder) to get through.

The area back from shore has the shade of kiawe and kolū trees, plus an old heiau. If it rains, the rock pools in the lava on shore collect fresh water. One larger pool, where fresh water floats in a layer on top of salt, has an underwater tunnel to the sea. It is recommended for slender, lithe swimmers only.

7. *Cove* (18 miles). This unnamed cove is where the Honokua lava flow of 1950 is marked on the Ka'uluoa quad map. It is a cliff-locked sand beach with no shade, no water, and no land access. No one will be concerned if you camp here.

8. *Pebble Beach* (Kona Paradise) (20 miles). This shore is not marked on the topo maps, but is four miles south of Kalāhiki and one mile south of Ka'uluoa Point. It is a privately owned development with a steep paved road up to the highway. No camping is permited here, but check one-quarter mile north for a tiny beach. Pebble Beach is also a possible put-in for day cruising.

9. *Kalaepa'akai* (22 miles). This pleasant small site has coconut trees and a table. It is used by fishermen, but their access is by land. Boats may not be able to come ashore except in very calm conditions.

Paddling On: Between Kalāhiki and Kīpāhoehoe you will pass three fingers of the lava flow of 1950, which came down the slopes from the southwest ridge of Mauna Loa 10,000 feet above. The enormous volume of this flow is hard to comprehend. Read *Volcanoes in the Sea* for the best account of the geological history of all the islands ("Further Reading"). On the Big Island, especially, you are aware of the whole volcanic process. If you haven't already learned the names for the two kinds of lava, now is the time. 'A'ā is rough and chunky, and tears up boots and feet. *Pāhoehoe* looks like black, ropy fudge. The Hawaiian names are also the scientific ones. There are no English equivalents.

Snorkeling is excellent among the arches and rock sea stacks in the five-mile stretch north and south of Kīpāhoehoe. Clip your lifeline to the bow and tow the boat for a while, using your fins to give your shoulders a rest.

10. *Kīpāhoehoe* (25 miles). This 5,000-acre wedge goes from the sea up above the highway. It is one of eight Natural Area Reserves on the Big Island. Hawaiians who once lived here filled hollows on the shore with water-worn stones to make a smooth landing place for canoes. Remains of the landing are still evident, but the strong surge may prevent safely landing your own boat. You could anchor out and swim ashore to explore. Anchoring can be as simple as diving down to tie a line to a big rock, or you could carry an hourglass-shaped rock with you to tie a line around. In Hawai'i, where the bottom so often has caves and tunnels and crevices, I prefer to use a disposable anchor, in case it gets jammed deeper than I can dive.

One of the most remarkable old trails is here, paved three stones wide instead of the usual one stone. The ancient Hawaiians carried up rounded beach boulders, one by one, so people could walk barefoot across the rough a'ā. The area is hot in summer, but trees have grown since I was first there, and the place has a pervading peace.

11. *'Ālika Bay* (27 miles). Evaluate carefully before landing at 'Ālika to see whether the surf is within your capability. The shore is all rocks, but at least they are rounded. Pāpā Bay Estates, a mauka subdivision, has beach access rights for its residents, but the rights are not exclusive. A flat, rock platform and a dry waterhole are nearby, the well with steps leading down into it, both indications of a former fishing village site. North of it and visible from the sea, but not from land until you are very close, is a big shelter cave that was probably once a burial cave, and later became a shelter for horses. Sleeping there at 3 o'clock one morning, I was awakened by "shots" moving north along the shore. No lights were visible and the sounds were moving faster than a man could run. It remained a mystery for years, until I learned that it was probably a pod of humpback whales thwacking their flukes as they swam by.

12. *Miloli'i* (30 miles). Here is a small harbor, a separate boat ramp, and the last paved road up to the highway, which is five miles *mauka*. If you go south from here, you may want to return here for take-out. Use the pebble beach near the dock to land and launch; leave the boat ramp for the many motorized fishing boats. Camping permits are issued for the little county park, with its new shelter, but bring your own water supply. Do talk with the Kaupiko family, long-time residents and owners of the small store in this last Hawaiian fishing village. Go humbly in Miloli'i; it is a special place, old style, not much changed since the lava flow of 1929 erased the neighboring village of Ho'ōpūloa. You will fit in much better as a low-profile visitor than as a blatant tourist. The village kids are superb water rats and, if you let them paddle your boat, will be great friends. More than in most places, residents are dependent on the fish of the area, so do your own fishing or spearing elsewhere.

I first landed here in 1974 on the way from South Point up to Hōnaunau. When I started to leave in the late afternoon, the mayor,

Use this coral and lava beach near the dock to land at Miloli'i.

Eugene Kaupiko, laughed and said, "You'll be back." He knew, but I didn't, that the local wind that arises just before sunset would blow me back. So I returned, had supper with Eugene and his wife, Sarah, and we talked until midnight about the days of fishing in outrigger canoes before the time of motors. When I left at 3 A.M., the winds were calm and the lop-sided moon was setting into the sea. A sudden rain pitted the water surface with sequins; then, as the sun rose, the fragrance of warmed kiawe and kolū blossoms came tumbling down over the cliffs.

13. *Honomalino Bay* (31 miles). Please do not intrude on the three private homes here. A pocket sand beach is at the north end of the bay, and the point to the west of it is state land. A trail leads from here to Miloli'i. There is no water supply except coconuts.

14. *Okoe Bay* (33 miles). Part of this is state land. The bay has a small black sand beach, and is much used by fishermen from land and sea who camp here. No water is available, but it rained six inches in six hours the last time I was here, a rare event on this dry side of the

island, and of course the best water supply is off the edge of your tarp. A privately owned house is now at Okoe.

15. *Kapu'a* (34 miles). A wealth of history, botany, and marine life is here, including the best-preserved example of a *hōlua* slide. These long, inclined rock ramps were covered with grass to make them slippery, then ridden with heavy sleds, a toboggan sport for ancient chiefs. John Clark's *The Beaches of the Big Island* is especially useful here. At Kapu'a you finally get a view of the huge expanse of Mauna Loa up to the northeast. This area is privately owned.

16. *No Name Cove* (36 miles). One-tenth of a mile south of Niuou Point is this tiny, one-canoe-wide opening to a small black lava and white coral pebble beach with a hook that hides it from the sea. There is no shade or water, but it is a magic place to spend a night on a solo trip. There is only enough space for one or two people. When I was there, the moon was so bright I had to turn the boat upside down and crawl under it to sleep out of the spotlight.

17. *Manukā Bay* (39 miles). This land is state-owned all the way up to the highway and beyond, over a very steep and rocky 4WD road. To find the road from the highway, go 1.6 miles north from Manukā State Rest Area. On the makai side is a black, steel pipe gate. This whole wedge of land, 25,550 acres is the largest of the Natural Area Reserves System. You could spend a month or more in just this area, sea level to 5,000 feet in elevation. The sand and rock beach has some surge and a shore break. An old heiau is just inland, sometimes with cans of beer as symbolic sacrifices. Island people come here frequently and you can learn much from them. You could go on further south for the snorkeling en route, return to Manukā to camp, and then go back to Miloli'i for take-out.

The island of Hawai'i does not have rivers to paddle or offshore islands to explore, but on any visit to the Big Island you may want to combine a shoreline paddling trip with some sightseeing or hiking. Hawai'i Volcanoes National Park has trails that include sea coast, the frequently active rift zone of Kīlauea, and the summit area of Mauna Loa, which last erupted in 1984, when both it and Kīlauea were

The heiau at Manukā Bay is beside an old fisherman trail of smooth stones.

pouring out molten lava at the same time. The summit will surely have snow from December to March. I remember testing out a sleeping bag between snow banks on the last day of May in a temperature of 12 degrees. At sea level it was 80. Other sightseeing can range from desert, to green sand beach, to waterfalls and orchid gardens on this most varied of all the islands in the state of Hawai'i.

Sources

For phone calls from outside Hawai'i use area code 808. From one island to another, dial 1, then 808, and then the local number. On any one island, all calls are local calls, 25 cents from a pay phone.

Shipping Your Kayak

Island	Airport	Barge Port nearest to airport	Miles airport to barge port	Paddle from barge port?
Kaua'i	Līhu'e	Nāwiliwili	3	Yes
	Princeville	Nāwiliwili	40	Yes
O'ahu	Honolulu	Honolulu	5	No*
Moloka'i	Moloka'i	Kaunakakai	9	Yes**
Lāna'i	Lāna'i	Kaumalapau	5	Yes
Maui	Kahului	Kahului	2	No***
	West Maui	Kahului	25	No
Hawai'i	Hilo	Hilo	2	No
	Kona	Kawaihae	35	Yes
	Kamuela	Kawaihae	11	Yes

Young Brothers, based in Honolulu, also has offices on Kaua'i, Moloka'i, Maui, and in Kawaihae on the Big Island. Their Honolulu phone is (808) 543-9331. The Hilo/Lāna'i Customer Service is in Honolulu, (808) 545-1852. Their address is 705 N. Nimitz Hwy, Honolulu, HI 96817

*Regulations have forbidden non-motorized craft in Honolulu Harbor, but check with harbormaster in Aloha Tower.
**Paddling would be upwind over reef flats.
***Paddling would be upwind, the reverse of the trip described. You could paddle to Kanahā County Beach Park to camp the first night and then transport your kayak to Hāna.

Local Sources

Places to Learn about Hawai'i

- Bishop Museum and Planetarium. 1528 Bernice St., Honolulu. Ph 847-3515.
- Hawai'i Visitors and Conventions Bureau. 2270 Kalakaua Ave., #801, Honolulu. Ph 923-1811.
- Lyon Arboretum. 3860 Mānoa Rd., Honolulu. Ph 988-7378.
- Sea Life Park. Makapu'u Point, Waimanalo. Ph 259-7933.
- The Waikīkī Aquarium. 2777 Kalakaua Ave., Honolulu. Ph 923-7941.
- Waimea Falls Park. 59-864 Kamehameha Hwy., Hale'iwa. Ph 638-8511.

Paddling Clubs

O'ahu:

- Hui Wa'a Kaukāhi ("club of single person canoes"). This sea kayak cruising club was named before the advent of the single person outrigger canoes. Any paddler is most welcome to join. The club makes almost weekly paddles on O'ahu and frequent ones to other islands. The address is PO Box 88143, Honolulu, HI, 96830, or contact them through Go Bananas Kayak store in Waikīkī, Ph 737-9514.
- Kanaka Ikaika. They sponsor two annual races across the Moloka'i Channel, one for surf skis and one for one-person outrigger canoes. Ph (808) 247-0838.

Maui:

- Kayak Association Hawai'i. See South Pacific Kayaking, below.

International:

- Paddlers International. 8 Wiltshire Avenue, Hornchurch, Essex RM11 3DX, England. Peter A. Clark, Secretary, Treasurer, Chairman, Director, etc. Eight-hundred paddlers corresponding through a quarterly newsletter, with questions, answers, and experiences. A wealth of information about world paddling. I stayed overnight outside London with an English kayaker who had placed a request for information about Alaska. I had brought those annotated charts and he shared his for my destination of Scotland.

Places in Hawai'i for Boats and Boat Gear

These are listed north to south by island, then alphabetical. Some companies just design and build boats; some just rent boats or give tours. Companies with an asterisk provide all or nearly all of the following: boats for sale, boat gear, rentals, instruction, guided trips, information on areas for paddling and more. This is not a complete list. See the Yellow Pages of the phone book.

Kaua'i:
- *Kayak Kaua'i. PO Box 508, Hanalei, HI 96714. Ph 826-9844.
- *Outfitters Kaua'i. 2827 A Po'ipū Rd., Koloa, HI 96756. Ph 742-9667. Rick and Julie Haviland. (Also bikes and mountains bikes.)

O'ahu:
- *Bob Twogood Kayaks. 171 Hamakua St., Kailua, HI 96734. Ph 262-5656. (Bob teaches basic kayak classes, designs, builds, and rents canoes and kayaks, and is very active in the racing scene.)
- 'Cuda Kayaks. 789 Kailua Rd., Kailua, HI 96734. Ph 261-8424. Karel Tresnak. (One person canoes, surf skis.)
- Fiberglass Shop. 91-291 Kalaeloa Blvd., Bldg. 85. Kapolei, HI 96707. Ph 682-5233. Walter Guild. (One person canoes.)
- *Go Bananas. 799 Kapahulu Ave., Honolulu, HI 96816. Ph 737-9514. Gary Budlong. (The widest range of boats, gear, and service.)
- Hunt Johnsen Designs. 50 C Sand Island Access Rd., Honolulu, HI 96819. Ph 847-4408. (Wave Witch, surf skis, wave skis.)
- Kailua Sailboard/Kayak Rental. 130 Kailua Rd., Kailua, HI 96734. Ph 262-2555.
- Pacific Map Center. 560 N. Nimitz Hwy., Suite 206A, Honolulu, HI 96817. Ph 545-3600. Maps and Charts. John and Ele Clere.

Moloka'i:
- Fun Hogs Hawai'i. PO Box 424, Ho'olehua, HI 96729. Ph 552-2761. Unit 256. Mike Holmes. (Guided trips south coast, rentals to experienced paddlers.)

Maui:
- Maui Sea Kayaking. PO Box 106, Pu'unene, HI 96784. Ph 572-6299. Ron Bass. (Trips, disabled paddlers, instruction.)
- *South Pacific Kayaks. 2439 S. Kīhei Rd., #101B, Kīhei, HI 96753. Ph 875-4848. Suzanne Simmins and Gordon Godfrey. (Trips, boats, gear, and more.)

Hawai'i:
- Kayak Historical Discovery Tours. 87-3187 Honu Moe Rd., Captain Cook, HI 96704. Ph 328-8911. Betsy Morrigan. (Trips, mostly South Kona.)

- *P & P Distributors. Keaʻau, HI 96749. Ph 966-4999. Peter Bukas. (Boats, gear.)
- Nautilus Dive Center. 382 Kamehameha Ave., Hilo, HI 96720. Ph 935-6939. (Two kayaks for rent; walk to the bay.)
- Ocean Safaris. PO Box 515, Kailua-Kona, HI 96745. Ph 326-4699. Mike and Carol Dennis.

Sources Outside of Hawaiʻi

Addresses for Catalogs for Inflatable, Folding, and Kit Boats

See also your local boat dealer, *Sea Kayaker* magazine, and annual *Canoe & Kayak Buyer's Guide*. Be wary, as many inflatable kayaks are yard-wide, beamy boats with upturned ends designed for river rapids, not for the sea. If the width is more than 30 inches or the width to length proportion is greater than one to five, it is probably designed for rivers. The following companies may make both river and sea kayaks. These are the U.S. addresses. (See also chapter 1.)

Inflatable Boats
- Aire. PO Box 3412, Boise, ID 83703. Ph (208) 344-7506.
- The Boat People. 1249 S. First Street, San Jose, CA 95110. Ph (408) 295-2628.
- EcoVision. Camelia #1326, Round Hills, Trujillo-Alto, Puerto Rico 00976.
- Grabner Inflatables. 9702 Gayton Rd., #153, Richmond, VA 23233. This is the address for the U.S. dealer. For the catalog and for direct orders from the European factory, use the following address: Wolfgang Grabner, Sportartikel Fabrik, Weistracher Strasse 11, A3350 Haag, Austria. Ask for the English language catalog. Ph 07434/2251, 2838.
- Innova. 180 W. Dayton, #202, Edmonds, WA 98020. Ph (206) 776-1171. (Also REI Camping Catalog, 1996. Ph (800) 426-4840)
- Jumbo. 1931 S.W. 14th St., #3, Portland, OR 97201. Ph (503) 274-2313.
- Sevylor. 6651 E. 26th St., Los Angeles, CA 90040. Ph (213) 727-6013.

All but the Aire and the EcoVision are made in Europe. Grabner European address is listed. For the others, call the U.S. dealers. See also "Buying A Boat Direct" at the end of this section.

Folding Boats

- Feathercraft. 1244 Cartwright St., Vancouver, B.C. V6H 3R8 Canada. Ph (604) 681-8437. Doug Simpson.
- Folbot. PO Box 7087 Dept. SK, Charleston, SC 29415. Ph (800) 744-3483.
- Klepper. 2075 S. University, Unit 119, Denver CO 80210.
- Nautiraid USA. Box 1305, Suite 238, Brunswick, ME 04011.
- Pouch. 1931 SW 14th St., Portland OR 97201.
- Seavivor. 576 Arlington Ave., Des Plaines, IL 60016.

Build Your Own (Kits or Plans)

- Chesapeake Light Craft. 1805 George Ave., Annapolis, MD 21401. Ph (410) 267-0137. Chris Kulczycki.
- Geodesic Aerolite Boats by Platt Monfort. RFD 2, Box 415, Wiscasset, ME 04578. Ph (207) 882-5504.
- Pygmy Boats Inc. PO Box 1529, Dept. 8, Pt. Townsend, WA 98368. Ph (360) 385-6143. Send $2 for catalog. Talk to John Lockwood.
- The Wooden Boat Shop. 1007 N.E. Boat St., Seattle, WA 98105. Ph (800) 933-3600.

Buying a Boat Direct

It's possible to purchase an inflatable kayak direct from the manufacturer in Europe. The best way to contact them is by fax. If calling by phone you may not reach someone who speaks English, and corresponding by mail can be time-consuming. Request a catalog unless you already know what model you want. Often the catalog will list models or spare parts that might not be imported by the U.S. distributor. Inquire about the current price, and get an estimate of the cost of shipping by air to a nearby airport that serves as an international port of entry, one that has a U.S. Customs office.

The cost will probably be quoted in the local currency, but you might be able to get a cost or at least an estimate in U.S. dollars. If the factory estimates a cost in dollars, it will be based on the current exchange rate that they get from their bank. Payment by mailing a check is possible, but the delays involved mean that the exchange rate may be different by the time your check arrives, leading to further delays if the change in rate is not in your favor. By getting the name of the bank and account number that the boat manufacturer uses, you can arrange a wire transfer directly to their account for a cost of about $30. You may need to check different local banks in your own area to find one that handles transfers to that particular European bank. If paying an estimated dollar price, add a little extra to allow for changes in exchange rate, and ask the factory to include some additional small parts, if the excess payment is sufficient.

The reason for shipping to an international airport is that for a personal shipment valued at $1,250 or less, U.S. Customs will figure any applicable duties and allow you to pay them directly. You'll need to go to the Customs office after the air cargo company notifies you that your shipment has arrived. Check with the air cargo company about the exact procedure they use. If the shipment is valued above $1,250, you need to hire a commercial customs broker to clear the shipment for you, which will cost an additional $100 to $200.

By wiring payment and having your boat sent air freight, you may get a boat faster than by ordering it from a U.S. distributor, and at a cost of from one-half to two-thirds of the U.S. dealer's price.

Buying a boat from the factory in Europe while on a visit is highly recommended. It's interesting to see how the boats are made, and the folks at the factory are quite interested in how their boats are being used. A chat with the repair department, even if you don't share a common language, can yield valuable tips on the best way of making repairs. Factories often have seconds, boats with cosmetic defects that are functionally perfect, that you can buy at very reasonable prices. And there are lots of great places to paddle in Europe.

Fax number for Grabner from the United States is 011-43-74-34-422513. (The source for this information about buying direct is Mark Rognstad of Hawai'i, who has been doing it for more than 10 years.)

Paddles

Thirty-five companies who make kayak touring paddles are listed in the *Canoe and Kayak 1997 Buyer's Guide*. See your local dealer or send for catalogs after you read the listings in the guide. Here is the one mentioned in chapter 1: Aqua-Bound Technology Ltd. 9520 192nd St., Surrey, B.C. V4N 3R9 Canada. Ph (604) 882-2052.

Other Information

Addresses for Camping Gear

O'ahu

- The Bike Shop. 1149 S. King St., Honolulu, HI 96817. Ph 596-0588. Attoman Kim. (Tents, stoves, half the stuff on the gear list, quality information, bikes.)
- Patagonia. 66-250 Kamehameha Hwy., Hale'iwa, HI 96712. Ph 637-1245. (Excellent clothing for the outdoors, plus some books and gear.)
- Hawai'i Outdoor World. 214 Sand Island Rd., Honolulu, HI 96819. Ph 845-2100.

Mainland (call for catalog)
- Campmor. Box 700-P Saddle River, NJ 07458. Ph 1-800-525-4784.
- REI 1700 45th St. East, Sumner, WA 98390. Ph 1-800-426-4840. (The Innova Helios inflatable kayak is now listed in their camping catalog.)

Airlines between Islands

- Aloha Airlines. Ph 484-1111. (Larger airports.)
- Island Air. Ph 484-2222. (Smaller airports.)
- Hawaiian Airlines. Ph 838-1555.
- TransAir. Ph 836-8080. (In and out of Kamuela, Big Island, from Honolulu.)

Ferries between Islands (Maui to Lāna'i and return; passengers and kayaks, no cars.)
- Lāna'i Ferry Shuttle. 658 Front St., Lahaina, HI 96761. Ph 661-3756.
- Maui Princess Interisland Ferry. 113 Prisons St., Lahaina, HI 96761. Ph 667-6165.

Freight Shipping by Barge
- Young Brothers. Pier 24, Honolulu, HI 96817. Ph 543-9385. (All sizes kayaks, canoes, cars. No passengers.)

Air Freight

- Polynesian Airways Inc. 471 Aowena Pl., Honolulu, HI 96819. Ph 836-3838.
- See Yellow Pages for other air freight listings and inquire about shipping kayaks. (Know the length, width, and weight of your boat.)

Government Offices—Camping, Permit, and Other Information

National Parks
- Hawai'i Volcanoes National Park, HI 96718. Ph 967-7311.
- Haleakala National Park. Box 369, Makawao, HI 96768. Ph 572-9306.
- Kaloko-Honokōhau National Historical Park. 73-4786 Kanalani St., #14, Kailua-Kona, HI 96740. Ph 329-6881.
- Kalaupapa National Historical Park. Box 2222, Kalaupapa, HI 96742. Ph 567-6802.
- Pu'uhonua o Hōnaunau National Historical Park. Hōnaunau, HI 96726. Ph 328-2288.

State Parks (Camping permits may be obtained at any state park office for any island.)

- Kaua'i. 3060 'Eīwa Street, Līhue, HI 96766. Ph 241-3444.
- O'ahu. 1151 Punchbowl St., Honolulu, HI 96713. Ph 587-0300.
- Maui. PO Box 1049, Wailuku, HI 96793. Ph 984-8109.
- Hawai'i (Big Island). PO Box 936, Hilo, HI 96720. Ph 933-4200.

County Parks

- Kaua'i. 4444 Rice St., Moikeha Bldg., Suite 150, Līhue, HI 96766. Ph 241-6660.
- O'ahu. 650 S. King St., Honolulu, HI 96813. Ph 523-4525. (Also available at nine satellite city halls.)
- Maui (includes Moloka'i and Lāna'i). 1580 Ka'ahumanu Ave., Wailuku, HI 96793. Ph 243-7389.
- Hawai'i. 25 Aupuni St., Hilo, HI 96720. Ph 961-8311.

See also the listing for *Camping Hawai'i* by Richard McMahon (under "Further Reading") for information about camping permits and about private organization or church camps.

Bus Schedules

- Kaua'i. Iniki Express. Ph 241-6410.
- O'ahu. The Bus. Ph 848-5555.
- Maui. Trans Hawaiian (shuttle only; airport to Kaanapali). Ph 877-7303.
- Hawai'i. Hele On Bus Service. Ph 935-8241.

Hostelling International

O'ahu:

- University: 2323A Seaview Ave., Honolulu, HI 96822. Ph 946-0591. (Price: $11.28 plus tax.)
- Waikīkī: 2417 Prince Edward St., Honolulu, HI 96815. Ph 926-8313. (Price: $14.44 plus tax.)

These are the only Hostelling International (formerly American Youth Hostel) inns in Hawai'i, but other hostel-type accommodations are on Kaua'i, O'ahu, Maui, and the Big Island. Look for card brochures in airport display racks or in the Yellow Pages of the telephone book. Ten are listed for O'ahu.

Glossary: Hawaiian Words and Boat Terms

‘a‘ā	Rough, chunky lava. In scientific terminology, simply written *aa*.
‘āina	The land.
aloha	Hello, goodbye, love, warm friendship.
‘ape	Large-leafed plant. Not edible.
bowline	A useful knot in a rope, pronounced bo-lin.
bow line	A line from the front of the boat for mooring, towing etc.; rhymes with cow line.
close out	When waves close out, they break all the way across a shore, leaving no access channel.
feather	A verb, to turn one blade of a paddle at right angles to the other.
gunwale	The upper edge of the side of a craft. Pronounced gunnel.
hala	Tree often found on the wet coasts; also called pandanus or screw pine, *Pandanus odoratissimus*.
hana	Work.
haole	Foreigner, Caucasian person.
hau	*Hibiscus tiliaceus*, a tree with useful wood, bark, and blossoms.
hāwa‘e	Short-spined sea urchin. *Tripneustes gratilla*.
he‘e	Squid, octopus. Two species in Hawai‘i: *Polypus marmoratus* and *Polypus ornatus*.
heiau	Place of worship.
hele	Move ahead, as in "hele on"—keep going.
hono-	Prefix meaning bay or place.
hula	Dance. Sometimes differentiated as old style, *kahiko*, and modern, *‘auana*.

hulaʻana	A place where it is necessary to swim past a cliff that blocks passage along a coast; a sheer cliff where the sea beats.
huli	Capsize (noun and verb). *Huli huli* chicken is roasted on a turning spit.
ʻiako	Connection between canoe and outrigger float.
ʻina	Small, short-spined sea urchin, *Echinometra mathaei*.
ka, ke	The (article).
kamaʻāina	Native, child of the land.
kapu	Taboo, forbidden, keep out.
kaukahi	Solo, alone, one person.
keiki	Child.
kiawe	Algaroba tree, related to mesquite. *Prosopis pallida*.
kikurage	Japanese word for tree fungus, *pepeiao*, probably *Discina perlata* or closely related.
knot	Measure of speed; 1 knot is 1 nautical mile per hour. A nautical mile is 1.15 land miles.
kōkua	Help, helper.
kolū	Thorny tree, *Acacia farnesiana*, known for its fragrant flowers and for the glue (*kolū* or *klu*) of its sap.
lanai	Stiff-backed, stubborn.
lanaʻi	Open porch or deck.
Lānaʻi	One of the eight main islands.
lau	Leaf.
laulau	Wrapping; package of *ti* leaves containing pork, fish, and taro tops, steamed.
laupāhoehoe	Leaf of *pāhoehoe* lava; often a peninsula at the base of a cliff.
lava lava	Samoan word for a wraparound garment, worn by males and females.
lee	Noun or adjective. Sheltered from the wind.
lei	Garland of flowers, shells, or ferns in sizes to fit a hat, a head, or around the neck and shoulders.
lilikoʻi	Passion fruit; *Passiflora edulis*.

limu	Seaweed, algae, mosses, and lichens.
lua	Hole that has a bottom, as contrasted with *puka*. Toilet, outhouse.
māhalo	Thank you. *Māhalo nui loa* means "thank you very much."
mainland	Continental United States, the North American continent.
makai	Toward the sea.
mauka	Toward the mountains.
mo'o	Legendary giant lizard or dragon.
moku	Island or district.
nā	The; plural form of the article *ka* or *ke*.
nautical mile	One minute of latitude, 1.15 land miles.
'ohana	Family.
'ōhelo	Shrub with edible red berries, sacred to Pele. *Vaccinium reticulatum*.
'ōkole	Buttocks.
'ono	Delicious.
'opihi	Limpet. Four species in Hawai'i of the family *Patellidae*.
pāhoehoe	Smooth, ropey lava, like billows of fudge.
pali	Cliff. *Nā pali* are the cliffs.
pareu	Tahitian word for lava lava or sarong.
pau	Done, through, finished. As in "pau hana time", end of the day's work.
Pele	Hawaiian volcano goddess.
pepeiao	Ear, fungus that looks like an ear when fresh. *Pepeiao akua* is ghost's ear.
pipipi	General name for small mollusks.
pōhaku	Stone, rock.
puka	Hole (through).
pūlehu	To broil on coals.
pūpū	Appetizer or relish; also a general name for shells.
pu'u	Hill, often used as a prefix in place names.
shōyu	Japanese word for soy sauce.

spray skirt	Covering for the cockpit of a traditional kayak, closely fitted around the paddler's waist and over the coaming (the edge of the cockpit opening).
spray deck	A larger covering for larger cockpits such as on Kleppers or inflatables, which changes them from canoe style to kayak. Also used on racing canoes.
tabi	A general term for a soft shoe or sock, some with split toes, some with felt or hard rubber soles. Old style tabi had hooks at the heel to fasten them.
tako	Japanese word for octopus.
taro	Low plant with edible roots and leaves; *kalo* in Hawaiian. A staple food, all parts edible. Needs long cooking to destroy oxalic acid crystals. *Colocasia esculenta*.
ti	Bush or small tree; *ki* in Hawaiian. Has a useful leaf and root. *Cordylene terminalis*.
tsunami	Large wave or series of waves, produced by a sea quake or an undersea eruption.
ulva	Sea lettuce, a kind of limu.
wana	Several species of sea urchin with long venomous spines.
wāwae'iole	Club moss on land, and an edible seaweed. *Codium reediae*.
zōri	Japanese name for split-toe sandals, also called go-aheads or slippers.

Further Reading

General

Burke, Katy. *Managing Your Escape*. 7 Seas Press, 1984.

Caldwell, Peter. *Adventurer's Hawai'i*. Taote Publishing, 1992.

Carroll, Rick. *Great Outdoor Adventures of Hawaii*. Foghorn Press, 1991.

Clark, John R. K. The Beaches series. See below under individual islands.

Daws, Gavan. *Shoal of Time: A History of the Hawaiian Islands*. University of Hawai'i Press, 1974.

——. *Hawai'i, The Islands of Life*. Signature Publishing, 1988.

Department of Geography, University of Hawai'i. *Atlas of Hawai'i*. University of Hawai'i Press, 1983.

Dowd, John. *Sea Kayaking*. University of Washington Press, 1988.

Kirch, Patrick. *Feathered Gods and Fishhooks*. University of Hawai'i Press, 1985.

Krauss, Beatrice. *Plants in Hawaiian Culture*. University of Hawai'i Press, 1993.

Macdonald, Gordon; Abbott, Agatin; and Peterson, Frank L. *Volcanoes in the Sea*. University of Hawai'i Press, 1983.

McMahon, Richard. *Adventuring in Hawaii*. Sierra Club Books, 1996.

——. *Camping Hawai'i*. University of Hawai'i Press, 1997.

Pukui, Mary, and Elbert, Samuel H. *Hawaiian Dictionary*. University of Hawai'i Press, 1986.

——, and Mookini, Esther T. *Place Names of Hawaii*. University of Hawai'i Press, 1974.

Stewart, Frank, ed. *A World Between Waves*. Island Press, 1992.

Washburne, Randel. *The Coastal Kayaker*. Pacific Search Press, 1983.

——. *The Coastal Kayaker's Manual*. Globe Pequot Press, 1993.

Chapter 1 The Many Ways to Paddle

Diaz, Ralph. *Complete Folding Kayaker*. Ragged Mountain Press, 1994.

Dyson, George. *Baidarka*. Alaska Northwest Publishing, 1986.

Haddon, A. C., and Hornell, James. *Canoes of Oceania*. Bishop Museum Press, 1975.

Seidman, David. *The Essential Sea Kayaker*. Ragged Mountain Press, 1992.

Chapter 2 Gear

Arbeit, Wendy. *What Are Fronds For?* University of Hawai'i Press, 1985.

Fletcher, Colin. *The Complete Walker III*. Knopf, 1985.

Getchell, Annie. *The Essential Outdoor Gear Manual*. Ragged Mountain Press, 1995.

Harrison, David. *Kayak Camping*. Hearst Marine Books, 1995.

Sumner, Louise Lindgren. *Sew and Repair Your Outdoor Gear*. The Mountaineers, 1988.

Chapter 3 Safety

Bezruchka, Stephen. *The Pocket Doctor*. The Mountaineers, 1988.

Burch, David. *Fundamentals of Kayak Navigation*. Pacific Search Press, 1987.

Hobson, Edmund, and Chave, E. H. *Hawaiian Reef Animals*. University of Hawai'i Press, 1990.

Nishida, Gordon, and Tenorio, JoAnn M. *What Bit Me?* University of Hawai'i Press, 1993.

Suiso, Kenn, and Sunn, Rell. *A Guide to Beach Survival*. Honolulu Water Safety Consultants, Inc., 1986.

Taylor, Leighton. *Sharks of Hawai'i*. University of Hawai'i Press, 1993.

Thomas, Craig, and Scott, Susan. *All Stings Considered*. University of Hawai'i Press, 1997.

Chapter 4 Wind and Surf

Bascom, Willard. *Waves and Beaches*. Anchor Books, Doubleday, 1980.

National Ocean Service, NOAA. *United States Coast Pilot No. 7*. U.S. Department of Commerce, n.d.

Sanderson, Marie, ed. *Prevailing Trade Winds*. University of Hawai'i Press, 1993.

Chapter 5 Food

Daniel, Linda. *Kayak Cookery*. Pacific Search Press, 1986.

Fortner, Heather. *The Limu Eater*. University of Hawai'i Sea Grant Program, 1985.

Gibbons, Euell. *Beachcomber's Handbook*. David McKay Co., 1972.

Laudan, Rachel. *The Food of Paradise*. University of Hawai'i Press, 1996.

Miller, Dorcas S. *Good Food for Camp and Trail.* Pruett Publishing, 1993.
Pill, Virginia, and Furlong, Marjorie. *Edible? Incredible!* Pill Enterprises, 1985.

Chapter 6 Planning, Packing, and Paddling

Balazs, George. *Hawai'i's Seabirds, Turtles, and Seals.* Worldwide Distributor Ltd., 1976.
Fielding, Ann, and Robinson, Ed. *An Underwater Guide to Hawai'i.* University of Hawai'i Press, 1987.
Hoover, John P. *Hawaii's Fishes.* Mutual Publishing, 1993.
Merlin, Mark. *Hawaiian Coastal Plants and Scenic Shorelines.* Oriental Publishing, 1986.
Pratt, Douglas, and Bruner, Phillip L. *Field Guide to Birds of Hawai'i and the Tropical Pacific.* Princeton University Press, 1987.
Randall, John E. *Waterproof Guide to Hawaiian Reef Fishes.* Harrowood Books, 1981.
———. *Shore Fishes of Hawai'i.* Natural World Press, 1996.
Shallenberger, Robert, ed. *Hawaii's Birds.* Hawai'i Audubon Society, 1997.

Chapter 7 The Voyages

Meyer, Kathleen. *How to Shit in the Woods.* Ten Speed Press, 1994.

Chapter 8 Kaua'i

Clark, John R. K. *Beaches of Kaua'i and Ni'ihau.* University of Hawai'i Press, 1989.
———. *Hawaii's Secret Beaches.*
London, Jack. "Ko'olau The Leper," from *A House of Pride.* The Macmillan Co., 1912. Published also in *A Hawaiian Reader,* edited by A. Grove Day and Carl Stroven. Popular Library, 1961.
Valier, Kathy. *On the Na Pali Coast: A Guide for Hikers and Boaters.* University of Hawai'i Press, 1988.

Chapter 9. O'ahu

Clark, John R. K. *The Beaches of O'ahu.* University of Hawai'i Press, 1977.

Chapter 10 Moloka'i

Bushnell, O. A. *Moloka'i.* University of Hawai'i Press, 1975.
Clark, John R. K. *The Beaches of Maui County.* University of Hawai'i Press, 1989.

Cooke, Richard A., III. *Moloka'i: An Island in Time*. Beyond Words Publishing Co., 1984.

Daws, Gavan, *Holy Man: Father Damien of Molokai*. Harper and Row, 1973.

Kepler, Angela Kay, and Kepler, Cameron B. *Majestic Molokai: A Nature Lover's Guide*. Mutual Publishing, 1991.

Summers, Catherine C. *Molokai: A Site Survey*. Bishop Museum Press, 1971.

Sutherland, Audrey. *Paddling My Own Canoe*. University of Hawai'i Press, 1978.

Chapter 11 Lāna'i

Clark, John R. K. *The Beaches of Maui County*. University of Hawai'i Press, 1989.

Emory, Kenneth P. *The Island of Lāna'i*. Bulletin 12. Bishop Museum Press, 1924.

Tabrah, Ruth. *Lāna'i*. Island Heritage Press, 1976.

Chapter 12 Maui

Clark, John R. K. *The Beaches of Maui County*. University of Hawai'i Press, 1989.

Kepler, Angela Kay. *Maui's Hāna Highway, a Visitor's Guide*. Mutual Publishing, 1987.

Sterling, Elspeth. *The Sites of Maui County*. Bishop Museum, 1988.

Chapter 13 Hawai'i, the Big Island

Apple, Russell A. *Trails, from Steppingstones to Kerbstones*. Bishop Museum, 1965.

Ball, Stuart, M., Jr. *The Backpacker's Guide to Hawai'i*. University of Hawai'i Press, 1996.

Bushnell, O. A. *The Return of Lono*. University of Hawai'i Press, 1979.

Chisholm, Craig. *Hawai'i: The Big Island Hiking Trails*. Fernglen Press, 1994.

Clark, John. *Beaches of the Big Island*. University of Hawai'i Press, 1985.

Periodicals

Atlantic Coastal Kayaker. PO Box 520, Ipswich, MA 01938.

Backpacker. 33 E. Minor Street, Emmaus, PA 18098.

Canoe & Kayak. PO Box 3146, Kirkland, WA 98083.

Hawai'i Paddler. 305 Hahani St., #245, Kailua, HI 96743.

Hawai'i Skin Diver. PO Box 0297, Kapolei, HI 96709.

Pacific Paddler. 287 Mokauea St. Honolulu, HI 96819.

Paddler. PO Box 1341, Eagle, ID 83616.

Sea Kayaker. PO Box 17170, Seattle, WA 98107.

Wave Length. RR-1 Gabriola Island, B.C., Canada VOR1X0.

Index